REFERENCE ONLY

HOW TO SET UP YOUR OWN SMALL BUSINESS

VOLUME 1
2009 Edition

ISBN 978-0-939069-29-3
0-939069-29-6

American Institute of Small Business

23075 Highway 7, Suite 200   800-328-2906
Shorewood, MN 55331   952-545-7001
                          Fax   952-545-7020
www.aisb.biz   info@aisb.biz

HOW TO SET UP YOUR OWN
SMALL BUSINESS

Kris Solie-Johnson

Published by
AMERICAN INSTITUTE OF SMALL BUSINESS
23075 Highway 7, Suite 200
Shorewood, MN 55331
(952) 545-7001
Fax (952) 545-7020
(800) 328-2906
www.aisb.biz

VOLUME I

ISBN 978-0-939069-29-3
0-939069-29-6
ISSN 1074-6080
Library of Congress Catalog Number: 94648091

CONSULTATION

CERTIFICATE

If You need help with
your current or new business, please call our
office for a **FREE** 15 minute consultation
with Chancellor Kris.

We will be glad to help
you any way we can.

952-545-7001

American Institute of Small Business

23075 Highway 7, Suite 200   800-328-2906
Shorewood, MN 55331   952-545-7001
                               Fax 952-545-7020
www.aisb.biz   info@aisb.biz

What Other Librarians Are Said about past Editions

"This comprehensive work offers objective accurate information, including the answers to real-life problems entrepreneurs face. The explanations are clear, and the filled-in-forms, addresses and samples that are included make this work invaluable. **Any public library** whose patrons include start-up or established entrepreneurs **should get their money's worth** from this set. Librarians would find it worthwhile to familiarize themselves with the contents, as it provides practical answers to so very many questions."

- Susan from Cuyahoga County Public Library, Maple Heights, OH

"Starting a business? **Here's all you need** - a 2 volume set, packed with vital information, yet easy to read and understand. What would our Business Resource Center do without it?"

- Linda from Aurora Public Library, Aurora, CO

"Anyone who is considering starting a business should **make this one of the first books they read**."

- Susannah from Norwalk Public Library, Norwalk, CT

"**Our Patrons use** "How To Set Up Your Own Small Business" **frequently.** It really gives the small business owner everthing they need to get their business up and running"
- Krista from Lisle Library, Lisle, IL

"The books are **very comprehensive**, written in language the average person can understand. I anticipate wide usage. **Previous editions have been heavily used** and appreciated by our patrons. I would recommend these books to anyone starting up their own business."

- Janice from Madison County Library, Madison, VA

"A readable introduction to the basics of all aspects of setting up a new business. This is a good general resources for people just getting started."
-Booklist

"Each step of setting up a small business is considered and covered in the two-volume set."
-School Library Journal

TABLE OF CONTENTS

VOLUME 1

About the American Institute of Small Business
Preface
Acknowledgements

Start-Up

The Business Plan

Finance and Accounting

TABLE OF CONTENTS

VOLUME 2

Marketing and Sales

Management and Operations

Appendices and Index

About the American Institute of Small Business

AISB's^{tm} mission is to teach entrepreneurs the skills needed to successfully start and run a small business by providing resources to librarians, teachers, current business owners, and others who serve as local advocates.

Formed in 1984, The American Institute of Small Business focuses on potential business owners with little or no small business experience.

Our publications are easy to understand and cover a wide variety of topics to help start and run a successful small business. A web site has been created at www.aisb.biz to help librarians, teachers and entrepreneurs find the additional information they may need. If you have comments about the web site, please contact us at info@aisb.biz.

The popular 2-volume set of books, written by Max Fallex, "How to Set Up Your Own Small Business" is currently in its 9th Edition since 1985. These books have been a foundation for many entrepreneurs when setting up their new businesses and a major focus of AISB's^{tm} goals as well. The information is regularly updated to keep small businesses competitive.

"A readable introduction to the basics of all aspects of setting up a new business." **- Booklist** (reviewing the 2-volume set of books "How to Set Up Your Own Small Business")

Owner and President, Kris Solie-Johnson, has been deeply involved with small business consulting since 1989. She received her MBA in Venture Management from the University of St. Thomas in 1996. While serving as a Strategic Alliance Account Manager at Residential Funding Corporation (RFC), she helped small companies receive new technologies in exchange for loans sold to RFC. She continued her career at a small Internet company offering financial reporting to small community banks over the Internet. Ms. Solie-Johnson purchased the American Institute of Small Business 2002 and created the largest school in the country for small business.

Chapter 1

Business Savvy Kids – Start At Any Age

"Much education today is monumentally ineffective. All too often we are giving young people cut flowers when we should be teaching them to grow their own plants." **— John W. Gardner, American Writer and previous Secretary of Health, Education and Welfare (1912-2002).**

In this chapter you will learn:

1. *How to find the perfect idea for you*
2. *Skills necessary for writing your own business plan*
3. *Finding money for your business if you need it*
4. *How marketing is the key to success*
5. *Resources for teen entrepreneurs*

First let's look at the childhood of most successful entrepreneurs in the United States. Warren Buffet stared multiple businesses before he was 10 years old, including selling pop at construction sites, multiple paper routes and selling a horse racing tip sheet that he and friend created. The last one only lasted until they were shut down for not having a license.

Bill Gates started his first business when he was 13 years old. He and a group of friends were paid in computer time to find bugs in a computer system for a company.

1

Many of the famous entrepreneurs had businesses before they were 14 years old. Like any other topic, business is best learned by doing it, by taking action. But where do you start?

In this chapter, you will discover the steps to create your own business including how to find an idea that works for you, how to get started and how to stay motivated.

FINDING THE PERFECT IDEA FOR YOU

Where do great ideas come from?

Ideas come from a variety of places. The best thing to do when looking for an idea is to take out a piece of paper and start brainstorming all the different businesses you could start. Research a wide variety of ideas from:

- Personal experiences -- hobbies, interests
- Work-related experiences
- Friends, family, teachers, coaches
- The Internet
- Library research

As you think about your idea consider these questions:

- What do I like to do with my time?
- What technical skills have I learned or developed?
- What do others say I am good at?
- How much time do I have to run a successful business?
- Do I have any hobbies or interests that are marketable?

Aha! The great idea. Now what?

Before starting out, list your reasons for wanting to go into business. Knowing why you want to start a business is one of the factors that will determine your success. The stronger your reason for starting, the more success you will have.

Some of the most common reasons for starting a business are:
- You want to be your own boss.
- You want financial independence.
- You want creative freedom.
- You want to fully use your skills and knowledge

Then identify the niche your business will fill. Conduct the necessary research to answer these questions:
- Is my idea practical, and will it fill a need or a want?
- What is my competition?
- What is my business advantage over existing firms?
- Can I deliver a better quality service?
- Can I create a demand for my business?

Consider the time it takes to run a business:
- Do I really want to give up baseball, hockey, soccer, basketball, football, dance, piano and voice, or hanging out with or going to the mall with my friends to run this business?
- Will I have to run my business every day or just sometimes?
- Will running my business have an effect on school?
- Will my family help me out?

Your pre-business check list
The final step before developing your plan is the pre-business checklist. You should answer these questions:
- ✔ What services or products will I sell? Where will I be located?
- ✔ What skills and experience do I bring to the business?
- ✔ What will I name my business?
- ✔ What equipment or supplies will I need?
- ✔ What insurance coverage will be needed?

✔ How much money, if any, will it cost to start my business? Will I need financing?

✔ What are my resources?

✔ How will I compensate myself?

Your answers will help you create a focused, well-researched <u>business plan</u> that will serve as a blueprint. The plan will detail how the business will be operated, managed and <u>financed</u>.

THE TEEN BUSINESS PLAN

Developing your business plan is your road map to success in the business world. A business plan is a written document that outlines measures and actions to define where you want to go and how you will get there. Without a business plan, you have no written goals or objectives to measure your success. Starting a business is a full of uncertainties. Developing a thorough business plan helps minimize those uncertainties.

Before you begin writing your business plan, consider these questions:

What service or product does your business provide, and what need does it fill?

Who are the potential customers for your product or service, and why will they purchase it from you?

How will you reach your potential customers?

Where will you get the financial resources to start your business?

Do you really want to give up baseball, hockey, soccer, basketball, football, dance, piano and voice, or hanging out with or going to the mall with your friends to run this business?

Will you have to run your business every day or just sometimes?

Will running your business have an effect on school?

Will your family help you out?

The business plan is your guide. You can adapt it to your specific business. Dividing the plan into several components helps make drafting it a more manageable task.

SAMPLE TEEN BUSINESS PLAN

Introduction
- Give a detailed description of the business and its goals.
- Discuss the ownership of the business and the legal structure.
- List the skills and experience you bring to the business.
- Discuss the advantages you and your business have over your competitors.

Marketing
- Discuss the products/services offered.
- Identify the customer demand for your product/service.
- Identify your market, its size and locations.
- Explain how your product/service will be advertised and marketed.
- Explain the pricing strategy.

Financial Management
- Explain your source and discuss the amount of initial equity capital you'll need.
- Develop a monthly operating budget for the first year.
- Develop an expected return on investment and monthly cash flow for the first year.
- Provide projected income statements and balance sheets for a two-year period.

- Discuss your breakeven point.
- Explain your personal balance sheet and method of compensation.
- Discuss who will maintain your accounting records and how they will be kept.
- Provide "what if" statements that address alternative approaches to any problem that may develop.

Operations

- Explain how the business will be managed on a day-to-day basis.
- Discuss hiring and personnel procedures.
- Discuss insurance, lease or rent agreements, and issues pertinent to your business.
- Account for the equipment necessary to produce your products or services.
- Account for production and delivery of products and services.

Concluding Statement

Summarize your business goals and objectives and express your commitment to the success of your business.

DO YOU NEED MONEY TO START?

Let's face it. Money matters. You can't start, grow or simply exist in business without sufficient money to pay the bills and provide some income. Here are some questions you should answer as you consider starting or growing your business.

- How much do I need to either get started or grow my business?
- Will I use my personal money?
- Should I ask someone else for a loan?
- Can I apply for a credit card?
- Will a vendor or a supplier be willing to give me trade credit? [This usually means that you have an extended period of time to pay your bill usually 30 days from time of invoice.]

- To minimize costs, should I start my business in my home?
- If I use someone's money, will my business generate enough money to be able to repay the loan (principal and interest)?

Funding Your Business

Many entrepreneurs start businesses at home using their own personal funds. Some ask friends and family to provide the initial or ongoing capital. When your business has been established for a while, you may want to go to your local bank for a loan.

You Can Bank on It

Developing a relationship with your bank and your personal banker is important. If you decide to seek a loan from your bank, your personal banker serves as your advocate supporting your application before the bank's loan committee. When you apply for a loan, you and your parents must co-sign the papers.

Before asking for a loan, you need to establish a savings or checking account. Banks generally prefer to lend to their existing clients who will bring the bank additional business -- other new clients or establish a number of accounts both personal and business. Once you have demonstrated that your business is successful, a bank may consider a line of credit or possibly a small commercial loan if you and/or your parents bank there.

Your Credit History is Your Rep

Finally, establishing and maintaining a good credit history is critical to getting money for your business. Always pay your bills on time and make sure that you periodically check your credit history. A credit report contains information on where you live, how you pay your bills, and whether you've been sued, arrested or filed for bankruptcy. Nationwide consumer reporting companies sell the information in your report to creditors who use it to evaluate your applications for credit. Your credit is like your name -- do not abuse it.

MARKETING IS WHAT DRIVES A BUSINESS

Marketing is the one thing that will bring you customers and will keep them doing business with you over time. Later in this book there are many chapters devoted to marketing, but the best way to launch your business regardless of what type of business you chose starts with one basic step – telling everyone you know what you are doing.

In the chapter on the Single Biggest Mistake, you will discover that the most valuable asset in any business, including yours is your customer list. You can build this list by starting with people you know and who know you. Even if those people are not part of your target market, you never know who they know that may be interested in your products or services.

The best beginning marketing for any teen business is an email to friends and family or a simple flier out to your neighbors. Both of these are relatively inexpensive to get the word out initially. After you have worked through these prospects you will need to develop a system to get others to try your product or service. You will want to break your marketing system into two main parts:

1.   How are you going to get customers who don't know you to try your product or service? You can do this by offering a free trial, a reduced new customer price or a guarantee.
2.   How will you get them to come back and make another purchase? Getting customers back to your business is a skill that anyone can do, but many do not do it. Marketing to your current customers is much easier than trying to find new customers and your current customers will spend more with you. Your customer list can become your own ATM.

Marketing is the lifeblood of any business. Most business owners do not put enough time into developing a marketing plan the works for them. They tend to think of an idea at the last minute to try to bring customers in the door. Normally by that time, it may be too late.

DO I NEED A LAWYER???

Do the Right Thing! Yes, it's not just director Spike Lee's first movie nominated for an Academy Award®, but also a best practice for everyone – especially entrepreneurs. Having a successful enterprise means being aware of relevant legal issues when organizing and growing your small business. (Academy Award® is a trademark of the Academy of Motion Picture Arts and Sciences.)
Below is a selection of resources which can help you manage common legal issues:

Organize your Business
www.business.gov
Get access to resources and services to help you start, grow, and succeed in business. The site gives you information on business laws, financing, government relations, taxes and much more.

Protect your Ideas
U.S. Patent & Trade Office: www.uspto.gov
U.S. Copyright Office: www.copyright.gov
Assist in protecting your investments, promoting goods and services, and safeguarding against confusion and deception in the marketplace.

9

Be Aware of Labor Laws

Department of Labor: http://www.dol.gov/

Find information on teen employment, wage and hour requirements, and providing a safe and healthy work experience.

Internal Revenue Service: http://www.irs.gov/

Starting a business can be one of the most rewarding experiences of your life. In addition you will be much farther ahead of your peers if you start to learn some of these lessons now. Business is not something you can learn in a book. The real learning comes from doing. So pick an idea and start now. It is the perfect time for you.

In this chapter you have learned:

1.   The perfect idea for you will come from your own experiences and activities you enjoy doing.

2.   Writing a business plan can put all your ideas on paper to make sure you didn't miss something.

3.   Depending on your financial needs for your business, you may have to take a loan from a bank.

4.   Being really good at marketing can make you more successful than you can imagine.

5.   Sometimes you will need to protect your ideas. It is good to know a lawyer and how to work with them.

Websites You May Find Useful

Small Business Administration Teen Site – www.sba.gov/teens/
Teen Entrepreneur Stories:
http://www.forbes.com/2008/02/09/teen-millionaires-startups-ent-success-cx-ml_0211millionaires.html
http://www.entrepreneur.com/startingabusiness/teenstartups/article69696.html
http://www.fastcompany.com/magazine/118/girl-power.html

Step To Success
One Action a Day Will Move You Forward

It is time to move forward. Complete the **Step to Success** Action and feel your progress. No matter where you are going, you can get there one step at a time.

The one thing that will separate you from the dreamers is to go and do something. So many people dream of owning their own business, but few do something about it. Quite dreaming and start doing. So pick an idea, tell everyone you know and start selling or performing your services.

Tell us about your business at Teen@teenbizclub.com

You can do it, so start right NOW!

Chapter 2

Time Management and Personal Development For Entrepreneurs

"You can't just sit there and wait for people to give you that golden dream; you've got to get out there and make it happen yourself."

– Diana Ross

Small business ownership isn't for everyone. All throughout this book, you have learned how to be successful regardless of what cards you have been dealt. Now is the time to set your fears aside and jump into an exciting adventure.

In this chapter, you will learn:

1. *How to think like a millionaire*
2. *To understand how you think and manage your time*
3. *Identify time wasters in your life*
4. *How to continue your education through other programs*
5. *Succeed beyond your current dreams*

THINK LIKE A MILLIONAIRE

Good habits are what will make you successful. This chapter is all about setting up those new habits and putting them to work for you and your business. Millionaires and successful business owners think differently than other "average" people.

Millionaires dream bigger. As Donald Trump has said, "It doesn't cost you any more to dream big." Allow yourself to dream bigger than you have ever dreamt before. Imagine yourself with everything you have ever wanted in life. Picture yourself traveling to exotic locations, enjoying your friends and family. Visualize how you would live if you had all the money in the world. What would you do each day?

Millionaires believe in abundance, that there is more than enough for everyone. Wealthy individuals do not think just because they made a dollar it is taking away a dollar from someone else. Millionaires believe that providing goods and services not only improves one person's life, but many people.

Millionaires see money as a tool and a measurement. Millionaires see money as a tool to use to make more money. Money is used the same way a hammer is used to build a house. It is a tool to be used. Money that is not circulated has no value. Money is meant to be used. But money is the one measurement everyone knows. Money is not evil. The higher power does not want you to be poor, but to have everything you desire.

Millionaires see challenges as something to be overcome. Poor people see challenges as blocks in the road. Wealthy people love a challenge and understand that part of the journey is in the challenges and the persistence in overcoming the challenges that brings joy.

Millionaires believe that they can accomplish whatever they set their mind to. Everyday millionaires create their goals and they set out to accomplish them. No matter what it takes. Persistence is one key to success.

TIME MANAGEMENT FOR ENTREPRENEURS

Rarely has there been an entrepreneur that has only one idea. Normally entrepreneurs have so many ideas and not enough time to fulfill them all. So how do you use your most limited resource, time, wisely? There are some consistent strategies that have worked for generation after generation of successful people.

First and foremost, time management and success are choices that you make. Every day you need to decide if you are going to make this day the best, most profitable day for you and your business. Are you going to use it to move closer to your goals or farther away? Time management is a CHOICE.

You only have 168 hours or 10,080 minutes every week. The same amount of time as everyone else. So why do some people get so much done with the same amount of time? First, what is your time worth? Have you ever calculated it? You can easily do it by taking the amount you want to work divided by the number of hours you want to work. But remember that the number of hours is dependant on the actual number of hours you are making money. If you are cleaning toilets and can not bill someone for that time or generate income from it, then it is not considered "making money" time.

Secondly, you need goals and objectives. You have probably heard about setting goals. But do you really take it seriously? Let's start with the proper way to set goals. Goals must meet the "SMART" factors.

➤ "S" is for Specific. Goals must state your desired result to be achieved.

➤ "M" is for Measurable. Goals must be measurable so that you know when you have achieved them.

➤ "A" is for Achievable. Your goals must be possible for you to accomplish.

➤ "R" is for Realistic. You must be able to achieve your goal in the set amount of time with the known resources.

➤ "T" is for Timed. If there isn't a timeframe for your goal to be achieved within, then you are just daydreaming. Without a deadline, it will take you much longer to achieve the goal, if it happens at all.

For example, a SMART goal would be exactly, how much, money do you want to earn this year from your business. Is it $30,000, $50,000 or $150,000? Write it down on a note card and carry it with you. Write it down on your bathroom mirror with a dry erase marker, so you see it right away when you wake up and the last thing before you go to sleep. Look at your goal each day to make sure everything you are doing is bringing you closer to result you choose.

Challenge yourself for the next 21 days to change your ways and try the following exercises:

First start with a blank spiral notebook or composition notebook. Write down your long term goal. What do you want your business to look like in 3 years? Write down as much detail as you can see and feel. Jot down what you feel like running your business at that time. What are your sales and profits at that time? Are you getting ready to sell your business?

Next, write down your mid-term goal, something to happen in the next year. What do you need to accomplish in the next year to move closer to your long term goal?

Finally, write down what you need to accomplish in the next week to move closer to the mid-term goal? Write down everything you can think of? Schedule or block out time on your calendar for the next week to accomplish all the things you need to get done. Make sure you start the day with this list before you get wrapped up into all the other things going on at work.

Each evening before you go to bed, think about the 1 or 2 items that you will work on tomorrow morning. Relax and then go to sleep. Let your subconscious work on your issues while you sleep. If you have a marketing letter to write or a presentation to give, your subconscious will prepare your mind for the event. But it is important to relax while doing this.

It is critical to your success to prioritize your day based on what you need to get done to bring you closer to your goal. Prioritizing and self discipline to stick to those priorities will make a huge difference in your results.

TIME WASTERS

Not only do you have to control your time, but you have to make sure others respect your time. One way you can determine if you are using your time wisely is to keep track for one week, in 15-minute increments how you spend each minute at work. You will be amazed at the amount of unproductive time that is wasted. And how you get side-tracked with things that do not move you to your long-term goal.

Many times your projects take as much time as you give them. The project fills the time. If you set an amount of time that it will take you to finish a project and stick to it, you will be amazed at how much time you have for other things.

Here are some more specific ideas for managing your time.
   1. Turn off your email for periods during the day. The way email is set up

lately is to beep in when there is a new message. This can interrupt your thought process or the project you are currently working on.

2. Work at home. Another time waster is other people who want to talk. If you track your time, monitor how much time is wasted by other people standing in your office.

3. Minimize meetings. If you work in a small office, limit the number of people in meetings. Make sure there is always an agenda sent out prior so people can prepare for the meeting and state an end time and a very clear objective of what will be accomplished at the meeting.

4. Be wary of interrupters. When anyone stops in or calls unexpectedly tell them that you have a specific amount of time and then you have to go. Most may try to take up as much time as possible. Also be aware of how much time you are losing to telephone interruptions. These calls can end up costing you valuable time.

5. Use To-do lists. Create a list every Sunday night of what you need to get done this week and stick to it until it is completed.

6. Procrastination. Procrastination and the inability to make decisions can have a dramatic effect on your business and how much you truly get done each day. Start each day with your most important task. Feel free to procrastinate on tasks that provide little to your business.

Time is the one resource no one can buy more of. We each get the same amount of time as everyone else. You must use this resource to preserve it in every way possible.

As a business owner, you should have a dollar amount you determine is your worth. If it is $60,000 per year, then your hourly rate is XZXX. Try everyday to quit doing jobs that do not produce XXX per hour. Hire the local high school student to type your mailing list, mow your lawn or clean your house. Your time is more valuable and you should protect it as such.

PERSONAL DEVELOPMENT FOR ENTREPRENEURS

Most self-made millionaires understand the value of continuing their education. The business world, your industry and technology are constantly changing.

Anyone who wants to achieve great wealth should continue their education through audio programs, seminars and mastermind groups.

In this chapter you have learned:

1. *Millionaires think differently. They believe in abundance and that there is enough for everyone.*
2. *Millionaires guard their time more than they guard their money.*
3. *Millionaires continue their education with audio programs and on-going training in their respective fields. They never stop learning.*

 ## Websites You May Find Useful

Earl Nightingale – Lead the Field – www.nightingale.com
Brian Tracey – www.briantracey.com
Napoleon Hill – Think and Grow Rich – www.naphill.org

 ## Step To Success
One Action a Day Will Move You Forward

It is time to move forward. Complete the **Step to Success** Action and feel your progress. No matter where you are going, you can get there one step at a time.

If you don't have a copy of Think and Grow Rich by Napoleon Hill, go to the library or order it online and start reading. The information will inspire you to think bigger and to follow your dreams like no one else in your life.

Do it now – It will make a difference in your level of success.

Chapter 3

MUST READ
The Single *Biggest* Mistake Small Businesses Make – And... How To Avoid It

"There is only one valid definition of business purpose: to create a customer."
     --Peter Drucker (1909-2005) Austrian-born management consultant and writer

---

In this chapter you will learn:
1. *The single biggest mistake small businesses make.*
2. *Importance of keeping your customers contact information.*
3. *How to create a profitable list.*
4. *How to manage the information on your customer list.*
5. *What information to keep about your customers.*

There is one secret reason, one secret formula that can make your small business a true success, faster and bigger than your current dreams. But rarely does anyone talk about this one factor that separates successful small businesses from the struggling others.   It is not taught in undergraduate or master's entrepreneurship programs.   The Small Business Administration doesn't mention it. Big business isn't using it except in rare cases. Bankers don't understand it. It is the most valuable asset a business can own, even though it is not on any financial statement.

Owners that know and understand the power of this one secret can generate money whenever they need or want it, can get clients to spend more and more with them on command, and can provide customer service

---

19

way beyond their customer's expectations.

This one asset is something that allows the business to keep running even though the business may have burned down, been ruined by hurricane or many other unforeseen events.

It is SO IMPORTANT that it is covered in detail in its own chapter. But what is it that creates a successful business?

The secret to small business success is... YOUR CLIENT LIST. Before you turn up your nose and quit reading, finish this chapter to understand the real power your client list holds for you. After reading, you can choose to follow your own path. But it will be the longer, more painful path to take.

Example #1

Martha opened up a store in October of this year. The store had makeup, hair accessories and bath products targeted at "tweener" (young people between 6-13 years old) girls. Martha was doing really well when she first  opened, even though the store was only open on Fridays, Saturdays and Sundays. Each weekend, Martha had at least 30-50 girls purchasing products from her store. In April, sales started to slow down. Martha needed to raise some cash quickly to pay her rent.

Martha was running out of cash quickly. After trying everything she could think of, Martha called Susan Johnson, a business consultant she had met at a conference. Susan figured out Martha had seen over 1,100 girls in her store since October.

"One of the fastest ways you can generate cash is to send a postcard to all the girls who had been to the store," suggested Susan. "These girls have been to the store and are familiar with all the great stuff there, they don't get a lot of mail, and if you offer them something special like: "Buy One lip gloss, Get One FREE", there will surely be many that come back into the store." After Susan had finished with her idea, she waited for a response from Martha.

After quite a while without an answer, Susan asked Martha if she liked the idea.

Martha quietly said, "I don't have any of the names."

The harsh reality is, without any customer names built over time, it is very difficult to generate sales whenever you want or need. It is very difficult and expensive to get new customers into your business without any prior relationship. If you start keeping your client list and continue to communicate with them, you will be more successful than you can possibly imagine.

Your most valuable asset in your business is **YOUR CLIENT LIST**. You could have the best employees, the best product, even one that cures cancer, but if you don't have customers, you don't have a business.

IMPORTANCE OF YOUR CLIENT LIST

Why is it important to keep your client list? As you saw above, it can keep you in business in slow times, and without a client list it can rapidly put you out of business. Having a client list gives you power and freedom that struggling business owners don't have and don't understand.

It is important to keep your client list for the following reasons:
1) Cheaper marketing
2) Current customers are more likely to spend again with you

3) You could be even more successful
4) Generate cash when you need it
5) Disservice to your customers if you don't keep it
6) Creates you in the toll-position

Cheaper Marketing

Many studies have been done on marketing to a "cold" (no relationship) and "warm" (established relationship). The "warm" list always outperforms the "cold" list. What does that mean to you?

If you examine a typical direct mail campaign, you will notice that a normal response is less than 1%. So for every 100 you mail, you will get about 1 interested person. But if you mail 100 postcards to your customer list, the response can be anywhere from 5%-50% depending on the offer. If it costs you the same amount to send the 100 postcards no matter who you send them to, then you will make more on your client list compared to the "cold" list. See below:

Your product is $10
You mail 100 postcards at 25 cents each = $25

Cold list return 1% or 1 which results in 1 sale = $10
Your customers list returns 25% which results in 25 sales = $250

The cold list will actually lose money for you:

$10 (for 1 sale) - $25 (postcard cost) = **- $15 Loss**

But mailing to your list generates a profit:

$250 (25 sales at $10 each) - $25 (postcard cost) = **$225 Profit**

As you can see, marketing to your own customer list can be the difference between success and failure to your business. It is much cheaper to market to your customer list than it is to a list of names that do not have a relationship with you and your business.

Clients are more likely to spend with you again

Why would your clients spend with you instead of someone else? When someone does business with you and becomes a customer, they have started to form a relationship with you. As long as you continue to meet their expectations, they will continue to do business with you.

Consumers like to know what to expect when they do business with someone. It is actually "risky" to do business with a new company. Since you have taken away the risk, your customers are more likely to continue to buy from you instead of someone else.

As you learned from the previous example, previous customers will more likely do business with you again and again and again if you give them a chance and a specific reason to come back.

You Could Be Even More Successful

If there was one secret you could learn from this book, it would be, the secret to building a business faster and more profitable than you have dreamed, you need a client list. Every business owner who does not keep this information is "leaving money on the table" every day.

Maybe your business is so successful; you don't think you need to keep your customer's information. But, what you don't realize is that if you continued to market to your customers, you would be making even more money than you are right now. You are actually losing money by not marketing to your list every month.

If you are in a business where you do not have capacity to service any new customers, then you need to increase your prices. You will actually make

---

some room for higher paying customers than the ones you are currently servicing.

Generate Money When You Need It Or Want It

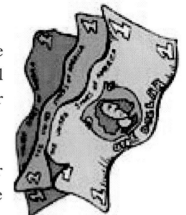

Having a client list gives you control over the business, instead of the business having control over you. It allows you to generate cash whenever you need it or want it.

With a client list, you can send them an offer whenever you want to generate extra cash. Maybe you would like to take a vacation with your family. Send a postcard or email with a special offer for your products or services if you customers act within a certain timeframe. If the offer is good enough, some customers will come forward and will purchase. A large enough customer list and an irresistible offer, will generate income almost every time.

Marketing to your list and not having to rely on bringing in new customers every day gives you the freedom to run the business instead of the business running you.

Disservice To Your Customers

In reality, when you don't market to your customers on a continual basis, you are really doing them and yourself a disservice. Although this may sound confusing, here is a quick story to explain.

There is a yarn shop down the street from Karen's office. Karen is a rookie knitter who only knows one stitch and has made only a couple of scarves. Karen has been into the store a couple of times, but they never ask her for her name, address or email. At this point, Karen couldn't go to a big craft store to buy yarn because once she finishes a project; she doesn't know how to get it off the needles.

Karen enjoys knitting, but doesn't even know what type of project people make after a scarf. All the projects that Karen knows about seem too complicated. So Karen is relying on the small yarn shop to help her. But Karen doesn't really know what questions to ask, so she doesn't ask any.

Little does the yarn shop know that if they send Karen a postcard or email about upcoming classes, new types of yarn, or other projects that one could do, Karen would be back to buy more yarn. But since the yarn store doesn't ask Karen for her contact information, they have no way to contact or find Karen again.

So Karen goes on to a different type of hobby and the yarn shop loses a valuable customer and sales. Karen would have continued to purchase expensive yarns, if the yarn shop would have helped her to enjoy the hobby more.

As you can see, NOT marketing to your customers is doing you and your customers a disservice because regardless of what business you are in, your customer do not know how you can help them further if you don't tell them. You lose sales, they lose the enjoyment of working with you or purchasing products that could make their lives better.

Once a customer has had an enjoyable experience with you, they trust you and would like to do more work with you. But you can't give them that chance if you don't continue to stay in contact with them through your marketing.

Key To Success

Your customer list is your Key To Success. Asking for and keeping your customer's information is the first step to being able to market to them long term. It isn't about the product they purchased today, it is about building a relationship where they will continue to purchase many more products in the future.

Your client list is really your Key To Success in any business.

HOW TO CREATE A CLIENT LIST

But where do you start with a customer list?

If you are still "thinking" about starting a business, you can start creating your client list. Everyone should start by writing down everyone you know personally. Make a list of the following people and their contact information.

- Family
  - Father, mother, in-laws
  - Everyone else – family tree
- Friends
  - Current
  - Past
  - College friends
- Mentors
- People you have done business with
  - Barber
  - Grocer
  - Pharmacy
- Teachers – your own and your children's
- Neighbors – old and current
- Business associates
- People you worked for
- People who worked for you
- People you worked with - colleagues
- Customers for your company
- Vendors for your company
- Consultants for your company
- Contractors for your company
- Professionals that work with your company
- People you worked with in the past
- Person who hired you
- Person who you hired
  - Do this for current jobs and past jobs

You may think that you can do it on your own. You may be able to, but why make it harder on yourself than you have to? The majority of people on your personal list will want to know what you are doing and will want to support you. Don't limit your success by keeping your friends, family and

acquaintances off your list. You never know who they know that could be your first million dollar client or that hard-to-find supplier.

After you have created a list of people you know, you will want to start adding customers who are doing business with you. If you don't have any customers yet, start creating a list of places you could connect with to build your list. Will you focus your clients on a

geographic basis or a demographic (characteristics like income level, gender age etc)?

HOW TO MANAGE ALL THE CLIENT INFORMATION

The first thing you will need is a system to keeping all the client information. This system should be easy to access with the data in a useable format. Basic systems can be started with 3 X 5 index cards or 3-ring or spiral notebooks. The biggest disadvantage with these systems is that it is difficult to print mailing addresses or emails in an electronic format. If you were doing a mailing, you would have to manually write all the names and addresses. If these systems work for you, then start using them. It is more important to start capturing your client's information than what format you keep the data.

If you want to try something more electronic, you could use anything from Microsoft Excel ™, ACT! or an online application. The best online applications for small businesses are email marketing services like Constant Contact (www.constantcontact.com) or Vertical Response

(www.verticalresponse.com). Or if you are a little bigger, SalesForce CRM (www.Salesforce.com) is another great option. ACT! and www.salesforce.com are also Customer Relationship Management (CRM) solutions. CRM is effective for companies that want or need to keep track of discussions with clients over a period of time. With both of these solutions, you can keep track of letters you sent customers and conversations. Many of these programs allow you to perform a mail-merge into a letter or to print labels, so you don't have to write the addresses manually.

If you have someone else keeping the information for you, make sure they understand the importance of gathering client information. Typically the owner understands the importance of gathering the data, but the receptionist at the front desk or sales clerks in your store do not fully understand and therefore do not follow through. Each client you miss will cost you later through lost sales.

The best way to add customers to your list is to make it a weekly goal. Create an incentive program for the staff person who adds the largest number of new client names and/or birthdays in a week.

WHAT INFORMATION SHOULD YOU GATHER

Whenever you are working with customers, you have to determine how much information to gather. The more the better for you, but not always for the customer. Although you may want to collect a lot of information, you may find your customers resistant to giving too much information.

The main reason you want to collect as much as possible is that marketing laws and rules change over time. Here are some examples:

- If you were only collecting consumer names and phone numbers, you lost your marketing in March 2003 when the do-not-call list came in to effect.

- In the business to business market, you could no longer fax without permission as of July 2005.

- Currently there is legislation about sending emails. The Can-Spam Act of 2003, effective January 2004 specifically addresses who you can send commercial emails. If you were collecting only name and email, your marketing would be negatively impacted.

As a basic rule, you should try to gather (but it will be based on your customer's thoughts also):

1) Name
2) Address (street address, city, state, zip, country (on the internet))
3) Email
4) Phone
5) Fax (For Business Clients)
6) Birthday (if you plan to use Birthday marketing)

Any information is better than nothing. Your collection of data should be what you feel comfortable with and how you plan to use the data. What types of marketing will be most effective for you?

WHAT IF CLIENT'S DON'T WANT TO GIVE THEIR INFORMATION?

Many consumers are tired of giving up their information to everyone. It seems that most of the large retail companies have been gathering information from clients and "over-using" the data.

If you find your customers are reluctant to give you their data, you can try a couple of different things.

- First, communicate your plans with them. Explain to them how you plan to communicate with them and how often. Unless you have a very targeted list of over 10,000 names, you probably wouldn't want to be selling or sharing the names with any other company. If you are sending a postcard quarterly or one about an annual sale, you will get more people to sign up. If you are doing a daily email, you will get less people to sign up.

- Second, give them an incentive. In the internet world, there is almost always an incentive. It may be a free, valuable e-newsletter (ezine) or a free report or another bonus gift. In a brick and mortar store, you can also use incentives. One store may use an annual 20%-50% off coupon. It may be advance notice of a huge sale. It may be priority access to an attorney, accountant or consultant. Customers always like something for free and therefore it is a good way to build up your customer list.

Always remember: your customer list is **YOUR MOST VALUABLE ASSET**. Even though bankers and educators don't fully understand the power of this secret, doesn't mean you shouldn't be using it. Having a customer list of people who know you and trust you can accelerate your success. It is much cheaper and more effective to market to this list. The clients will spend more with you over time and will be there whenever you need or want more cash. In reality, not keeping your customer's data and continuing to communicate with them, is doing not only your business a disservice in lost sales, but is a disservice to your customers. They don't know the questions that they need to be asking, so help them.

Finally, keeping the information and what to ask for may be challenges along the way. But try to give your customer comfort by communicating with them how you plan to use the information and perhaps giving them an incentive to help you build your business.

> ### In this chapter you have learned:
> *1. The value of YOUR CLIENT LIST.*
>
> *2. How to start creating a list from your own personal contacts and then build it over time with repeat customers.*
>
> *3. How to use a manual or electronic system to keep the data.*
>
> *4. Name, Address, email are basics.*
>
> *5. How to give an incentive if customers are not leaving information.*

Websites You May Find Useful

Constant Contact – www.constantcontact.com

Vertical Response – www.verticalresponse.com

SalesForce CRM – www.salesforce.com

Step To Success
One Action a Day Will Move You Forward

It is time to move forward. Complete the **Step to Success** Action and feel your progress. No matter where you are going, you can get there one step at a time.

After reading this chapter, take out a clean sheet of paper and a pen and start making your own customer list. Although you may not be able to get this accomplished in one sitting, try to get as many names and contact information down in the next 20 minutes. You will be amazed at how many people you know.

You can do it, so start right NOW!

Chapter 4

Choosing the Right Business for YOU!

"What is it that you like doing? If you don't like it, get out of it, because you'll be lousy at it. You don't have to stay with a job for the rest of your life, because if you don't like it you'll never be successful in it. " Lee Iacocca

What is the most challenging part of running a business? If you ask most entrepreneurs it is about making decisions. There are so many decisions to make in one day that sometimes it gets overwhelming. The biggest challenge in running a business isn't making decisions, it is when you chose NOT to make a decision. The in-decision can cost you more than a decision.

Now is the time to make a decision that will impact you and your business. What path do you follow?

WHICH PATH SHOULD YOU TAKE?

Making the all-important decision to go into business for yourself is only the beginning. Whether running a small operation in your own home or managing a giant corporation being in business involves constant decision-making. Right off the bat, there are decisions you must make just in getting started. And there are many paths. Getting you on the right path is what the rest of the chapter is all about.

WHAT BUSINESS IS RIGHT FOR YOU?

Selecting a business that's right for you really involves two questions:

1.   What **kind** of business to choose?

2.   What **business** opportunity to choose?

At first glance, these two questions may appear very similar. But they are quite different.

What kind of business means: What is the **nature** of your business? What goods or services will you offer? Where and how will your business operate? Small businesses typically fall into one of three types: personal services, retail merchandising, and light manufacturing. And no two businesses are the same; each has its own requirements for capital investment.

What business opportunity is concerned with **how** you are going to get into your particular business? Will you start from scratch? Or will you buy an existing business or franchise?   Where and how will you get the money?

These are questions you don't answer by flipping a coin, or drawing them out of a hat. This chapter will show you how to arrive at the right answers, how to choose the right business, and the right opportunity. You'll see how to arrive at sound decisions logically and systematically, using a proven method of gathering and analyzing data. The techniques you'll learn will help you to continue making sound decisions in your business during the months and years ahead.

CHOOSING THE RIGHT BUSINESS

Choosing a business is one of the most important decisions of your life, yet many people do it by chance or coincidence. Some get lucky and succeed. Some even get rich. Those are the stories you hear about.

But for every lucky break success story, there are hundreds of disillusioned people who've gone broke, or sold out, or are still struggling just

---

33

to make ends meet. Too often, these are people who started the wrong business, in the wrong neighborhood, at the wrong time, in the wrong way.

Too often, the eager entrepreneur chooses a particular kind of business that's right for someone else, but totally wrong for them.

For example, you may have a friend or relative who's making a bundle as an independent sales rep, and so you're tempted to give that a try. But unless you really enjoy meeting people, and enjoy selling, and don't mind traveling, your career as a sales rep would likely fail or be an unhappy struggle at best.

There are four types of commonly accepted businesses including:

1. Retail or Product companies
2. Service companies
3. Combination of retail and service companies
4. Manufacturing companies

Retail companies sell physical products to end-users like consumers or business for their own use. Product companies can either be a retail or wholesale establishment. Examples of retail businesses include stores such as clothing, giftware, hardware, sporting goods, drug stores, or grocery stores. Wholesale establishments such as plumbing supply, electrical supply, or medical equipment.

Service companies are the second type of business. For example, restaurants, dry cleaners, insurance agents, automotive repair, consulting companies and tree trimming firms. These companies offer a service rather than the sale of a specific product or group of products.

Combination companies offer products and service to end users. Examples include landscape and garden centers, computer sales and service, gasoline service stations, import and export companies, and swimming pool companies.

Manufacturing companies includes any type of company that builds a finished product that is ready for sale, or takes a product, adds value to it for resale to another company that may possibly use it in their making of a finished or semi-finished product. Examples of products made by such companies include computer casings, electric motors, plastic components, and construction materials.

One day we were having lunch with a friend, Jane, and it was obvious she was wrestling with some problem. When we asked what the trouble was, Jane replied: "Oh, I've just had it up to here with working for somebody else. I'm tired of company politics, and being controlled and exploited by my boss, and waiting for an annual raise. I've got to get out on my own, start my own business, be my own boss."

When we asked Jane what type of business she was considering, she answered: "Well, I really haven't made up my mind yet. Maybe a pizza place ... or a McDonalds ... or maybe manufacturing of some kind, if I can raise the money. What do you think?"

We could have pointed out that Jane knows nothing about the food business or about manufacturing. But, instead, we thought of a business more suited to his background and interest. You see, Jane is an avid sports "nut." She was an all-around athlete in school and is still active in many sports. For three or four years she's been a volunteer coach in Little League Baseball and PeeWee Football. "How about a sporting goods store?" we suggested. Jane

admitted she hadn't considered that idea, but said it sounded interesting. In a few minutes we had a list of about ten more types of businesses that might be right for Jane. We arrived at our list of possible businesses by discussing Jane's interests, her background and experience, and her skills. We also discussed her personal goals and the kind of life style she envisioned for herself. And whenever we came up with an idea that Jane shrugged off with obvious lack of interest, we immediately discarded it. Our "top ten" were all ideas that Jane could consider with **enthusiasm**.

It's extremely important to select a business that satisfies your personal goals, that suits your life style, and that involves the kind of work you like to do and are good at doing. If you enjoy and find fulfillment in your work, you are much more likely to do an outstanding job. And if you do an outstanding job, you are much more likely to succeed.

Up to now this chapter has dealt mainly with personal qualities and traits, motives, success formulas, and good habits. Consciously or unconsciously, you've been "taking inventory" of your own personal qualities, motives, and mental attitude. You've been sizing yourself up as to whether or not you have what it takes to go into business. We'll assume the answer is definitely **"yes."**

Now we want you to get down to the nitty gritty about "who you are" in a different kind of self inventory. We're going to select the business **that's right for you** based upon who you are and what you are. Our objective is to come up with businesses you're likely to succeed at, and rule out those in which you'd be more likely to fail.

Using the questionnaire below, prepare your own "resume" of experience, hobbies, interests and acquired skills. In a way, you're "hiring yourself" for a career job. So take care that you don't lie to yourself or exaggerate the truth. Be honest and objective.

> * What skills do you have?
> * What knowledge do I have in finance, accounting, marketing, sales, and management?
> * What experience have you acquired that could be applied to your own business?
> * What are your three most satisfying accomplishments?
> * What are your hobbies and interests?
> * What knowledge expertise have you acquired from schools, seminars, and special training?
> * What do I like to do with my time?

- What do others say I am good at?
- Do I have hobbies or interests that are marketable?
- Will I have the support of my family?
- How much time do I have to run a business?

Armed with the information from your resume and the above questionnaire, you now have a good picture of your strengths, your skills, and your acquired knowledge. It should be fairly evident what you can bring to your new business and where your interests lie. Keep this inventory handy, for it will be an important tool in selecting your business. For areas that you do not feel comfortable, find someone who can teach you about those areas.

WHAT DO YOU WANT FROM THE BUSINESS?

It's important to know what you can give to the business. It's equally important to know what you expect the business to give you. You may be thinking, "That's easy". I want independence, wealth, and status. But which of the three is most important to you? How important is personal satisfaction? How about creative expression? And how about the impact your business may have on your family? These considerations, and more, are all important when selecting a business that's right for you.

You'll want to look at both business goals and personal goals. You may find a business goal contradicts a personal goal, and you'll have to make a choice between them, or at least modify one or both. For example, you may list "spend more time with my family" as a personal goal and "build a national franchise operation" as a business goal. Chances are, your business goal of developing your operation nationwide will involve considerable travel and working longer hours. Thus, you would likely be spending less time at home, not more. So you may decide, instead, to develop a local business close to home and perhaps even choose one that gets the family involved in its operations.

WHAT ARE THE BUSINESS POSSIBILITIES?

Now it's time to go shopping. First, we need a shopping list. What are the **kinds** of businesses you might consider? Now, we don't want you to start **evaluating** the possibilities yet, except in a very general way. What we want you to do is come up with a **long** list of businesses you could possibly consider, eliminating only those that are obviously not for you. In other words, rule out the ones that: (a) demand obvious talents or qualifications you don't have; or, (b) ones you would definitely **not** enjoy being associated with.

Where do you look for types of possible business candidates? Here are some of the places you might look:

1. Search the Internet. Search "small business" or "home based business" on www.google.com or www.yahoo.com or other search engine. Two other sites that will give you a wealth of ideas are
   www.frachise.org where you can research all different franchises and www.bizbuysell.com where you can find different businesses for sale.

2. Your telephone yellow pages.

3. Your own neighborhood business community or shopping center.

4. Your public library. Consult Thomas Register, and other business directories. Also, a directory of FRANCHISES is available and may give you some ideas. But remember, you're just looking for **kinds** of businesses at this point, not specific business opportunities.

5. Entrepreneurial magazines, such as "Income Opportunities," "Entrepreneur," "Inc.," "Fortune," "Small Business Opportunities," "Success," "Money" and similar publications. Some of the magazines are only available on the Internet.

---

6. Networking with friends, associates, neighbors, relatives. What businesses are they in? There are also many free networking groups around the country. See if there is one in your area.

7. Inside yourself. You may have an original idea for a business that no one has thought of, or for a product that doesn't exist. But don't limit your thinking only to this new business or product. You want to see how your idea "stacks up" against other possible businesses.

THE CRITERIA RATING SYSTEM

Ever notice how Consumer Reports goes about rating a product? Notice they don't come right out and say a product is excellent, good, fair, or poor and expect you to take their word for it. Instead, they take a systematic approach to rating products by considering certain criteria they feel are important to consumers. They then compare products to each other based on the selected criteria, and allow readers to make evaluations of their own. Readers can select their own criteria the things most important to them and select one product over another accordingly. In other words, Consumer Report researchers recognize that you may give different value points to one feature or another based on what's important to you.

We're recommending that you follow a similar process in selecting the kind of business that's right for you, and apply the process again later in selecting the specific business opportunity for you. You want to find a business that "fits" with you. You don't want to open a coffee shop if you can't get up in the morning. Even if everyone is making lots of money at coffee shops, you will end up hating it and not doing very well. You want to find a business that fits with your personality, family and financial limitations.

GIVING VALUE POINTS TO YOUR CRITERIA

The first thing you should do is take 20 minutes and write down all of your goals. Try to write 50 goals the first time you try this exercise. You should try to get up to 100 goals. After writing down your goals, break them into Personal Goals and Business Goals. With the summary of the things you're looking for in a business; your personal goals, and your business goals, now you can rate these goals in order of importance and assign a point value to them.

Use the following procedure:

1. Reduce your list of personal goals to the top six or less goals, and list them in order of priority.
2. Do the same with your business goals.
3. Divide your lists in half and assign a rating scale to the upper half that is twice the range of the scale applied to the lower half.

For example: Items 1-3, (upper) rate on a scale of 1-6.
                 Items 4-6, (lower) rate on a scale of 1-3.

Personal Goals	Rating
1. Use my creative talent	(1-6)
2. Use My past experience	(1-6)
3. Enjoy my work	(1-6)
4. Meet people	(1-3)
5. Spend more time with my family	(1-3)
6. Get more exercise	(1-3)
Business Goals	**Rating**
1. Limited investment needed	(1-6)
2. Good growth potential	(1-6)
3. Non-seasonal business	(1-6)
4. Total independence of management	(1-3)
5. Minimum government regulation	(1-3)
6.Local outreach	(1-3)

Thus, a number three goal with a four rating (on a scale of one to six) would outweigh a number four goal with a three rating (on a scale of one to three). (See example illustration.)

Using this rating method, higher priority items will usually count for more than lower priority items. You will better appreciate the importance of this distinction when you work out your rating chart and add up the scores.

MAKING YOUR OWN RATING CHART

Following the example in the illustration below, make your own rating chart using the following procedure:

1. In the left column, list the business possibilities you've come up with. There's no limit to the number of businesses you might consider. They can be listed in any order. Don't try to prioritize them.
2. Make vertical columns to the right of your list of businesses, one for each of your personal and business goals. (Maximum of twelve columns.)
3. List your personal and business goals across the top, along with their assigned scale. (one to six or one to three.)
4. Evaluate each of the businesses you've listed according to the criteria you've listed across the chart, rating how they measure up on a scale of either 1-3 or 1-6.   Enter the score in the appropriate box to the right of each business.
5. Add up the points from left to right horizontally after each business listing. Enter the total score in the far right column.
6. Narrow your possible business candidates down to the top five which will be the five that scored the highest totals.

SAMPLE CHART OF GOALS & RATING SCALES

	PERSONAL GOALS							BUSINESS GOALS						
	#1 (1-6)	#2 (1-6)	#3 (1-6)	#4 (1-3)	#5 (1-3)	#6 (1-3)		#1 (1-6)	#2 (1-6)	#3 (1-6)	#4 (1-3)	#5 (1-3)	#6 (1-3)	Total
Business A	5	4	2	3	1	2		6	5	5	3	1	2	39
Business B	6	5	2	2	3	1		5	4	6	2	3	2	40
Business C	2	4	5	2	2	1		3	4	4	2	1	2	32
Business D	6	6	5	3	3	2		5	6	3	3	2	2	46
Business E	3	2	2	2	1	1		4	3	2	2	0	1	23
Business F	4	3	4	2	3	1		4	5	2	2	1	1	32
Business G	5	6	5	3	3	2		6	5	6	3	2	2	48

How did your selections come out? Did you have some surprises? Did you eliminate some that you considered favorites? If you did, take a good look at your list of goals again and the way you prioritized them. Maybe you left some important goals off your list. Or maybe you underestimated the importance of some. If you end up changing your list, or their order of priority, you'll have to go through the rating procedure all over again. It's worth doing until you feel your rating system is accurate, objective, and "feels right."

This type of rating system can help you evaluate different areas of your business. But in the end, you must also listen to your "gut feeling" in addition to the cold, hard facts. There's something mysteriously powerful about our intuition sometimes.

MAKING THE FINAL SELECTION

You may not end up going with the kind of business that scored the highest. You may select number four or five on your list. The rating method is not totally conclusive. But what you have done is eliminated those businesses that only stand a remote chance of being "right" for you when considering your priorities. Now that you have narrowed the possibilities down to five good candidates, you can go about the selection process in more depth. Here's the procedure we recommend in making your final selection:

1. **Talk to people in the same or similar business.** Seek out people who are operating businesses like or similar to the ones you're considering. Most people love to talk about their businesses. Select people outside of the area in which you are considering locating your business. Be frank and honest with them. Let them know you're considering a business similar to theirs and you would value their advice. Usually, these contacts will be flattered and willing to share their experience and advice. Meeting at their place of business is best, unless your presence will inhibit their operation or the activity would not allow for a relaxed conversation. You may want to consider meeting the business owner for lunch or for coffee or dinner after hours. **Note**: While talking with these people, you may conduct some market research. Be sure to come prepared with written questions and take notes of responses.

2.   **Check success and failure reports.** Articles are written each year on small businesses, and most of them list the ones most likely to succeed and those most likely to fail, based on recent data. These articles are usually available at your public library. If you know of businesses like the ones you're considering that have failed, try to contact former officers or employees of the company and inquire about **what happened.**

3.   **Ask professional advice.** There are three professionals you should get to know if you are to succeed, and you might as well start now. The professionals are: Lawyer, Certified Public Accountant (CPA), and Banker. These people work with business owners every day, and have a good knowledge of the ins and outs of most of them. Share your thoughts with them. Tell them what businesses you're considering and why. They will likely point out factors you haven't thought about or share with you specific knowledge about the particular businesses. You'll want to consult these same people later when you come to select your specific business opportunity.

4.   **Share your thoughts with your family, friends, and associates.** Your family members, friends and associates may point out some considerations you never thought about. They may come up with significant thoughts that would discourage you from one idea, or, they may offer real encouragement for pursuing another idea. An added benefit is the comfort you feel in getting others who are close to you involved in your big decision.

5.   **Make the final decision yourself.** If you've followed all the steps faithfully and carefully, and thoroughly investigated the "top five", you've done all that you could to prepare yourself. You have given yourself the benefit of ample data, advice, and knowledge from which to make your decision. The rest is up to you. You're on your own. If, for a specific business type, you can answer yes to all three of the following questions, you're ready to make

a commitment:

1. Does the business satisfy most of my wants and desires? (That is, business selection criteria.)
2. Do I know how to be successful in this type of company?
3. Do I have, or can I develop (or hire), the attributes and capabilities that are required for success in this business?
4. Is the current condition and outlook for this type of business favorable?
5. Am I and my family willing to make sacrifices to achieve business success?

If you can answer yes to all five questions, you're in great shape. But what if the best you can do is two out of three and one maybe? Or, what if all five rate the same? What then? At this point, it boils down to going with your "gut feeling." Remember, there probably is no perfect business. None will suit you exactly; you're going to make some compromises. But if the choice is between remaining a frustrated and unhappy employee, or making a few compromises so you can be in your own business, then you will probably be much happier in the long run if you make the compromises.

When you've made your commitment, you're halfway home. You've finished Step One of the business selection process. Congratulations! Now you can go on to Step Two: Selecting your Specific Business Opportunity.

SELECTING YOUR SPECIFIC BUSINESS OPPORTUNITY

You've selected the kind of business you want to go into. That is, you know what product or service you want to market. But now what?

Basically, you have three options

1. You can buy a franchise business.
2. You can buy an existing business.
3. You can start your own business from scratch.

Each is a different kind of venture. Each has its own advantages and disadvantages, its own risks and rewards, and its own financial requirements so each option will be covered in detail in the new chapters.

ANALYZING YOUR START UP OPPORTUNITIES

Even after thorough investigation of selected business opportunities, using the expert help of your lawyer, banker, and marketing consultant, you may come up with several "good" possible opportunities in your chosen product/business area. How do you decide which one is best for you? We recommend you go right to your list of business goals and personal goals and see which business opportunity satisfies your priorities best. Use the same kind of chart analysis you used to select the kind of business that's right for you. List the possibilities, rate them according to your priorities, and add up the scores. (But don't forget to listen to your "gut feelings" too.)

THE DECISION IS YOURS

In this chapter you have learned how to build a firm foundation for your business venture, how to select the kind of business that's right for you, and the options available to you in business opportunities. There is no single right way of getting into business. Buying an ongoing business is right for some people in some situations. Starting from scratch is right for other people in other situations. We've pointed out the different options you have and **how to go about** selecting what's right for you. But the final decision is yours. The important lesson here is that you take a careful, logical, systematic approach to making your decision, giving yourself the benefit of as much information as you can gather. With the proper information, self-analysis, and the principles you'll learn in this manual, we are confident that you will succeed if you have the desire to succeed.

Here are a couple of other thoughts on how to create a truly successful business:

1. **Know your business inside and out before you start**. The more you learn the better you will be to handle the different decisions that need to be made. Contact anyone that you can think of in the industry to gain more education.

2. **Prepare a Business Plan**. This will help you understand the areas of your business that you may need more help from outside advisors or consultants. If you have trouble creating the financial statements, and this is very important to running a successful business, you will need to take a class or get help from someone to understand financial statements before you jump into your own business. This is a major reason for failure in small businesses.

3. **Manage your money**. Many entrepreneurs lose sight of the cash in the bank account and the amount that they will need to fund upcoming purchases and bills. It always costs more to start a business than most entrepreneurs prepare for.

4. **Understand financial statements.** You can not learn enough about managing money in a small business.

5. **Learn to Manage Your Employees.** Employees will make or break your business. The best way to make them effective is to train them well and make sure they are motivated to help you reach your goals.

6. **Make Your Business Different than the Competition**. In competing with the large companies, try to give better customer service, better quality, better pricing or whatever will make your customers happy.

7. **Keep Your Mind and Body in Shape**. You can not perform at the level you need to on a daily basis if you are constantly run down, drinking too much or too stressed. The decisions you will make will not be in the best interest of the company.

> *In this chapter you have learned:*
>
> 1. *Choosing the RIGHT business for you can be an easy task when you use a process for ruling out businesses that do not "fit" with your personal and business goals.*
> 2. *The final selection of a business is ultimately up to you alone.*

 Websites & Books You May Find Useful

1. **Start Up Nation -**
   http://www.startupnation.com/articles/1179/1/AT_6-Steps-to-Choosing-the-Right-Business.asp
2. **All Business** - http://www.allbusiness.com/business-planning-structures/starting-a-business/1436-1.htmlSalesForce CRM –
3. **Yahoo Small Business** - http://smallbusiness.yahoo.com/r-article-a-57788-m-1-sc-13-choosing_the_right_business-i

 Step To Success
One Action a Day Will Move You Forward

It is time to move forward. Complete the **Step to Success** Action and feel your progress. No matter where you are going, you can get there one step at a time.

As we discussed in this chapter, to find the perfect business for you, you'll want to create your own chart of personal and business goals and business opportunities. If you haven't already done so, start by creating your own list of personal and business goals. Weight them according to their importance to you. Next, make a list of different businesses that interest you. Then test the business options with your own chart of goals and ratings scales.

Then tell us your findings at <u>Mentors@aisb.biz</u> .

Chapter 5

QUICK START GUIDE
7 Days to Your Own Business

"No one lives long enough to learn everything they need to learn starting from scratch. To be successful, we absolutely, positively have to find people who have already paid the price to learn the things that we need to learn to achieve our goals."
- Brian Tracey, Motivational Speaker

In this chapter you are going to learn about what other successful business owners do to jump start their businesses for immediate success. No point in trying to reinvent the wheel, let's just use the techniques that has worked for others.

Why This Chapter Was Added

When people think about starting a business, rarely do they know what they need to do first, second and third. This chapter is for all the struggling entrepreneurs who really want to start a business, but don't know what to do first.

I have been where you are now: reading books about small business. Most of them are written by MBA graduates with more theory than actual down to earth, practical experience. This chapter has been written just for you.

Many times small business is like bungee jumping. Some people think about climbing the ladder to get to the platform and never do it. These are the dreamers. They will always dream and never act. The next group is a form of the dreamer, the one that stands on the platform but never jumps. They are always checking the ropes, the height of the platform, their harness – research, research, research, but still never jump. This group ends up in "Analysis Paralysis".

You are never really in small business until you take a step off that platform and have a few minutes of a scary free fall until you believe with every bone in your body that everything will be fine and you can find any answer you need to be successful.

Our minds control a lot of the success we have. "If you can believe, you can achieve."(Napoleon Hill) Believing is the first hard part.

The smart entrepreneur looks at every situation and tries to figure out how to make the most of it. How can you maximize the use of your limited resources? My small business education has taken over 20 years and tens of thousands of dollars. I want to pass on the short cuts to small business success through this chapter. I truly believe that everyone should have a side business. A job working for someone else is too uncertain in these economic times.

My Assumptions About You

Before we get started, let's talk about you. I have made a few assumptions about you and your small business dreams.

1. I assume you have (or can find) some money to spend, whether it is your own or borrowed. You will need some money, although not much to start any business. If you can not find "some" money, go get a job, until you have some saved up.

2. You have an incredible "burning desire" to be successful in business. This will take shape in many different ways. Starting a business is not all fun and games. There will be times that it looks like you should hang it up. That is why you need a deep desire to succeed. If you make a half-hearted effort, you will only

get marginal results or no results at all.

After the First 7 Days

This is NOT a get rich quick scheme, it is the process any business owner should go through to start a business. After the first 7 days, you will need to continue to market your products and services and continue to grow your business until it fulfills your personal and lifestyle goals. As you continue to grow your business and you have tasted success, you will want to devote as much time as necessary to its on-going success.

Let's get started – your life is about to change forever.

Day 1 - The Right Frame of Mind

Before you get started, let's schedule time out for the next 7 days to work on your business. Take your TV time at night and devote it to your new business. What you miss in reality TV will not help you as much as an hour spent on a new business.

Next, let's get the necessary materials. Get a notebook, either a 3-ring or spiral to keep all your notes.

Let's get started. First you need the right frame of mind. Let's make sure you have "enough" reasons to start a business. Take out a notebook and write at the top of page # 2 "Everything I Want". Leave the first page blank for right now. Then start to list everything that you want to own, everyplace you want to go, everything you want to do that money will allow you to have.

After the first list create a short list of **"Why Am I Really Starting A Business"**.

Next think about what your life is like when you have achieved your business goals. What happens on a day-to-day basis? What do you feel like? How do others treat you differently? Remember those feelings and use them to your advantage. Write them down so you can refer to them again. You will meet your goals. You can do it.

The biggest reason is the same for most people. You want FREEDOM. Financial freedom, time freedom and freedom to make your own choices. Write down the top reason you want to go into business on page 1 in BIG LETTERS. Remind yourself often why you started this journey.

Day 1, Step 2 – Find Customers You WANT To Work With

The first day is a lot of brainstorming and thinking instead of "doing". The first thing you are going to do is to brainstorm different markets or groups of people that you want to service. Let's take, for example, you think you could help the people in your neighborhood or at your church but maybe you don't know how. That's OK, we will talk more about an actual product tomorrow.

We want to think of a group of people that will buy from you. They either know you or have something in common with you. There are also groups that "know" you by association. If you have trouble with this exercise, try thinking of all the groups that you are a part of, like:

1. You have a group at work
2. You have a family and relatives group
3. You have a friends group
4. Maybe you are part of a bowling team or other sport team
5. You may have a church or religious group
6. Maybe a group of small business owners
7. Consider groups by town, state or country
8. Consider different cultural groups
9. Consider groups of income level
10. Same lifestyle groups like 2 kids both parents work, or over 65 years old
11. Consider school groups

Most successful business people would agree on the fact that if you had 2,000 buying customers, you should be able to earn $1 million per year.

So it is very important to keep track of each and every customer you have.

Day 1, Step 3 – Ask the Group

Once you found your group, go and ask them what is their biggest problem. Take out your notebook and keep notes on their comments. This will help you to create a product or service that will fit the needs of your group.

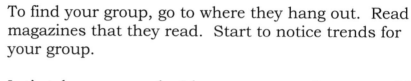

To find your group, go to where they hang out. Read magazines that they read. Start to notice trends for your group.

Let's take an example: I have a community group. My community typically "hangs out" at home at night. So I go door-to-door for a little bit one night and ask them about their biggest problem or service they want to see in your community. Do they want or need any services that are not currently available? If they compared your neighborhood to a perfect neighborhood, what would be different?

The answers that come back may surprise you. Some neighbors may want more communication with each other, some may see a need for a new dry cleaning shop or home delivery of evening meals.

Keeping notes in your notebook to look at later will help when you are searching for product ideas. It is important in this step to realize that the most successful businesses will be the ones that address the wants of their customers. If you start with the customer's wants, you have a better chance at success. It is sometimes much easier to sell something that people WANT versus what they need. We all know we NEED certain things, like a family will, but we don't always prioritize it. If we only bought what we needed there would be no one selling tattoos. Does anyone really NEED a tattoo?

One more example. If my group was African American women between the ages of 18-30 because those are my friends and family. In the 1970's I would have heard about the lack of makeup available for ethnic women. This may have been the start of a very lucrative cosmetic line targeted at this market. These women would have gladly paid for makeup made especially for them and their skin tones. The cosmetic industry has gotten better in more recent years, but they are still behind the times for Asian skin tones and colors.

Day 2, Step 1 – Analyze the Answers

The next part of your journey will be analyze the answers you received and to look for some trends. First try to group the answers into common ideas. For small business clients, the ideas may be around: marketing, money, operations. But there may be other topics that were mentioned like health insurance.

Make a short list of the most common issues that you found in your research.

Day 2, Step 2 – Brainstorm Products or Services

Today is a day that is always fun. Take the most popular item that was on the list yesterday. Relax and ask yourself silently, "How could I solve this problem for my group?" When you relax it allows your mind to use the power of the subconscious.

Let's work with a couple of examples. Maybe on your list was your church group. The most popular issue was fundraising. Everyone wanted to know how to raise more money for mission trips. It is important when you are doing these brainstorming exercises that you do not throw out any ideas no matter what they sound like when the come to you. So, if you relax and think about solution, you may come up with a list like:

1. Special events for church members
2. Special events for non-church members, but community members
3. Creating a marketing campaign to ask community leaders and corporations for donations or money or supplies
4. Creating a product the church could sell to other churches (maybe a book on fundraising ideas)

Sometimes you will think of so many ideas it will amaze you. If you have trouble with this part, create a get together of friends and family. One of the best ways people brainstorm is in groups. Have only your most open-minded friends and family members over for dinner. Before they come to dinner tell them to think of different ideas for your group's most common issue. Be sure to pick only one issue. If you pick more than one idea the conversation may get out of control.

Before dinner, start making a list of everyone's ideas. No idea will be thrown out at this time. You can always throw it out later. Then after dinner, continue with the exercise. This is a really fun way to create product ideas.

Day 3, Step 1 – Analyze Your Product Ideas

Today is the day you let your mind think about all your ideas. You want to look for one that you can get behind 100%. You want to be passionate about the product/service idea. Which ones do you like more than the others? Start by ranking them in order from 1-10.
The top 5 ideas you will research further. Make your final list of the top 3 ideas.

One caution here: **DO NOT** toss out product ideas at this stage. Even if you feel you could never deliver the product or service that you are thinking about, keep it in your notebook. There are so many resources available that you can always find a way to bring the product to the group. The group and its needs are much more important than your ability to create the product.

Day 3, Step 2 – Ask The Group Again

Today is the day that you go back to your group. You want to make sure if you are going to put time, energy and resources into a new business that someone will buy from you.

First you want to reconfirm that the issue you identified is really important to your group. Here is a series of questions you want to ask your group:

1) Is this an important issue to you that you will be willing to pay something for it to solve the problem?
2) How much would you be willing to pay?
3) Where would you expect to find this item?
4) Since you are not using it now, what are you doing to solve the issue?

Tally the results in your notebook and look for the most common answers. This exercise will help you to define pricing, true needs of the group and possible marketing strategies.

Day 4, Step 1 – Back to Day 2 or Forward to Day 4, Step 3

Review your notes from yesterday and see if you need to go back to Day 2 or head on to the next step. If you need to go back, don't get frustrated. Making sure you are identifying the needs of your group will make you more successful sooner rather than later. Spending time on this area is important.

In addition, be sure that your product idea is one that you can be passionate about. That will help you through the tough times that come with every business.

Day 4, Step 2 – Product Specifics Brainstorming

Once you have a good product idea that has been confirmed from your group, it is time to figure out how to deliver the product or service. Again relax and think about all the different ways to deliver your product or service. You have two ways to do this:

1) You create the product or service
    a. Pros of creating:
        i. You control the product
        ii. It's YOUR baby

    b. Cons of creating:
        i. Typically need more money to create product
        ii. Slower to market and positive cash flow
        iii. Need to create marketing materials and process

2) Someone else creates the product or service – You only USE their product or service
    a. Pros of Using:
        i. Faster to market and positive cash flow
        ii. Marketing materials may already be created
        iii. Need less cash and resources to start

    b. Cons of Using:
        i. You do not have control of product features, pricing etc
        ii. Success of your business relies on someone else

There is no right or wrong way of doing business. Both options are very successful business models when used in the right situation with the right partners. In addition, just because you start doing business one way in the beginning does not mean that you are permanently stuck in that way of doing business.

If you have limited resources, start by USING someone else's product or services until you have enough resources to do it on your own. Let's go through some examples:

Let's say, your group talked about the need for a dry cleaner in the community. Starting a dry cleaning business is very expensive. You have the costs of the building, the equipment, employees and much, much more. But, you could always provide a delivery service for your community to a dry cleaner in the next town. You could pick up and drop off. When you have enough money you could always build a dry cleaner in your town.

 In the makeup example from before, you could find a current cosmetic manufacturer that is producing this type of product. Maybe it is overseas in Asia. You could then agree to sell their products in the United States. You would buy the products at a discount and then mark them up when selling to your customers. Depending on your resources, you could sell them door to door or to larger accounts like major department stores. Either way would be USING someone else's product.

In creating your own product, you would need to do more research on the exact costs it will take you to start that type of business. Before you invest thousands of dollars, it may be beneficial to do some more market research with your group before you commit dollars.

Day 4, Step 2 – Research Again

If you are creating a product, start researching everything you need for your product or service. Start creating a business plan for your business to make sure you address all the important issues.

If you are using someone else's product, this is a day to research different vendors that you could use. In your previous examples, you would want to look for dry cleaners. Who has a good reputation? Who does the best work? Who may help you promote your business? Remember in a using relationship, both parties win. You win by making money selling their products and the vendor wins because they sell more without having to hire more employees.

If you are looking at the cosmetic example, you will want to head down to your local library and start searching on the Internet for possible vendors. Once you find them, you need to contact them about selling their products. If you contact a company and said, "I want to help you sell more product", it would be a very foolish company to turn you away. But sometimes businesses are not very smart in marketing and sales. Don't be surprised if you get turned down, just move on to the next possible vendor. Someone will be smart about your offer.

Day 5, Step 1 – Your Client List

Today is the day you start your marketing efforts. Take out your notebook and start making a list of everyone you know.

Use the following categories:
- ❖ Family
- ❖ Friends
- ❖ Neighbors
- ❖ People I Worked With
- ❖ People That Worked for Me
- ❖ Vendors I Know
- ❖ Old Friends from School
- ❖ Groups that I am In (sports, church, etc.)
- ❖ And any others that you can think of.

Be sure to keep the following information on people you know:
- ❖ Name
- ❖ Company they work for
- ❖ Address, City, State, Zip
- ❖ Phone Number
- ❖ Fax Number (for business to business sales)
- ❖ Email (if they have one)

The majority of these people want to support you in your new venture. It will be important to tell them what you are doing at a later time.

Concentrate on making the list of everyone you know.

Now it is time to list everyone that you think would be interested in your product or service that is not on your previous list.

In the previous examples, the delivery for dry cleaning would consist of a geographic area. How could you get the names and addresses of each person? For business to business products, you could use the yellow pages. Time to take another trip to the library. Ask your librarian to help you find the information you need for your group. They have some wonderful resources and would be glad to help.

The larger the list the better as long as the list includes people that will typically buy from you.

Day 5, Step 2 – Unique Selling Proposition (USP)

Today you will focus on your USP. A USP is a statement about you that tells a customer why they should buy from you rather than any other option available to them. Domino's Pizza had great success with their USP: "Hot Pizza in 30 minutes or less, guaranteed." Before Domino's, pizza delivery was so slow that many people received cold pizza for dinner. What is your unique selling proposition? What makes you completely different from every other option available? Why should a customer do business with you? Understanding your unique USP will help you to develop your first marketing message.

Brainstorm many ideas and then decide which one fits your business the best. Focus on the biggest benefit that you bring to your customers.

Day 6 – Setting Up The Business

Step 1 – Naming Your business. Today you will focus on setting up your business. First decide on the name you will be using to conduct business under. Will you use your own name, or an assumed name?

Brainstorm as many ideas as you can. Try for 20 minutes to list all your ideas. If you get writer's block, just keep writing anything such as: blah, blah, blah until your thoughts start again. It is important to keep your pen moving. That will help your mind to keep moving.

Step 2 - Filing Your Name and Business
The next thing you need to do is file your business with the state and federal agencies. First you need to decide what form of business yours will be: sole proprietorship, partnership, LLC or corporation. Consult the LEGAL Chapter and an attorney and accountant for more information in deciding.

Typically you will then need to contact your Secretary of State office for an "Assumed Name" form. This form will need to be filled out and the fee paid (around $40, unless incorporating) before your state will let you do business.

The Secretary of State will send you a confirmation form in the mail.

Next is Tax ID numbers and sales tax numbers. Ask the Secretary of State office which numbers you will need for your business. You can file you Federal Tax ID by phone, mail or Internet.

Step 3 – Setting up your office
Even if you do not have a formal office for your business, you need to set some space aside for your business. This may be a drawer in a desk or even a dresser. Keep a couple of folders in there to keep your information together. Start with simple folders labeled: Sales - Done, Receipts, Orders to be Filled and any other that would be helpful.

Day 6, Step 4 – Estimate Start Up Costs

Make a list of all the items you need to start your business. These are probably one-time expenses only at start-up. Be sure to include computer, new phone installation, Internet costs (if you use it), office supplies, or other equipment (car?) etc.

Have it listed on a piece of paper as follows:

Start-Up Costs
Car (use my own)	$0
Computer	$500
New Phone	$35

If you have a few minutes and are really tight on cash, brainstorm how you could get each item without paying for it. For example, most libraries have computers that you could use for a short while if you needed it. Maybe you know someone that owns a business that would be willing to let you use their office computer at night when they aren't using it. The smart entrepreneur is going to find ways to meet their goals, even if they have to do business a "different" way in the beginning from everyone else. Really think about who has the resources you need and how could you "borrow" them.

 Now it is time to start doing some projections for your business. In all of your responses to group questions, try to determine how much of your product you can sell. One way to do that is take how much people thought they would buy and cut it in half. Some people will tell you they will buy, but then never do.

Estimate how much it will take you to either produce that product or buy that product from your vendor. You should have something like this:

Sales	$500
Expenses	
Cost of product (50%) $250	

Next determine what other monthly expenses you will incur including: phone, fax, Internet access (AOL), supplies, gas etc.

Be sure to add in a dollar amount for marketing. This number is typically 3-5% of your sales. In the above example, the amount for marketing would be $15- 25. It will be important that you spend that each month on

---

59

marketing, because you can never stop marketing. Even if you have too much business you should raise your prices instead of stopping your marketing.

This list becomes your first projection for your business. It tells you what you think you will make. It also gives you a benchmark to achieve on an ongoing basis.

Day 7, Step 1 - Setting Your Price

Pricing can be tricky. You have a choice at this point that you need to decide before pricing your product or service. Do you want to be the highest price option or the lowest priced option? Some considerations in thinking about this choice would be your service level, additional things you can offer that the competition does not, and where you feel comfortable. Most entrepreneurs and typically women entrepreneurs tend to price their products too low. It is important to understand your costs of doing business. Luckily you calculated that above. You need to make sure that you cover all the expenses of the business in your pricing.

Brainstorm some prices and see how the work with your projections. Compare your pricing with what you market research said they would be willing to pay.

Day 7, Step 2 – Marketing – The Offer

Now is the time you start your marketing process. Even if you only have $5, you can market you business, but first you need an offer. What are you going to offer your first customers? Will it be a discount, free delivery with a paid month, or free samples? There are many different types of successful offers. When you determine your basic offer, try to add items that are inexpensive for you to add, but have a high value to the customer. For instance in the dry cleaning example, you could add in a coupon for a discounted car wash from the local car wash. Or how about a restaurant coupon or a small gift?

In our business, at the American Institute of Small Business, we give our clients small gifts like chocolate, cookies or other small goodies. Food items are very well received. There are really endless possibilities where you could offer value, where it does not cost you much.

Day 7, Step 3 – Marketing – The Sales Medium

Now that you have a good, solid, valuable offer, let's chose a sales medium. A sales medium could be anything that gets your message to your customer. Some examples would be flyers, postcards, newspaper advertising, yellow page ads, Internet ads, billboards, telemarketing, or faxing. There are almost too many sales mediums to list. What is easy for you to get in front of your customer? If you had the dry cleaner delivery or a landscaping business, flyers may be the best way to get in front of clients.

The cosmetic business may be best by door-to-door sales. Pick a sales medium to try. Remember to chose one that will be easy and inexpensive to get your message in front of your customers.

Day 7, Step 4 – Marketing – Writing Your First Marketing Piece

Start with a blank piece of paper and start jotting out your marketing piece. Or to get some ideas, start with a marketing piece from your own mail that

caught your attention. Start with your offer. Place it on the page to get the most visibility. Then create a headline for your piece. Think of a compelling reason that your customer should continue to read your marketing piece. This is the same for almost any marketing piece you create.

Finally, create an action step. Tell your customer exactly what you want them to do: Call you, mail you, visit your website.

To get your customers to act more quickly, put in a deadline, a time when the offer will no longer be available. Or you can make the offer only available to the first 25 clients that call.

Review what you have created. Change items as necessary to help it read better or easier.

Don't forget to include information on how your clients can contact you. It is very important. Customers will not go too far to find you to buy your products or services. Make it easy for them.

Day 7, Step 5 – Delivery of Marketing Piece

Send out/deliver your marketing piece to your prospective customers. The next step will separate you from almost all other struggling entrepreneurs. You need to track your responses. To do this, make a chart in your notebook that looks like this:

Description of Piece	How many pieces sent?	How many responded?	How much did it cost me?	How much did I make in sales from piece?

Why do you want to do this? Many small business owners have no idea if their marketing efforts are paying for themselves. I see so many expensive yellow pages ads that never pay for themselves. If they do, the entrepreneur does not know that they do and then cancels the ad because it is so expensive. You need to track your marketing pieces and their effectiveness.

Also make a list of things you would do differently in the next marketing piece. We have learned by trial and error some very valuable mistakes. The first mailing we did was too wide for standard postage. The main post office called us to come re-stamp about 200 letters. What a waste of time and money.

End of Day 7 - CELEBRATE

By this time, you have done market research, set up your business, found a product or service you could offer and sent out the marketing. Very soon, you should have some customers calling you for your product or services. Take some time to recap all of the things you have accomplished over the past 7 Days. You will be successful if you follow this process.

Beyond Day 7

As you continue with your marketing efforts you can purchase business cards to give to people when you meet them. There are thousands of ways to market your new company, but the most important thing is to prioritize the methods that will make you money quickly.

GOOD LUCK!
Tell us about your progress
info@aisb.biz

Chapter 6

Start Right and Start Right NOW!

"You see, in life, lots of people know what to do, but few people actually do what they know. Knowing is not enough! You must take action." - Anthony Robbins

Build a bridge, and then take it

This chapter is about getting you off on the right foot. It's about decisions that have been made up front **before** you actually get into the thick of running your business.

In this chapter you will learn:
1. Characteristics that make up the successful entrepreneur.
2. How to measure your own success potential.
3. How to arm yourself with the tools of success.
4. How to select the business that's right for you.
5. How and where to get the help you need to start and operate your own business.

You may have already selected the kind of business you want to go into. **We urge you to read this chapter anyway.** If you have gone through the selection process properly, this chapter will confirm in your mind that you're off to a good start. Knowing you're off to a good start, that you've done things right, will boost your confidence and help you succeed.

If you have not selected your business opportunity yet, this chapter will show you how to examine your thinking and weigh the many alternatives available to you. Better to pause now than plunge ahead in the wrong direction.

This chapter is probably the most important one in the manual, because it is concerned with getting you started in the right direction. Take your time. Do all the exercises and quizzes. This is one of your first giant steps on the road to success.

Fasten your seatbelts and hang on, because you're about to start on one of the most exciting journeys available in life. Your destination is a business of your own.

There is a special brand of opportunist known as the Entrepreneur or, the Small Businessperson. A dictionary definition of an entrepreneur is "one who manages, organizes and assumes the risk of a business or enterprise." The entrepreneur represents freedom: freedom from the boss, freedom from

the time clock and - with some strategic work and a little luck - freedom from the bank.

Now, if America is the land of the free and the home of the brave, too few of us are brave enough to venture out on the road to freedom. But, those of us who have ventured, very few of us would choose to go back.

The road to success in small business ownership is full of potholes, bumps, and pitfalls. But if you have the motivation and the will to succeed, you're off to a good start. This manual, written by fellow entrepreneurs **who have achieved success**, will give you the information you need to plot your own course for success. You'll understand how and why things happen ... and how to apply that knowledge to ANY business you choose.

PREPARING FOR THE JOURNEY

Most people spend more time planning a vacation than they do planning their lives. Many float aimlessly through life, taking its ups and downs as they come, getting by, living from day to day. If they become even moderately successful, or even comfortable, it's more by accident than by plan.

Achieving success in small business, however, is not a matter left to luck or chance. You may know of successful entrepreneurs who were "lucky" or "in the right place at the right time" -- but it's not something you can count on, nor will luck or good timing carry you through years of operating a business successfully.

You wouldn't think of starting out on a vacation trip without knowing where you're going, how you're going to get there, and having adequate money and provisions to see you through to your destination. In other words, you must **plan and prepare** for your journey.

That's what this chapter is all about. You select your destination; but we help you make the choices. You plot your own course, but we show you how to avoid the dead ends, the rough roads, and obstacles in your way. In short, we show you how to get there successfully.

PROFILE OF AN ENTREPRENEUR

American entrepreneurs number in the millions. Of the approximately 20,000,000 small businesses in this country, more than 12,000,000 are operated as sole proprietorships - in other words, "entrepreneurs in the business for themselves."

So, who are these people we call entrepreneurs? While there are no absolutes, there are some general observations you can make about entrepreneurs:

1. **We love to make money.** With some, it's the things that money can buy. With others, money is just a way of measuring success.

2. **We have bigger dreams than other people.** We challenge ourselves to do more because we want more. More of the money, freedom and status that accompany entrepreneurship.

3. **We are very success oriented.** We have a need ... sometimes a burning desire ... to succeed. We need to prove ourselves to everyone who knows us, to our families, and to our toughest critics ... ourselves.

4. **We work smarter than most people.** Some of us even think working eighteen hours a day is fun. We don't mind putting in extra effort when we get to reap the rewards. What we don't like is working hard so someone else can reap the rewards. Maybe that's why - as a group - we don't like working for other people.

5. **We are better at something than most people.** Some of us have great artistic talent; some are brilliant marketers. Many of us have a natural gift for organizing; most are born leaders. We all have something extra that helps us succeed. And we're smart enough to make the most of it.

6. **We look at risks differently than most folks.** We understand the basic risk and reward ratio of life: the greater the risks, the greater the

rewards. In other words, no guts, no glory. We can't win if we're not in the game. But, it's not just rolling the dice. Our risks are almost always carefully calculated, and supported by confidence and belief in ourselves. We reduce the risk by knowing what we're doing.

7. **We are proud.** Proud of our abilities and our achievements. Our success proves to us that we are not average or mediocre. Success gives us great satisfaction - and pride!

1. **We respond to challenges in a positive way and learn from our mistakes.** We never give up! Challenges are exciting and we feel the need to conquer them.

9. **High Level of Integrity.** Entrepreneurs know that every person holds a success key for the future. Treating people like they were your biggest client can dramatically influence your business. The billionaire Oprah Winfrey says it best, "Real integrity is doing the right thing, knowing that nobody's going to know whether you did it or not."

Joseph Mancuso, President of The Center for Entrepreneurial Management, in a recent survey, came up with the following additional common traits and profiles or successful entrepreneurs:

1. **One or both parents were self-employed.** The child who grows up in a home where at least one parent is self-employed is more likely to try his hand at his own business than children of salaried parents.

2. **They have been fired one or more times.** The entrepreneur's brashness and almost compulsive need to be right often leads to dismissal, usually by a superior who wants less conflict and/or less competition. But, this need to be right often turns rejection into courage and courage into authority.

3. **They were in business at a young age.** Mowing lawns, shoveling snow, or peddling papers - the enterprising adult first appears as the

enterprising child. Michael Dell and Oprah Winfrey had businesses before the age of 12. Learning business concepts when they are young, give these entrepreneurs a huge advantage.

4. **They are in their 30s or in their 60s.** The age range is down from the late 1950's and early 1960's, when it was found to be between 40 and 45. The younger generation seems to be doing almost everything sooner. There is a movement for older, partially retired individuals to start businesses.

5. **They are usually the oldest children in a family.** Perhaps it has something to do with being a leader rather than a follower.

6. **The majority are married.** A spouse can be an asset by providing support, encouragement, love and a possible second income. Also, bankers and venture capitalists look more favorably on entrepreneurs who are married because they regard it as a sign of stability and commitment. Fair or not, that's the way it is.

7. **Most have a bachelor's degree,** and the trend seems headed toward the M.B.A. Few entrepreneurs have the time or the patience to earn a doctorate.

8. **They are very sociable people,** and more often than not, charming as well. Which better equips them to charm the right banker or supplier and get what they want.

9. **They are super-organized.** Organizational methods and systems may differ, but you'll never find a successful entrepreneur without one.

10. **They are highly competitive.** Entrepreneurs tend to be participants,

not observers; players, not fans. They like challenge, and they like to win. The greater the challenge, the more glorious the victory.

HOW DO YOU MEASURE UP?

After reading the profiles of entrepreneurs described above, how do you stack up against them? If you can say "Yes, that's me", then you're feeling pretty good right now. But, if your profile is vastly different from the people we've described - don't let it get you down. There is no absolute profile of the successful business owner, it only means that you may have to balance it with other strengths, or that you may need the help of others who have certain talents that you lack. The most important factor in success is the reason you are going into business and your level of desire to succeed. If it is high enough, you will not fail.

Many high achievers become entrepreneurs, but it is not a requirement by any means. Most people have a good amount of hidden entrepreneurial instincts in them - and most people want to make a lot of money, too. What you do with what you have will make the difference.

Take the following Entrepreneur's Test:

	ALWAYS	SOMETIMES	NEVER
I am persistent.			
When I like a project I am working on, I tend to sleep less and lose track of time.			
I have clear, written goals.			
When I make a mistake, I can learn from it.			
I achieve my goals when I create them.			
I want to succeed above everything else.			
I am creative and have new ideas.			
I can find a path to solve a problem.			
I am interested in how things work.			
I am insightful.			
I can always find a solution to a problem.			
I see problems as opportunities & challenges.			
I take calculated risks.			

I don't need all the answers before I start. I will find them.			
I like learning about things I don't know about.			
I can continue after setbacks.			
I believe in myself and my abilities.			
I'm a positive person.			
I experiment until I find a solution.			
I'm willing to endure hardships for possible long term rewards.			
I usually do things my own way.			
I tend to question authority.			
I often enjoy working by myself.			
I like to control things around me.			
I can be stubborn.			
Totals			
	X 3	X 2	X 1
Total Score			

Multiply the number of times you chose column one, by 3 to get your first column total. Then do the same for column 2 and 3. Then add your three columns together to get your final score. If you scored between:

60-75   You should start your business. You have the traits of a successful small business owner.

48-59   You have the potential, but you need to keep yourself focused and on task. You may want to take some classes to improve your skills in your weaker areas or look to hire someone with these skills.

37-47   You may not want to start a business by yourself. Look for someone who has skills that would complement your knowledge.

Below 37   Small business is very challenging and may not be for you at this time. Work toward getting some experience that your don't currently have and learning more about how small businesses succeed.

MOTIVATION - THE FUEL THAT KEEPS YOU GOING

 You may have just recently **discovered** that you have the clear-cut desires and ambitions to succeed as an independent business owner. But, the personality trait or inspiration may well have begun when you were a child. That doesn't necessarily mean that you've wasted all the years in between. Everything seems to happen for a reason, and chances are you'll find a way to apply all the experiences and lessons of the past years.

What's important now is to recognize that, today, you **have** the motivation to start your own business and to succeed. Hang on to that determination that you're feeling now and use it to keep you going through the anxieties and tough times that may come your way. If you have a **good** reason for wanting the life of the entrepreneur today, it will be a good reason tomorrow, next week, next year, five years from now. It may be a time-worn cliché, but **the power of positive thinking really works!**

> An entrepreneur is the kind of person who will work 16 hours a day just to avoid having to work 8 hours a day for someone else.
>   -Anonymous

WHY PEOPLE GO INTO BUSINESS

You may have decided to start your own business after an external event triggered your entrepreneurial abilities. The event may have been a very positive occurrence, such as inheriting a family business from an uncle. Or, it could be a traumatic event, such as being fired or laid-off. In either case, you should look upon what has happened as an opportunity. Seize it, and make the most of it. This may well be the most significant time in your life.

There are many reasons why people go into business for themselves. But, they usually fall into one of two categories: concrete **practical** or abstract **personal**.

2009 © Copyright of the American Institute of Small Business

Some of the **concrete, practical** reasons include:

1. To make a living and/or get rich.
2. To prepare for retirement. That is "something to do" in retirement, or to provide additional income, or both.
3. For supplemental income and equity building, such as in real estate.
4. To use as a tax shelter or business write-off.
5. To have something to occupy spare time. To relieve boredom.
6. To create a common cause for the whole family, thereby building togetherness.

Some of the **abstract, personal** reasons include:

1. Freedom & Flexibility – The New American Dream is not to work more hours. The New American Dream is to make more, play more while working less. Small Business gives you financial freedom, time freedom and the flexibility to spend time with people and places you chose.

2. For emotional rewards; a realization of self worth self-image, seeing your creativity develop and expand.

3. To escape working for someone else.

4. To have flexible working hours - the freedom to do what you please, when you please.

5. To stop having to take orders.

It's important that you go into business with your eyes open and not kid yourself. Emotional rewards are certainly worthwhile motives, but you should understand that they sometimes are a long time in coming. The emotional rewards are worth working towards, but don't expect them right away.

Working for yourself, instead of someone else, may be a welcome change for you. But be prepared for challenges. In some businesses, it means doing what your employees don't get done, which may mean working on nights and weekends.

If you never want to take orders again, then you'll need a business that doesn't involve serving customers. Because customers tell you what they want, and if they don't get it they don't do business with you. So be prepared to jump through hoops just to keep your customers happy so you can stay in business.

EXAMINE YOUR OWN MOTIVES

It's important that you examine your own motives for going into business. Identify them. Make your desires part of your goal plan. But be sure they're realistic. You want to avoid setting yourself up for a letdown early in the game. If you expect too much or expect something not easily attainable, you only run the risk of early discouragement.

Going into business is a lot like going into marriage. If you do it for the wrong reason, or with unreal expectations, you increase the chances that it won't survive. Marrying because of superficial physical attraction, or because it's "convenient," or because one person has a lot of money, practically guarantees failure.

Like marriage, a business needs a firm foundation, realistic expectations, and a total commitment in order to succeed.

WHEN TO START A BUSINESS

When to start

Since the middle of 2008, the United States has been in a recession. Many people are concerned about starting a business in this economic time. In reality, the best time to start a business may be in a recession. The theory is, if you can make it now, you can make it when times get better.

Seth Godin, known as America's Greatest Marketer (www.sethgodin.com) is the author of many best-selling marketing books and founder of numerous businesses says the best time to start a business is when:

- **The best time to start** is when you've got enough money in the bank to support all contingencies.
- **The best time to start** is when the competition is far behind in technology, sophistication and market acceptance.
- **The best time to start** is when the competition isn't *too far* behind, because then you'll spend too long educating the market.
- **The best time to start** is when everything at home is stable and you can really focus.
- **The best time to start** is when you're out of debt.
- **The best time to start** is when no one is already working on your idea.
- **The best time to start** is when your patent comes through.
- **The best time to start** is after you've got all your VC funding.
- **The best time to start** is when the political environment is more friendly than it is now.
- **The best time to start** is after you've got your degree.
- **The best time to start** is after you've worked all the kinks out of your plan.
- **The best time to start** is when you're sure it's going to work.
- **The best time to start** is after you've hired the key marketing person for the new division.
- **The best time to start** was last year. The best opportunities are already gone.
- **The best time to start** is before some pundit declares your segment passe. Too late.
- **The best time to start** is when the new generation of processors is shipping.
- **The best time to start** is when the geopolitical environment settles down.

Actually, as you've probably guessed, **the best time to start** was last year. The second best time to start is *right now.*

No matter what you are feeling right now, whether it is fear of success or fear of failure, it is time to start a business RIGHT NOW! The updates to this book are being done during one of the most challenging economic times since the great depression. Just as many people created successful business in the Depression, the time is now to create your business.

WHY DO BUSINESSES FAIL?

Businesses, like marriages, fail for many different reasons. But generally, most of them are related to going into business **unprepared**. Or, put another way, usually a case of **not enough of something.** Not enough money, not enough skill, not enough experience or just plain not enough planning before starting. Many business owners underestimate the difficulty of starting a business. But with patience and hard work and the right planning, most anyone can start a business.

A recent survey of why businesses fail lists the following reasons:

- The owner doesn't see themselves as the main salesperson.
- Lack of experience
- They start with too little money.
- Their industry or market is dying.
- They don't understand their customers' needs.
- They don't know their product.
- They merchandise poorly.
- They merchandise the wrong products.
- They're poorly managed (accounting and personnel are the most common trouble areas).
- Their inventory is out-of-date.
- They don't know their true costs of selling a particular product.
- Their businesses grew too fast to control.
- Poor locations.

You have already taken perhaps one of the smartest steps to avoid all the problems people will warn you about: you have recognized the need for this manual, to teach you what you need to know. Together, we will build a well-thought out, carefully constructed plan for your business.

Businesses do fail, but there is no reason why you should fail if you know what you're doing. **Success will come through knowledge, proper preparation, and perseverance.**

If you want to see a future successful entrepreneur, look at yourself in the mirror. Know thyself and be honest about your true needs and desires. Unless you genuinely feel a deep motivation to go into business for yourself, you are better off doing something else. But if you want the life of the successful business owner, we'll help you prepare so that you will not fail.

WHAT MAKES A SUCCESSFUL ENTREPRENEUR?

One of the "formulas for success" is the 5 D's that makes an entrepreneur successful.

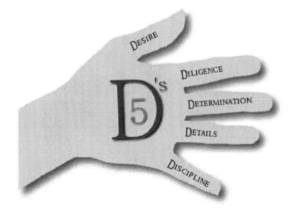

The Five D's are:

- Desire
- Diligence
- Details
- Discipline
- Determination

Without these five qualities, the entrepreneur is not going to reach his full potential.

Desire is the carrot out in front of you. Desire is the vision that burns in the heart of the entrepreneur. If your desire is strong enough, it will point you toward success and provide the fuel to get you there. Desire is the vision that you see in your mind about what life is like when you have achieved your small business dream.

Diligence is making the most of your opportunities and options. It's developing your strengths and overcoming any lack of skill, education, space, or money. You learn what you need to learn, do what you have to do, to get the job done. This takes diligence.

Details, especially focusing on details, is a special skill of most entrepreneurs, who are usually excellent organizers. Some can do it with a simple "To Do" list on their desk. Others employ a battery of computers and electronic or paper organizers. Organizational systems may differ, but you'll never find a truly successful entrepreneur without one.

Discipline is the sister of detail because it's hard to have one without the other. One of the nation's most successful salesmen attributed his success to doing the things that other salesmen don't want to do in other words, doing things that are difficult, or uncomfortable, or that require some sacrifice. Your success will require that you discipline yourself to do the tasks you'll be tempted to put off or avoid altogether.

Determination is closely related to Desire and Diligence. But it's more than the two combined. Determination is what keeps you going when the going gets tough. Determination is a measure of your character. It's seeing your dreams through to completion and not letting others get you down.

The entrepreneur-in-motion is a joy to watch. He exploits the products and services he offers. He is unrelenting in his attack. He goes after the exposure he needs. He builds bridges between clients, suppliers, business contacts and other entrepreneurs.

The entrepreneur also trains himself for success by getting into everyday success-oriented habits:

1. Get to bed early, get to work early, and keep yourself physically fit and mentally alert. Ben Franklin was right!
2. Manage your personal finances properly. Keep accurate checking and savings account balances.
3. Dress to do business. Keep a neat appearance; you never know when you're going to meet a customer.
4. Keep your appointments and always be on time.
5. Call everyone you say you are going to call; keep all other promises, too.
6. Strive to be happy in your work and friendly, fair and honest in your personal and business dealings. Running your own business is a highly personal matter, and people will judge your business by how you conduct yourself.
7. Learn to love your hard work and achieve your goals.
8. Set goals and create a plan to achieve them.

You learn these habits through practice; you go over them in your mind and imagine yourself becoming better and better. Whatever you do, work them into your system in such a way that they become second nature to you.

Making money is only part of the success formula. Feeling good about your business is part of it, too. At the beginning, that may be all you have. In the end, it is not enough to sustain you and your family, but if you believe you will succeed, you stand a good chance of making it happen.

DRAWBACKS OF SMALL BUSINESS OWNERSHIP

Along with the opportunity to gain control of your destiny, to make a difference in a cause that is important, to reach your full potential, to reap unlimited profits, to contribute to society and be recognized for your efforts, and to do what you enjoy, there are some disadvantages of small business ownership. These include:

1. **Unknown Income** – Owning a small business is no guarantee that you will earn millions of dollars in the next year. To reach your financial goals, careful planning is necessary.

2. **Risk of Losing Your Own Money** - Almost every financing source will require you to put money in for initial costs. Your initial money shows them that you are serious enough to invest in yourself and that you have something to lose if the business is not run well.

3. **Long Hours and Hard Work** – Most small business owners will agree that they put in more time than they ever did working for someone else. The work is also more difficult with many more decisions to be made. You may even have to clean the bathrooms.

4. **Changed Life** – Because ownership takes longer hours and more work, many of the typical duties with being a mother, father, wife or husband get put on the "back burner" until the business gets started.

5. **Higher Levels of Stress** – The higher stress level comes from longer hours, harder work and your new work lifestyle. These can all take a toll on your mental attitude and your physical well-being.

6. **Complete Responsibility** – This is also an advantage. But with complete responsibility comes more pressure to make decisions faster and with less information.

In this chapter you have discovered the advantages and disadvantages of owning your own business. If you are still reading, you now need to decide the best type of business for you which will be discussed in the next chapter.

> ### In this chapter you have learned:
>
> 1. *Entrepreneurs come in all shapes and sizes but most have an overriding desire to make lots of money.*
> 2. *People go into business for a variety of reasons including practical and personal reasons. Understanding your own reasons for starting a business is very, very important for the success of your business.*
> 3. *Advantages & disadvantages to owning your own business.*

Websites & Books You May Find Useful

Here are some Entrepreneur Quizzes to see if you have what it takes to be an entrepreneur. If you get a low score on any of them AND you believe them that you will not be successful, then you are not ready to start your own business. You need to have enough passion to follow your dream no matter what anyone says. Most successful entrepreneurs know that the skills, passion and idea can not be measured through a standard test.
Georgia State University - http://www2.gsu.edu/~wwwsbp/entrepre.htm
CNN -
http://www.cnn.com/2009/LIVING/worklife/01/07/entrepreneur.quiz/
Forbes Magazine - http://www.forbes.com/fdc/welcome_mjx.shtml

Step To Success
One Action a Day Will Move You Forward

It is time to move forward. Complete the **Step to Success** Action and feel your progress. No matter where you are going, you can get there one step at a time.

Time to take another step forward. Take out a sheet of paper and write down all the reasons you want to do this. Write as many as you can in the next 10 minutes and then take a break for 5 minutes and then write some more.

Chapter 7

How to Legally Set Up Your Business

"The future depends on what we do in the present."
   --Mahatma Gandhi (1869-1948) Indian political and spiritual leader

This chapter is by no means meant to give any legal advice. Be sure to always contact a competent attorney for all legal questions.

What you need to know about your business and the law

Business people are often overwhelmed by all the decisions that have to be made in so many unfamiliar areas of business operation. Even the simplest one-person operation eventually comes up against the need for informed, intelligent help. An individual's judgment, personal experience and the advice from counselors and professional consultants, especially lawyers.

One thing is certain; sooner or later, the day will come when a lawyer will be needed; to help set up the structure of the business, to legally protect your ideas, prepare contracts or defend against legal actions.

Chances are, at the beginning, you will be dealing with a small one or two person law firm. The good news is that computer technology has made it possible for the smallest firms to put out the same quality product as any large firm. A small firm, at its best, offers flexibility and closer one-on-one contact with clients at a cost more small businesses can afford.

You have plenty of choices. There are a lot of lawyers out there – over one million in the United States, and it is expected to increase over the next few years.

This chapter is not intended to replace your lawyer. Don't mistake it for that. But you will find that after you have read and understood this chapter you will be more confident about talking to a lawyer and asking the right questions or raising the right objections if some of his or her explanations seem like Greek to you. As an independent business person, you should know there is no mystery in our legal and fiscal system. You can make it work for you.

In this chapter you will learn:

1. *How to make an intelligent choice in picking the right form of business (sole proprietorship, partnership, corporation or limited liability company); how to evaluate different forms of organizing your business.*
2. *How to come up with a successful name for your business; and how to protect it.*
3. *How to act responsibly as an employer.*
4. *What to watch out for when you think buying a business is better than building one.*
5. *What to watch out for when you have to deal with corporate landlords.*
6. *How to choose a lawyer.*
7. *How to maintain a solid working relationship with your lawyer.*

SELECTING AN APPROPRIATE FORM FOR YOUR BUSINESS

General Considerations

Making a choice as to the legal form of your business involves choosing to protect your personal assets and, in most cases, enhance your personal wealth by selecting tax efficient methods of withdrawing capital from an enterprise. A choice has to be made though. The absence of choice is, in and of itself, a choice to conduct your business as a sole proprietor or partnership (if you are in business with someone else who ignores the decision). As you will see, sole proprietorship and partnership forms are not particularly efficient form an asset protection view. Unless you are judgment proof, you expose your personal assets to liability. While there are some opportunities to efficiently enhance your wealth as a sole proprietor or partnership, they are normally outweighed by the tremendous exposure to liability.

Before we go into the details, let's look at the most basic questions to ask before you start:

- To what extent are you personally able and your family willing to be responsible for business debts and losses?
- Are you judgment proof or do you have assets that exceed your state's asset exemption laws?
- How much profit do you expect to make –the more profitable the more issues there are with the withdrawing the profits with tax efficiency?
- Will you be employing family members?
- Are you in a profession where liability can't be shielded?
- How likely is someone to assert a claim?
- How important is the ability to deduct your health insurance or other fringe benefits?

Sole Proprietorship

The oldest and simplest form of business entity is called "sole proprietorship". Under this framework no other owners or partners are involved. At any time you can transfer funds into or out of the business from your personal assets. It is all yours, the good and the bad. In legal terms, you and the business are identical.

Setting up legally is very simple; you start conducting business in your own name. If you want to conduct business under something other than your own name, usually it's a matter of getting a DBA ("doing business as") or similar form from the state. The advantages and disadvantages are considerable. A sole proprietorship involves the least amount of bureaucratic red tape; it is the least expensive arrangement to set up your business initially and needs the least amount of paperwork to get started. Its simplicity and convenience make this the usual form for the small business at inception. Sometimes you also need (or may want) to file an assumed name and to obtain a license. Both of these formalities are very easy to take care of.

Other advantages to a sole proprietorship are:

1. First and foremost, you alone are the boss. You make the decisions. No one is second guessing you or vetoing your decisions.
2. In a sole proprietorship, you have the opportunity to reflect your personality in the business. You can mold it in any manner you wish.
3. Filing federal and state income tax returns, bookkeeping, and accounting can be quite simple. No fancy accounting is necessary. You simply keep track of your expenses and deduct them from your sales to determine your profit and/or loss. All one needs for filing with your Federal Tax return is an IRS Schedule "C".
4. In the event that you may want to close down the company, it is a relatively easy thing to do with no partners or shareholders to be concerned about.
5. You have the opportunity to set up a simple retirement arrangement such as a Simple IRA or a Keogh Plan.
6. You can pay your immediate family wages without paying a FICA or other wage withholding obligations. This can amount to a 15.3% benefit.
7. You can initiate a Medical Expense Reimbursement Plan, employ your spouse and deduct expenses.
8. Sole proprietors who employ their spouse and the spouse elects

family coverage can also deduct health insurance.

However, if you are planning to expand, the sole proprietorship can lead to problems. The biggest disadvantage is that you also have <u>unlimited personal liability</u>.

Since there is no firm separation between your business and your personal assets, business liabilities are completely yours. Creditors can take your personal assets, including the equity in your house which exceeds your state's homestead exemption, as well as non-exempt equity in your car. Creditors can garnish or levy upon your car or bank account if the company's funds are inadequate to pay them and if they have a judgment. Since you, as the owner, are personally subject to unlimited liability for the company's obligations, you will probably want to use sole proprietorship only if you intend to operate very conservatively.

Sometimes even the most conservative person can get into trouble, consider the following:

> Your planning was good, the advice you got was excellent. You start your retail business by shelling out about $25,000 for leasing space, ordering supplies and merchandise, and so on. Before you really get started there happens to be an economic down turn in the economy and people (your prospective customers) stop spending disposable income. There has not been any substantial business income to pay the bills. Now you are personally stuck. Your creditors want cash, no returns. You have to sell to a liquidator (if you can find one) at a substantial loss. Beyond your business, you may lose your personal bank account, your car, maybe your home!

Another equally scary scenario: Your employee engages in inappropriate conduct leading another employee to claim sexual harassment. The victim sues for lost wages. You are not adequately insured (many business policies now exclude sexual harassment coverage unless specifically included).

And there are more specific disadvantages. The income of a sole proprietorship is taxed when it is earned and it is all considered wages, even if you have a substantial investment in the business. Wages are subject to 15.3% self-employment tax. This is generally the case, even if the income is really a return on investment from the assets you placed into service. You also get taxed, even if you do not withdraw the profits from the business. There are no retained earnings for a sole proprietorship. If your income increases you become a candidate for a higher tax bracket. If you need to withdraw money to satisfy the tax payments, those earnings will not be available to the business for expansion.

Also, as a sole proprietor, you don't qualify for tax advantages which corporations get when you offer fringe benefits, such as insurance programs and some medical reimbursement plans.

General Partnership

Formerly, a very popular method of operating a business, especially service based professional organizations, has now been largely replaced with the limited liability company and limited liability partnership.

Perhaps the single best feature of a partnership is the ability to distribute partnership assets (as with a sole proprietorship) to the owner without creating tax consequences. For example, if the partnership acquires an interest in a condominium in

Florida, rents that condominium over the course of 20 years and then decides to make personal use of the condominium in retirement, unlike a corporation, the distribution results in no tax consequences.

Most states have adopted what is called the Uniform Partnership Act ("UPA"). It defines a partnership as "an association of two or more persons to carry on as co-owners a business for profit". <u>No legal contract between the partners is required since the UPA will supplement the disputed terms of the relationship</u>. Needless to say, you would be wise to have one anyway. You and your partner(s) can define your relationship just about any way you wish. The partnership agreement stipulates how much capital is contributed by each partner, what duties each will perform and how the profits will be distributed.

In a partnership each partner "acts as the agent" of all the other partners. Each one can "bind the partnership". This means no matter whether Jill, your childhood friend and business partner, signs a $500 or a $500,000 contract on behalf of the partnership, each partner has unlimited liability for the company's obligations. It does not matter whether or not you had given prior consent. Again, as with a sole proprietorship, you have personal liability exposure. This time though, the exposure is magnified by your partner's conduct. On the other hand, no one can join the partnership without the permission of all the other partners.

Partnerships don't have to be 50-50 deals. For instance, you may have ten slices of the cake and leave just two or three for your companion. Or, if you are bold, you may even consider your mother-in-law as a third partner.

An important consideration in a partnership is that each partner is entitled to full information, regardless of subject, about the affairs that concern the partnership. The partners are bound by a "fiduciary" relationship. Each partner owes the other the highest possible duty of good faith, loyalty and fairness. The notion of "conflict of interest" becomes quite important: Your partner Jill could not run a competing business as a sole proprietor without your consent.

In many respects, a partnership is not much different from a sole proprietorship. Your personal assets are in jeopardy, in addition to any assets of the partnership. Also, death has a critical impact. Legally, a partnership dissolves upon the death or withdrawal of any partner; thus, its duration is uncertain. As far as taxes are concerned, a partnership cannot take advantage of planning flexibility and fringe benefits offered by a C corporation. It does not pay any income taxes. But don't jump to premature conclusions: Profits or losses have to be reported, along with information that determines each partner's share. Now each partner is taxed on his or her share (along with income from other sources), whether or not the money was actually distributed during the year.   Payroll withholding taxes are owed on the partner's share of profits.

Because of the risks involved, partnerships now are rare between natural persons. There are far more efficient methods of operating a business than in a partnership. You should exert your energies on finding the appropriate entity to form rather than operating as a partnership.

Limited Partnership

Under this type of agreement, the **limited** partners share in the partnership's liabilities only up to the amount of their investment in the limited partnership. There must be one "general" partner and at least one "limited" partner. The general partner is exposed to all the liabilities of the limited partnership. In contrast, a limited partner is more like a stockholder. The limited partner does not have unlimited personal liability. Limited partners are only responsible for the amount of money they paid into the business. Normally the limited partners do not participate in day-to-day activities of the business. If a limited partner participates in the day-to-day activities, he or she may lose the limited liability status they enjoy. The death or withdrawal of a limited partner has little impact on the survival of the partnership as a legal entity.

While this may sound like a perfect solution for your business ambitions, there is a catch. A limited partner faces no restriction if she wants to sell her partnership interest to somebody else. No consent by the other partners is typically necessary. Since limited partnerships can accommodate many interests, objectives, different characters and personal backgrounds, state legislatures keep a special eye on this form of business. If you are selling stock to a limited partner, you may have to file special forms with the Securities and Exchange Commission. Be sure to consult a lawyer before deciding on this type of business structure to make sure you are in compliance with regulations.

Limited Liability Partnership

The Limited Liability Partnership is a blend between a General Partnership and a Limited Partnership. It has the unique advantage of limited liabilities to the business just as in a corporation. It permits that same tax status as a partnership at both the state and federal levels.

For example, in the past, the partners of a general partnership have automatically been responsible for the total liabilities of the enterprise, regardless of the extent of involvement by each of the partners. The Limited Liability Partnership does what the name says; it operates in much the same way as a corporation-like shield against liability.

However, in order to obtain such protection, the partnership must include in its name the phrase "Limited Liability Partnership" or the abbreviation "LLP". And in most states, the "LLP" must register each year with the appropriate State department office in order to maintain this status.

The other major advantage of the "LLP" is that it still permits the enterprise to file state and federal partnership tax returns. Each state has its own registration procedures including an annual filing fee.

Limited Liability Company

The limited liability company (LLC) is an unusual mix that combines the structure and attributes of partnerships and corporations. In its simplest sense, it is like a partnership in which all of the partners have limited liability. Limited liability companies are, generally, regarded by the federal government as a partnership for tax purposes.[1] For the purposes of liability exposure, Limited liability companies are treated as the equivalent of corporations by state law.

The creation of the limited liability company business form has its origins with enhancing domestic oil exploration opportunities. Investors sought to create a business form that had the limited liability features of a corporation with the tax features of a partnership. For example, the assets of the company can be distributed to the owners without the tax consequence, even if the assets have appreciated in value. Other countries had created business forms similar to the current limited liability company's, i.e. Panamanian limitadas. An oil exploration investment group approached the state Legislature for Wyoming (after being unsuccessful in Alaska) and successfully passed a limited liability statute in 1977. More than 10 years later, in 1988, the Internal Revenue Service issued an interpretation which allowed limited liability company's two have partnership tax classification despite the presence of limited liability. In 1990, Colorado in Kansas each passed limited liability company statute's authorizing the creation of a limited liability company. By 1994, 48 states have adopted the limited liability company form.

---

[1] With the onset of "check the box" regulations, a limited liability company can choose to be taxed as an S corporation, a partnership or even a traditional corporation.

There is much less complexity, tax and organizational baggage in the limited liability company organization. In short, the LLC is an efficient and flexible form of business that allows its members many worthwhile benefits plus partnership federal income tax treatment. There are some differences in the way various states operate their LLCs but there has been a movement to make this more uniform. Information about your state's LLC requirements can be obtained from the state authority that oversees corporate affairs.

Limited liability corporations are quickly becoming the preferred entity among small businesses because of their simplicity to form and manage. But an LLC is not the best choice if you are professionally licensed and live in California or you are enticing employees with stock options or stock bonuses. Always consult with a tax advisor on specific issues.

The Corporation

When the term corporation is used, you may think of IBM or Shell Oil. A corporation is in many ways the ideal business form even if your business is tiny in comparison to the ones above. Think of a corporation as an artificial person with a separate existence for legal, tax and economic purposes. In a corporation, investors have limited liability; they can lose no more than they initially invested in the company. A corporation allows you to control the financial risks of owning a company.

There will be no nightmares involving your house, car or personal bank account. Even if some of your employees have made costly mistakes, have been careless or negligent, there is no need for total panic. Along the same lines, if your company receives a loan from a bank, but cannot repay the loan for some reason, the bank must take the loss on your loan. Yet those instances would be rare. Most banks will require you to co-sign or guarantee with your personal assets, which puts your assets at risk. Even though you own all the stock of the corporation and you may be its only employee, you and the corporation are separate for legal, financial and tax purposes.

The liability granted to investors within the corporate form applies only to conventional business debts. If the corporation goes bankrupt, creditors cannot recover their bills out of personal assets of the stockholders. But the liability is limited in that it does not cover criminal or improper actions. The corporate form does not automatically protect the management of the company from lawsuits directed against them personally.

A corporation is not difficult to set up. Do-it-yourself kits and books are available. The cost of incorporating is much lower than most people think. For non-complex corporations that have few shareholders, many of the forms are available from your Secretary of State offices. It is likely that you can set up a corporation for less than $1,000. If your corporation is complex, consult with a lawyer for direction and the proper forms.

 There are certain differences between a public and a closed (closely held) corporation. We will focus on the Closed corporation. This is an enterprise that you own either by yourself or with a few other people. We base our arguments and reasoning on the assumption that all the owners of the corporation are involved in the day-to-day management and that no stock is sold to the general public.

The most important feature of a corporation is that it is a legally separate entity from the individuals who own and operate it.

Legally, a corporation has a definite, eternal existence. This means that even if the owner dies, the business does not. It does not matter who owns the stock. And, it is very easy to transfer ownership. If this is done within your family, you might want to include in your will that your shares (which may actually account for 100%) will be taken over by your spouse, child or whomever you have in mind. If later on this becomes a burden for the heir, he or she can give away or sell the shares of stock.

Previously, establishing a corporation required six people -- three incorporators and three directors. Today most states have changed their legislation to allow for only one incorporator and one director.

It has become easier to run a closely held corporation. Formalities have been substantially reduced. While it is normally a prudent practice to institute bylaws to govern the operation of a corporation and require  shareholders two entry into a subscription agreement evidencing their investment intent, in many states, shareholders meetings and boards of director meetings can be by unanimous written consent instead of holding formal, expensive, time-consuming meetings. They can also be held by phone.

As for corporate taxes, the corporation must pay income taxes on its earnings. In addition, when you withdraw some or all of those earnings as dividends, you must include them in your individual tax return and pay taxes a second time for the same item. But this in itself is no reason to avoid corporation status. With a little thinking and a little advice from your lawyer or accountant, the double-tax issue can be minimized or completely eliminated.

You may want to consider having a corporation adopt a preemptive right for shareholders. Preemptive rights allow shareholders to acquire a fraction of the unissued shares, or a right to purchase unissued shares, before the corporation may offer them to somebody else. It is intended to provide original shareholders the opportunity to preserve their control. Another important right to consider is cumulative voting. Cumulative voting allows minority shareholders to determine one or more of the members of the burden of director pursuant to a formula which allows them to cumulative votes. This ensures that they have representation of the Board of Director level. Most states allow cumulative voting for directors.

"S" Corporation (Formerly Subchapter S")

Most small businesses can opt to be treated as an "S" corporation. This is a straight-forward and inexpensive procedure, requiring only one form (Form 2553) to be filed with the Internal Revenue Service. It must be signed by all stockholders. Other requirements are that you must opt for the "S" designation within the first 75 days of any tax year or within the first 75 days of business operations.

Your company can only issue one class of stock. For instance, you cannot make a distinction between voting stock and nonvoting stock. If somebody has the right to control 40% of the corporation, they must generally own 40% stock. Another requirement is that there can be no more than 75 stockholders. The shareholders also have to be natural persons (the breathing individual), resident aliens or a qualified subchapter S subsidiary or trust.

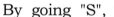

So when it's "your" corporation, you can get away with only one signature. Being the owner of such a corporation means being free of any corporate income taxes! The corporation serves basically as a vehicle for establishing income (or losses). It only files an information return and the income or loss becomes part of your personal tax return.

By going "S", you kill more than one bird with one stone. You enjoy immunity from unlimited personal liability and you avoid double taxation. Furthermore, you are able to determine what your reasonable salary is and make distinctions between the income which is subject to the ordinary income tax and wage withholding tax of 15.3% versus that which is subject only to ordinary income tax.

What's the catch? There are cases when

shareholders/owners may actually want to have their corporate income taxed separately. This is especially the case during growth periods, when it is to the advantage of the corporation to retain some of its earnings for expansion purposes. If it does take this route of financing, the benefits or savings result from the fact that the tax rate on corporate earnings is lower than the tax rate on individual earnings. Had the owner declared the corporate profits on his personal tax form, not only would he have been taxed at a higher rate he would not have the advantage of using the money for personal purposes. You probably will not be able to claim your health care costs as tax exempt, if any of it.

Stockholders working for their company are considered employees. As an employee, you are eligible for insurance programs and similar fringe benefits. For the corporation, these fringe benefits turn into tax-deductible expenses of doing business. Thus the financial effect for you should be clear: The company writes off those costs as expenses before paying taxes.

As you probably see by now, this issue can be a rather complex one, especially when you are determined to use the sharpest pencils to maximize your profits. That's another way of saying, "Have a very good lawyer and accountant help you."

Summary of Business Entities and Pros & Cons

Entities	Sole Proprietor	Limited Liability Corp (LLC)	C Corp	S Corp
Owner Rules	Only one owner	Unlimited number of owners allowed	Unlimited number of shareholders and classes of stock	Up to 100 shareholders and only one class of stock
Personal Liability of Owner	Unlimited personal liability	Generally no personal liability	Generally no personal liability	Generally no personal liability
Tax Treatment	Added to all other personal income	Entity not taxed. Profits and losses passed through to owners	Corporation taxed separately from owners	Profits and losses are passed through to shareholders
Key Documents Needed	None unless using a business name other than your own name	Articles of Organization and Operating Agreement	Articles of Incorporation; Bylaws; Organizational Board Resolutions; Stock Certificates, Stock Ledger	Articles of Inc; Bylaws; Board Resolutions; Stock Certificates, Stock Ledger; IRS & State S Corporation Election form
Manage-ment of Business	Owner makes all decisions	Operating Agreement states how business is to be run	Board of Directors has overall management responsibility, Officers have day-to-day responsibility	Board of Directors has overall management responsibility, Officers have day-to-day responsibility
Money Contributions	Owner puts in all money	Members typically contribute money	Shareholders typically purchase stock in the corporation	Shareholders typically purchase stock in the corporation

How to Incorporate

Setting up and operating a corporation requires special arrangements to assure that your business will be recognized as a corporation under the laws of the state or states in which you operate.

1. Apply to your state corporation authority (often the Secretary of State's office) for a corporate charter.
2. File articles of incorporation with the state. This operation varies from state to state. Some states have a reasonable simple fill-in-the-blanks form, so you can choose to seek a corporate charter yourself. If the procedure is complex in your state, you may need the services of a lawyer.
3. Even if you do not use an attorney to file the necessary papers with the state, you should have an attorney review your stockholder agreement – unless you are the only stockholder.
4. The choice of name for your corporation may present problems. Your state authority will not grant a charter to your corporation if your intended name duplicates, or is close to, the name of another corporation chartered in your state. However, once you have submitted an acceptable name, the protection will be on your side.
5. File the annual registration forms with the corporation authority.
6. If you are going to operate in several states, you need to register in each state as a "foreign corporation".
7. Pay the necessary fee to the state or states, whether they are called registration, franchise or some other name for the fees.
8. Make sure the state of states has the correct name and addresses of directors, officers and in particular, the registered agent (may be you).

A business operating as an S corporation not only has to fulfill state laws, but it must also satisfy the IRS requirements.

You may also use a variety of internet based filing services. Typically it will be cheaper for you to file on your own if your business in not complex with many owners. Call you state offices for forms.

Why and When to File A Name For Your Company

If you do not incorporate your business and use your full legal name to identify your business, there are no special filing requirements. Ralph R. Randall's Realty as a business name would not require filing procedures if Mr. Randall is the owner of the business. In contrast, "Triple R Realty" would have to be registered, as would "Randall Realty". The reason for this rather stringent regulation is to provide better information on the identity of the business owner or owners' -- not only for the customers, but for business partners (creditors) as well. The important thing to remember is that as soon as you want to use only a part of your legal personal name, i.e. the last name, as your business name, it's technically treated as an adoption of an assumed name and filing procedures apply.

Officially, this filing serves identification purposes only. It does not provide official protection against other persons filing the same name. It's the responsibility of the entrepreneur to take legal action if a duplication of names occurs. However, most states will notify the original filer of later filings that seem to constitute a problem.

On the other hand, there may be instances where your unregistered full legal name is duplicated because someone else (a corporation, for example) claims it as an assumed name. Although the authorities would most likely not prevent this (because they don't have you on their records), you do have certain rights in such a case because it's your name and you have had it longer. It's considered a matter of common law and would largely depend on an individual ruling by a judge.

There is another interesting aspect to the name game: You cannot "sneak in" on a corporate name hoping that the name you intend to file for your sole proprietorship business will be confused by many customers with the name of your famous competitor.

For example, if your name happens to be John Target and you wanted to name your gift store "Target's Store", you would be in a heap of trouble. The same would be true for names like "The Hallmark Card Shop", "Windy's Hamburgers", "Gen'ral Motors".

An assumed name must be "free of conflict". This means it is already turned down when it comes close to those of corporations. This, of course, is a matter of judgment. Therefore, you should check with the appropriate state offices before you go through the preliminary filing motions. You may also want to consider registering your name through the United States Patent and Trademark Office.

How to File an Assumed Name

The actual filing procedures may vary slightly from state to state. The following account is based on Minnesota law and should give you an idea of what is involved:

Get a "Certificate of Assumed Name" form from the Office of the Secretary of State. Complete it; and sign it and send it to the appropriate government office for certification. Have the approved Certificate published in two successive issues of a newspaper qualified to publish legal notices in the county serving as the principal place of the business. The ad must appear in the legal notice section, not as a display or classified ad. The notice must contain the same information that is provided on the Certificate.

After the paper has printed the information shown on the front of the Certificate, it will send you an affidavit stating that the Certificate was printed for the specified time. Make sure this affidavit bears an original signature and has a copy of the actual publication attached to it. All in all, your total cost for the application fee and the newspaper filing may reach about $100. If you try to get by without filing, you risk a fine and you make it impossible for your business to initiate lawsuits and other legal proceedings. As a general rule, your filing, if there are no changes, remains valid for 10 years. You will be notified six months prior to expiration.

What You Should Know About Copyrights, Trademarks And Patents

Many businesses have been built on the legal protection of ideas. There is enough difference among copyrights, trademarks and patents that you should be familiar with the basics of what they are, how they guard property rights and how you can use them. Copyrights, trademarks and patents can be searched at: http://www.uspto.gov/ebc/indexebc.html

Copyrights

A copyright protects the original effort you put into the development of a literary, musical, artistic or other creative work. Copyrights cover various forms of expression such as books, films, computer programs, data bases, semiconductor chips, works of art, promotional brochures, product drawings, architectural plans and advertising copy.

The creators ("authors") and other rights holders of a copyright have the exclusive right to duplicate, sell, license, display, publicly perform and distribute all or part of a copyrighted work.

An idea, in and of itself, cannot be copyrighted. A copyright is created only when a person utilizes an original idea in an actual form of expression.

Registration with the United States Copyright Office is not necessary to establish an author's rights. Registration does, however, afford you certain clear legal advantages if you want to stop someone from copying your work or protecting it from unfair usage.

The term of a copyright (with some exceptions) is the life of the author(s) plus 50 years--instead of the previous term of 28 years (renewable for another 28)--measured usually from the date of first publication.

Trademarks

A trademark is a word or words, name, symbol, label, device, or picture attached to a manufacturer's or merchant's product to identify it and distinguish it from similar products. Its most common form is the brand name. A trademark is different from a copyright in that the protection is in the trademark symbol that distinguishes the product, not in the product itself.

A trademark comes into being as soon as and for as long as it is used - and if the legal requirements of proper trademark usage are observed. Registering trademarks does help protect them but only if they are strictly defended.

Trademarks that are not properly protected may become generic terms and available to all manufacturers. That's how Xerox almost went from being a trademark to a generic term for dry copying. That's how the term aspirin moved into the public domain.

> Some examples of other trademarks are:
> Intel, *The Computer Inside*
> IBM, *Solutions for a Small Planet*
> Pfizer, *We're Part of the Cure*
> Sherwin Williams, *We Cover the World*
> Lincoln, *What a Luxury Car Should Be*
> Ford, *Have You Driven a Ford Lately?*

A service mark is the same as a trademark except that it identifies and distinguishes the source of a service rather than a product. Normally, a trademark for goods appears on the product or on its packaging, while a service mark appears in advertising for the services.

For current copyright and trade mark information and registration contact the United States Patent and Trademark Office at (800) 786-9199 or on the World Wide Web at www.uspto.gov.

Patents

A U.S. patent gives its owner(s) the right to keep others from making, using, and selling the owner's invention in the United States for 17 years (14 years for design patents). Patents are not renewable, but a new and useful improvement of something already patented, as well as a new use of an old device, may be the subject of new patents.

Patents are granted only to the true inventor. Like a copyright, a patent cannot be obtained on just an idea or suggestion. Patents are issued only after a complete application is filed in the Patent Office, an official search of the prior process, machine, or composition of matter has been conducted, and the Patent Office is satisfied that all the claims are allowable. A patent may not be obtained if the invention was in public use or on sale in the United States for more than one year prior to the filing of the patent application.

Because a U.S. patent does not confer rights abroad, application must be made anywhere protection is sought.

You can now file your trademarks online at the United States Patent and Trademark Office at www.uspto.gov.

The legal aspects of any business can be frightening and even intimidating, but it doesn't have to be. Nor does good representation have to be expensive. In the next chapter, you will discover how to find an attorney that you can work well with and the basics on contracts so you know the right answers to ask.

In this chapter you have learned:

Business Forms
1. *Selecting the right form for your business requires close cooperation and coordination between you, your lawyer and your accountant.*
2. *The main disadvantage of a sole proprietorship as well as a partnership is that the owners face unlimited personal liability if the business goes belly-up, or if threatened by a substantial lawsuit.*
3. *The main advantages of forming a corporation are limited personal liability and flexibility in tax matters.*
4. *Incorporating has become rather easy in recent years, making it an ideal form of business even for small businesses.*

The Business Name
1. *As soon as you use anything but your full name for doing business, you are required to file an assumed name.*
2. *Filing an assumed name does not protect your name against usage by others.*

Websites You May Find Useful

IRS SS-4 Form – www.irs.gov

How to Form A Corporation - www.nolo.com

US Patent & Trademark Office – www.uspto.gov

Step To Success
One Action a Day Will Move You Forward

It is time to move forward. Complete the **Step to Success** Action and feel your progress.

Start collecting the forms you'll need to file. Even if you're not ready to file your paperwork, you'll be prepared for when the time comes. If you plan to operate under an assumed or fictitious name, you'll also want to search your county's records to see if the name you've selected is already in use. Using a search engine such as Google, search on the keywords *fictitious business name (your county)*. You can do it, so start right NOW!

Chapter 8

The Ultimate Home Based Business Guide

"Success is liking yourself, liking what you do, and liking how you do it."

--Maya Angelou (1928 -) American poet, writer, historian, educator

Working at Home

Sometimes it's necessary, sometimes it's a choice. Working out of the home has become the established way of making a living for millions and millions of Americans. For some it is the practical answer to the problem of where to work between outside jobs or when the budget is too tight to afford rental office space. For others, and these are in the majority, the home office offers the best way to spend the working day.

A Growing Trend

 In a recent report commissioned by the Small Business Administration titled: Home-Based Business – the Hidden Economy, author Joanne Pratt found over 20,000 home-based businesses had sales over $1,000,000.

In addition, home-based businesses represent 52% of all small firms and provide over $314 billion in receipts to the United States.

According to IDC, a national research firm, there are between 18 and 20 million income producing home offices.

"The number of U.S. households that have a home-based business currently exceeds 12%" stated the Small Business Administration Office of Advocacy. In 2005, A.C. Nielsen conducted a survey and found that over 724,000 Americans use eBay as their primary or secondary source of income.

Federal government figures indicate a growing trend. With an average of 4.2 million people starting up home businesses each year, it is now expected that the home-worker population will increase by roughly 15 percent a year, to eventually reach 56 million.

Like anything else, there are plusses and minuses on both sides and that's what we'll be discussing in this chapter. Whatever else they are doing, the home-based professionals are changing the way Americans are looking at work and the workplace.

THE HOME BASED BUSINESS VS. THE TRADITIONAL BUSINESS

The latest force for the growth of home based businesses came in the early 1990s as America went through a new kind of recession. Unlike other

business slowdowns, in which "blue collar" workers were most affected, this recession touched middle and upper management as well. Tens of thousands of "white collar" people were put out of work.

Since many companies in a particular industry were likewise affected, there weren't enough jobs available to take up the slack for management people. This was something totally new for people born after World War II and it was a shock.

Only two choices were left for "white collar" workers: moving to a new industry, which meant changing careers, or setting up their own business. At the same time, the computer, the fax and other electronics, started to make home-based business a very attractive alternative. The growth of these businesses continues at a rapid pace.

What Goes Around Comes Around

Home based businesses have been on the American scene ever since the Pilgrims landed at Plymouth Rock. As recently as the beginning of the century most people worked out of their homes, which were usually farms or ranches. They raised their own food, made what they needed at home, repaired the machines they used at home and took care of their finances on their own.

Today, home-based businesses are making a major comeback. But this time they tend to be efficient, well-run businesses such as consulting firms, advertising services, publishing companies, bed and breakfast inns, photography, free-lance writing businesses and event-planning services, to mention just a few.

It's a Business Trend to Be Taken Seriously

For some people working at home is definitely no substitute for working in a large office. They consider it a halfhearted, dead-end, lonely attempt to make ends meet while they look and hope for a "real" job to come along.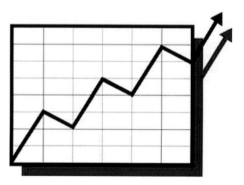

The truth of the matter is that plenty of energetic men and women have discovered that they can make as good a living as they had in a corporate job and even increase their take home pay as a self-employed person. As an extra benefit, they avoid costly commuting time, energy consuming office politics, sometimes unreasonable bosses, and gain more time with the family.

The constantly rising cost of housing forces many people to live far way from their jobs. Two hour commutes each way has become acceptable for many people. Now, it has become obvious that many jobs, usually done in an office, can be performed just as well at home - anywhere a telephone line can reach. Many of these same jobs can be done by individuals or small businesses. Even large companies have encouraged employees to go "out on their own" and operate right out of their homes.

According to the National Center for Policy Analysis, 70 percent of home-based businesses are run by women, in part because of the expanding number of mothers who prefer to stay at home to raise their children while having a career.

Retirees form another large group of likely home office workers. The downsizing of American business has forced many employees to take early retirement from companies that are anxious to cut their payrolls. Then there are large numbers of people in their fifties and early sixties, retired before their time, who aren't satisfied to sit back and watch the world roll by. They have the energy and drive to run their own companies. And, the logical and most economical place to work is in their own homes.

ADVANTAGES OF A HOME BASED BUSINESS

There are a great number of advantages of having a home based business. The list is as varied as the number of people who work at home. Some are:

1. **PERSONAL FREEDOM:** Personal freedom consists of all the items in the list below. But really personal freedom gives us the ability to keep

the money we make. Your earnings potential is directly connected to your performance. Personal freedom is also about doing what we love to do. Working from home allows you more flexibility to come and go as you please.

2. **TIME SAVINGS:** Getting to work is never a problem - neither rain, nor snow, nor dark of night, can keep a home office worker from getting the job done. It's no problem to arrive at the office early and stay late. You can turn on the radio, or even the TV, listen to music while you work, without any complaints. Americans spend 348 hours commuting each year according to the Federal Highway Commission.

3. **WORK WITHIN YOUR OWN TIME FRAME:** Do you want to get up and work at midnight, or start to work at 7:00 in the evening? You can come and go as you please. This is the kind of time shifting you can enjoy easily when you run your business out of your own home.

4. **COST SAVINGS:** This is one of the biggest single factors why people set up home based businesses, rather then operating out of a conventional office. There are many fiscal savings. Rent is just the beginning. Typical office space can run from $10 per square foot all the way up to $30 depending upon the location. And retail space, in a shopping mall, can begin at $30 per square foot. But in addition to rent savings there are several others: utilities, parking (a costly factor for many people locating in a downtown building), restaurant lunches, car expenses or train, bus or subway costs.

5. **TAX SAVINGS:** A home based business offers distinct tax advantages. You can deduct a portion of your mortgage, including interest on the mortgage at tax time. Your home office can be located in your basement, den, study, garage or a spare bedroom. Or, it could include a number of these spaces in your home. But you must use the space just for your business. One important note: KEEP TRACK OF ALL YOUR EXPENSES AND SAVE YOUR RECEIPTS FOR TAX

PURPOSES.

6. **<u>DECORATING AND MAINTENANCE</u>:** Many people who rent office

space discover that the landlord will not handle redecoration or fix-up costs. They are confronted with "lease hold improvements," added expenses at their new location. By operating out of one's home numerous costly maintenance expenses can be avoided.

7. **<u>SET YOUR OWN DRESS CODE</u>:** Want to wear blue jeans to work? Is it a hot day and you want to wear shorts? Too early to change out of your PJ's? If your answer is YES, then put your formal business outfits in mothballs, except for client meeting attire. If, on the other hand you want to wear a tux or a ball gown to your home office you won't be out of place.

DISADVANTAGES OF HAVING A HOME BASED BUSINESS

For as many advantages there are to having a Home Office Business, there are an equal number of disadvantages. These include:

1. **<u>A BUSINESS AWAY FROM HOME</u>:** It is truly a business place, all business with no home interruptions. Distractions from the significant other, the children, the personal telephone calls and visits from neighbors stay safely at home.

2. **<u>A HOME AWAY FROM HOME</u>:** Everyone needs diversity. This is true for all members of a family. Many people cannot be with their families 24 hours a day. It has nothing to do with love and caring but simply

that some people need their own space for some part of the day. So, for some, a home office could introduce troublesome interpersonal pressures that don't arise when business is separated from personal life.

3. **BUSINESS PEOPLE NEED BUSINESS PEOPLE:** Operating a business out of a standard business setting provides the opportunity to come in daily contact with other business people. In friendly discussions and "brain storming." this contact can often lead to valuable ideas, suggestions and support for one's business.

4. **CREATING THE BUSINESS IMAGE:** Having a standard business setting location conveys the message that you are serious factor in the market at a permanent business location. It never hurts to show customers, clients and suppliers that yours is a successful enterprise. There is a certain prestige reflected on a businessperson who presents a prosperous appearance.

5. **LACK OF ACCESSIBILITY:** Having your business in a conventional business location usually means you will probably be close to the local office supply store and other suppliers. It means you will have ample parking for customers and any employees. Further, it you have a business that is dependent on pick-up and deliveries by UPS, Federal Express, U.S. Mail and suppliers, then operating out of your home can be a cause for concern since your home may not always be accessible.

6. **FAMILY AND NEIGHBOR HARMONY:** Having a home-based business can lead to problems not only with one's own family but with neighbors and friends. Frequently family members feel their own sense of privacy is destroyed. Or the wife and children simply may

be upset at having a business mixed in with their lives. Likewise, for neighbors, a home based business may bring forth feelings of envy, jealousy, sense that their neighborhood is being converted to a commercial area, thus affecting their real estate values, or they may feel their own privacy is being invaded.

TOP 10 HOME BASED BUSINESS OPPORTUNITIES

If you are looking for home based business opportunities and are tired of all the "get rich quick" schemes that come up when you are searching online, then here is a great list of current and future trends that may fit your idea of a perfect business.

1) Home Renovation Services
Home renovation services are hot, hot, hot - and there's no sign of this trend slowing down. On the contrary, as the population ages, even more individuals and couples are going to want to make their homes more livable by investing in the home renovations they need to stay where there are. The best home renovation to focus on for the long-term? Bathroom and handicap renovations.

2) Pet-Based Products
Is there anything that indulgent pet owners won't buy for their pets? If you can come up with a product for dogs or cats that you can produce in your home, you'll have a real winner of a home business opportunity on your hands. From designer collars to "organic" pet foods, the sky's the limit. For a great story about a home based business in the pet industry, look at the top money maker for home based businesses at Start Up Nation (www.startupnation.com).

3) Catering Services
Think dinner for eight. Not just delivered, but served. Catering services aren't just for big parties any more. Career couples are having almost every social occasion catered, and busy families who are tired of living on take-out are spending more on having food brought in or even pre-made for them. If you have a knack for planning and preparing nourishing, appealing food and can deliver it hot (or frozen), this is the home business opportunity for you.

4) Cleaning Services

Along the same lines, there's currently a heavy demand for cleaning services, and the demand for domestic cleaning services will only increase. If you're good at organizing and comfortable with the thought of running a crew, this home business opportunity has the potential of turning into something big.

5) Fall Prevention Products

Did you know that falls are the leading cause of fatal injury among the elderly? The trend of hip and replacement surgeries from falls is on the rise. What if you developed or distributed a product related to helping seniors prevent falls? Think of the growing size of the potential market!

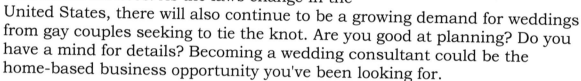

6) Wedding Consultant/Planner Services

More people are opting to get married which means growing opportunities for wedding consultant services. As the laws change in the United States, there will also continue to be a growing demand for weddings from gay couples seeking to tie the knot. Are you good at planning? Do you have a mind for details? Becoming a wedding consultant could be the home-based business opportunity you've been looking for.

7) Dietary Consultant Services

Another growing trend that's only going to get larger is the perceived need for dietary advice. People are increasingly concerned about the food they put in their mouths and increasingly aware of the connection between dietary habits and their general health - and they're increasingly prepared to pay for personalized dietary planning and advice.

8) In-Home Beauty Services

This home-based business opportunity combines two trends; the insatiable demand for services that make people look and feel younger and better and the growing desire to have those services delivered. And why not? Having someone come to your home and cleanse and tone your skin and do your makeup is the height of luxury.

9) Sewing and Alteration Services

Sewing is on the way to becoming a lost art as more and more people find they have less and less time. But as not everyone is the regulation size, the demand for other people to provide these services will only increase. If you're really skilled, tailoring is another good home-based business opportunity.

10) Life/Business Coaching Services

Coaching has been hot for a while now, but I think this new industry will continue to grow. Remember when everyone had or wanted a personal fitness trainer? Now everyone has or wants a personal coach. If you have the skills and training necessary, this is a great home-based business opportunity because it can be done remotely as well as in person.

Most of these home based business ideas do not need formal training. If one of these ideas sounds exciting to you, find someone that can teach you the ropes and get started.

HOME OFFICE BASICS

All your life, your home has been a place to - well, come home to. As a student, you got up, ate breakfast, and went to class. You did your work and then came home. When you went into the work force, you followed pretty much the same routine. When it comes to working at home, you don't usually

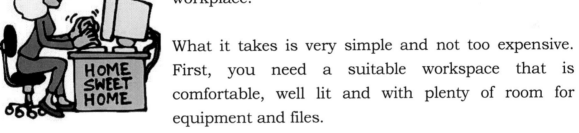

associate your living room or spare bedroom with a workplace.

What it takes is very simple and not too expensive. First, you need a suitable workspace that is comfortable, well lit and with plenty of room for equipment and files.

According to your needs you may have to start with, or will be satisfied with, a small corner of a room and a computer on a folding card table. But the possibilities for today's home-based office can match anything you can think of in layout, design and technology. There are furniture, lighting, and fabric designs intended specially for offices that must make the most of every inch of space. The newest developments in home-office furniture have an impact on both your personal comfort and professional image. Setting up your office right means investing in the right equipment from copiers to telephones, fax machines to computers.

Margaret expects to retire in only a few years from her job with a major food corporation. She has gotten an early start with a party catering service that runs right out of her own kitchen.

Wesley, a Certified Public Accountant who took early retirement keeps quite busy with his tax and financial advisory business. Interestingly enough his business is such that most of his work takes place in his clients' offices, so the subject of Wesley's office space rarely comes up.

Setting Up for Business

It's important to choose the right office location within the home, but it's equally important to design the right setup for the business functions you will have to perform.

If you will be selling by mail you'll need space to store, package and wrap items for shipping. When choosing the area for your office notice the sunlight patterns. Morning sunlight hitting your computer screen can make work impossible. Incidentally, standard bulb light fixtures are generally preferred for room lighting and halogen desk lamps for task lighting.

Keeping Comfortable and Efficient

If possible, it is best to work in a room with a door and to establish firm rules about visiting. It's especially important to have it understood that you cannot drop work and run out to perform an errand during business hours. Remember, even if your work space is merely a card table in a corner of a recreation room it's your office and must be treated as such if you're to get your work done and keep your business growing.

An important consideration is having a well-designed desk, chair, and filing system. It's worth taking a fair amount of time with these choices because they can make a real difference in your day-to-day business effectiveness. You've heard about all those painful joint and nerve conditions that office workers can suffer from. Well, you'll be working longer hours than the average office worker but still in roughly the same situation.

Furnish for Comfort and Convenience

Your office chair should be chosen for long term support, so it should offer height and back adjustments. The more prongs on chair's base the more

stable it will be, especially if you like to wheel between desk and file cabinets. It's also a good idea, if you have a rug, to get a plastic rug protector or a remnant to cover any parts of your office that will get extra wear.

If possible, position your desk in a space that has natural light. Add soft overhead bulbs and strong task lighting, (halogen is warm and inexpensive). If you're using a computer, situate your monitor to reduce the kind of eye strain, which glare from windows or other reflective surfaces may cause.

If you have enough room, consider horizontal file cabinets. They hold legal-size file folders and allow for easier access than vertical cabinets. And make sure you position the cabinets so you can reach vital information without racing across the room.

Handling Business Visitors

You may need a waiting area. You may want a completely private place for meetings with customers. If, for example, you're setting up a crafts business you'll need a studio where you can attractively display your output.

If you want customers to come to your home, you'll have to design your office and workspaces to accommodate them while not disturbing the normal

---

operations of your house. The best way to do this is to spend some time observing the activities of the other family members. Where do the children usually play? How does your husband or wife conduct his or her activities during the day? When and how do members of the family come and go, through which rooms? Listen for the noise tendencies in the house and outside. You can't get much done over the telephone if there are constant noises coming from the street or from children at play.

If you don't want business visitors coming into your home on a regular basis or at certain times, there are a few options you can try: Rent a conference room or office space just for the time you need it. These professional suites are offered by office buildings or leasing services. You'll find them listed in the Yellow Pages.

Another idea is to join a club which has facilities for meetings and entertaining clients or potential clients.

Conduct business as much as possible by fax, telephone or mail. Use a courier service to pick up and deliver materials. Today people expect to work at a distance easily and conveniently. You could work by telephone, and send documents by fax to a client for months without knowing that he works out of his home office.

Tell the World

Working out of your home doesn't mean working at a disadvantage. Although as a home-based business you'll be competing against larger and better established firms, you will still be known and valued by the quality of the work you do, and by the face you present to your public. You can be just as impressive as your bigger competition in some important ways.

Choose a company name that conveys what you do with strength and distinction. For example, United Consumers Club, a consumer buying club has a name that tells exactly what their business is and indicates they offer a special consumer benefit. In Denver, The Secreteam company's clever name invites interest in their word processing, transcribing, desktop publishing and other office support services.

In Sonoma California, The Screen Machine is a mobile service business specializing in making and repairing window screens. A good name is a good start for any business.

Incidentally, all of these companies are run out of their owners' homes.

After you settle on a name you'll want to project a stylish look through your company logo and the look and feel of your business cards, stationery and business brochures. It's important that these should all look attractive and professional because they are, in many cases, the first impression customers get of your organization and abilities. It's worthwhile to get in touch with an artist or graphic designer (there are plenty who work out of their homes too!) and get a first class set of images for your company.

Where Do Nice Guys Finish?
Take the case of Al Riggins, a representative for an industrial computer software firm, who decided he didn't need a large office. His selling was mostly through personal contact, over the phone, or in his clients' or prospects' offices. He set aside part of a guest room for his work, installed separate business phone lines, and bought a fax machine and a computer.

In the beginning things went fine. Al would get out of bed - an hour later than when he had gone to his office. For several hours, he made phone contacts, starting with his East coast clients and working across the country. Then he would do his computer work, preparing estimates, proposals and billing.

But eventually a problem arose. Al's friends, neighbors, and even former co-workers started dropping in for visits. Being friendly, Al at first welcomed the sociability. But soon, the time Al had set aside for calling and preparing projects began to be displaced by social phone calls and unexpected visitors.

At first Al accepted the phone calls and visits as welcome breaks in his work day. He soon realized that something would have to change. The sad fact is that Al was such a nice, friendly guy he was unable to make the necessary changes. A few months later he was back in an office but he still hoped to realize his dream of working out of his home.

What could Al have done? He could have stopped the interruptions at the beginning. Unfortunately Al was new at the home office business and didn't see the problem coming. In his old job he was used to having a buffer, in the form of a secretary, who constantly screened calls and visitors. It was now up to Al to be strict with social callers and that was a skill he had to learn.

A Home Office is Not a Prison

Al's example is only one of the downsides of working at home. Emotional problems are among the most critical because they concern how you handle working alone, how you get yourself to work against deadlines, or how you resist the urge to constantly overwork.

One of the biggest blocks to people who must be self-starters is lack of concentration. Working at home demands independence and self-discipline, two qualities that may not be quite as important when you are working for a salary in an office. But when you are on your own, no two ways about it, you've got to have them.

Get Out of the House

Working at home doesn't mean never leaving home base. When a prominent television script writer, who usually works at home, has a major project, he takes off to a cabin, far from Los Angeles and his family, in order to write without distractions.

Only a short time ago I received an agitated phone call from another friend who had quit his job and started working full time at home. After cruising through the first three months, suddenly he was feeling solitary and shakily upset. Worst of all, he wasn't able to manage his time and get his work done on schedule.

"There are many days, he told me, Awhen I find myself working into the early hours. Next morning I come right downstairs to my office, and get right back to work. But some days, I may not even leave the house. I can spend the whole day working in my robe. I start to feel isolated and uncomfortable. I don't want to go back to an office job, but I'm having difficulty managing by myself.@

There was nothing unusual about my friend's experiences. When the office is only footsteps away, it's always too easy to slip into the office to get some

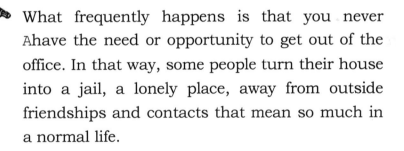

details out of the way before breakfast, and get lost in the serious need to complete some jobs.

What frequently happens is that you never Ahave the need or opportunity to get out of the office. In that way, some people turn their house into a jail, a lonely place, away from outside friendships and contacts that mean so much in a normal life.

This is the kind of problem that often arises for self-employed people who must take on the tasks that were handled by others in their previous offices. Suddenly they become their company's secretary, cashier, marketing expert and salesperson. They do whatever needs to be done, because they have to, at least until they grow large enough to afford to hire help.

The Secret is Organization

There are ways for even the busiest self-employed people to cut down the time they spend isolated in the office, at home. Here are a few suggestions to make more time to enjoy all the good things in life you're working so hard to achieve:

Keep a careful record of your projects. Note down the time it takes to complete each of your activities. Then, after a week or two, look over the list. Consider - did you waste time on "busy work" - unimportant tasks you could have done without? Were all your phone calls necessary? Are you setting up barriers for yourself by spending time on one new business idea after another - without completing projects already scheduled? Eliminate such time-wasting activities, and you'll shorten your work day.

If you feel the pressure of too much work and you can see your way clear to hiring a full or part-time assistant. High school students, women who want to work while their children are in school, and retirees often are interested in part time work for very little money. They either want to gain job skills or keep busy. Even an inexpensive helper will reduce your work load, and help you to maintain a more business-like attitude.

The Challenge is Isolation

There are various ways home workers can challenge feelings of solitude and loneliness, if they occur. Here are a few suggestions:

> Resolve to have business lunches or even dinners at least a few times a week. Contact your competitors. You will not only get out of the house, you will also be building a system of contacts with whom you can share common interests.

> Join trade and professional organizations. Their meetings,

seminars, and dinners are ideal places to meet, greet, be seen and pick up the latest business news. In a slightly different way and just for relaxation join a club that involves a hobby; woodworking, for instance, or photography. In one of these groups, away from usual problems, it will be easier to relax. You may even find a new interest that could lead you into a profitable business some day.

➤ Take courses at your local university or trade school. Business connected or just interesting, it's always enjoyable to learn things and meet new people.

➤ Arrange business calls to take you out of the house fairly frequently. Even if it takes a little more effort, it's always a good idea to go out and visit with your clients or prospects face to face.

➤ Make good use of the time you spend away from work. Keep up your social contacts and go out and meet with new people. Consider scheduling free time for yourself during the day. Make sure you stick to the timetable by making appointments to meet others for lunch, tennis, golf, even walking. You might want to get a dog, so that you'll have the perfect excuse to take a daily walk. There are plenty of dog walkers in every community. Anything that will get you out of the house and preferably in contact with other people is good.

While you may feel uneasy about the interruption to your day at first, eventually you'll find that you will accomplish more when you take a break than you do when you work nonstop to exhaustion from morning till night. And, remember the old adage - haste makes waste. Take the time to do the job right the first time.

Licenses, Permits, Taxes and Zoning Regulations

Before you start to work in your home office there are a few items that you had better look into. First, you should check out what your community requires concerning licenses, permits and zoning regulations for the business you're planning. In most cases regulations will offer no problems, and those that do will be easy to take care of.

Some Yellow Pages telephone books have a special section under Agovernment offices@ devoted to small business. It may not be immediately clear which agency can answer your questions. Try one that sounds logical and if it doesn't have the information you need, the people there can direct you to an office that will help.

Check In To Any Special Taxes.

Contact your city or town hall or the appropriate regulatory agency for information about any occupational license you may need. For example, if you intend to make or distribute food you may need approval from the local health department. Don't ignore this kind of requirement. You don't want to grow to success and suddenly find that the city can close you down because of a trivial technicality.

Such businesses as child-care services may also require special licensing. Find out before you jump in.

If there is a sales tax to be collected, make sure you contact the proper authorities to determine what your responsibilities are. Too many small businesses have been hit years after they started with tax bills they didn't know they owed.

Zoning

Zoning regulations may be a little trickier. They tend to concentrate on the impact of particular activities. They are often called Anuisance laws@ by the business people who have to abide by them. But you must realize that they are designed to protect neighborhoods from annoying noise, traffic, odors, and other things that would tend to bother people where they live.

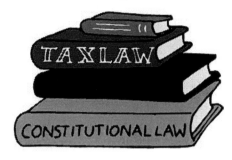

In some places, especially rural or far suburban areas, there's usually nothing to worry about. In more heavily populated areas, however, there are often special conditions in the zoning laws concerning home occupations. A great deal depends on the nature of your home-based business, the neighborhood you live in, and local and state ordinances.

The Financial Picture

Independent Contractors
Home office workers are usually paid as independent contractors. This means that you are considered a kind of company of your own and are financially entirely responsible for yourself.

Self-Employment Tax
There are benefits and disadvantages in being an independent contractor. The most important requirement, as far as the government is concerned, is that you'll be responsible for your own taxes, especially the ASelf-Employment Tax@ which is really your Social Security tax.

Business Expense Deductions
A major financial benefit from Uncle Sam are the business expenses deductions you'll be entitled to under tax law. But, to get the most value at tax time, you will need to keep a record of every business expense item right from the start. You can get more detailed information on what these deductions are call the IRS for their detailed list of business

deductions allowed. Remember, there can be changes in the list from year to year.

The Home Office Deduction Benefit

The Home Office Deduction is the most valuable because it generally offers most home workers the most substantial way to reduce their federal taxes. In order to claim this deduction, you must show that your home work space is used regularly and exclusively as your principal place of business.

Home office expenses are deductible mostly based on the percentage of square footage of your home that you use as a workspace. If your home is 1,000 square feet and you use 200 square feet exclusively for workspace you can normally deduct 20% of your total mortgage or rent payments on your tax return.

But, be careful: if you use your workspace for any other purpose than work, you cannot deduct any of these expenses. For example, working on the kitchen table is a bad idea, as far as tax deductions go, unless you really don't have any choice.

The last time we looked, there were some 23 possible tax deductions for a home office. To make sure you don't miss any, get a copy of IRS Publication 587. It is available free online at http://www.irs.gov/publications/p587/index.html or from an IRS office and is updated annually, so if you don't use the latest year's publication you may be missing a valuable deduction.

A Major Change

Working at home changes the standards. You're up in the morning and at work after a very short walk to your office. There's no boss to tell you what to do, except that small voice inside your head that says, get going, get earning.

There are no dress codes - you can wear anything you want. In your home office it's just you, the phone, the fax and your computer.

At the start you may just need a small corner of a room and a computer on a card table. However, as your business grows, you will have to invest in equipment - from computers to copiers to telephones and fax machines that will help you maintain a professional operation without more paid help.

Unpaid Help

If you're used to working in a corporate office environment you'll have to learn how to handle your own communications; and scheduling. However, there are plenty of computer programs that can do a pretty good job of helping manage your record keeping and communications.

Personal computers have made it possible for one man or woman to do the work of two or three people. Specialized software is available that's like having an expert and a secretary at your side. Electronic communications can now keep you in regular contact with your clients and suppliers and cellular telephones keep you available whenever needed. There are very few things a standard office can offer that you can't match at home these days with relatively inexpensive business equipment. In fact many stores, these days, offer long term, interest free payment programs for the electronic equipment you'll need.

It's All Up To You

There can be times when working at home can feel lonely. However, there are some things you can do to avoid feeling isolated. Have business lunches or even dinners at least a few times a week. Join trade and professional organizations. Arrange business calls to take you out of the house fairly often.

Working at home demands independence and self-discipline - two qualities that may not be quite as important when you are working for a salary in an office. But when you are on your own, no two ways about it, you've got to have them.

> *In this chapter you have learned:*
>
> 1. *The home office offers many benefits and can provide a satisfying experience.*
> 2. *You are the boss; in business for yourself and by yourself.*
> 3. *The home office offers just about the best opportunity for getting started in your own business with the smallest amount of capital and the lowest overhead.*

Websites & Books You May Find Useful

Following are some of the organizations that can be helpful to you as you pursue your career in your home office. For further help there are also plenty of books with good ideas on being able to work more effectively.

Start Up Nation – www.startupnation.com
Small Business Administration – www.sba.gov
Home Based Working Moms – www.hbwm.com
Small Office Home Office America - www.soho.org

Step To Success
One Action a Day Will Move You Forward

It is time to move forward. Complete the **Step to Success** Action and feel your progress. No matter where you are going, you can get there one step at a time.

If you are considering a home based business, make a plan of how you can separate your business work with file folders, a desk or whatever else you need from your home work. Thinking about this in the beginning and communicating it with your family will help you in the long run to stay organized and moving forward.

Chapter 9

Franchising For Fun And Profit

"The will to win, the desire to succeed, the urge to reach your full potential... these are the keys that will unlock the door to personal excellence."
   --Eddie Robinson (1919 -) Hall of Fame college football coach, with 408 career victories

How to be in business for yourself, not by yourself.

The business pages of newspapers are full of success stories. All about people who got an idea, got financial backing and started their own enterprises. It's an old story, yet always new and fascinating, especially to people who have decided it's time to stop working for a boss and start working for themselves, taking a chance for independence.

Take caution not to overlook the other stories farther down the page announcing business failures, i.e. bankruptcies. These people devoted money and effort to create businesses but, for one reason or another, couldn't make a go of it. The news articles hardly ever tell you the real reasons businesses flop--inexperience, lack of knowledge of the market they put themselves in, and lack of understanding basic merchandising principles. It's a sad story, but one you don't have to repeat. There is a way to get the training and continuing guidance that can remove many of the uncertainties of starting and operating a business.

Take the example of John and Mary Samples, a two-income family in their 40s. John was a draftsman, had a pretty good job and had been with his company for fifteen years. Mary was a librarian, worked for the city and had excellent job security. They had two children and an average income. About ten years ago they got the itch, they wanted to start an enterprise of their own.

Neither of these people had the kind of background giving them any specialized know-how for a venture that would provide them a better income or a better life than they already had.

John and Mary had a dream; they talked for years about owning a restaurant. They went to the library and took out a stack of books on small business in general, and restaurants in particular. They discovered a lot of things they never expected pertaining to the pitfalls of running a restaurant. They became aware that restaurant operation was risky--too complicated to give people with their background a good chance at success. It appeared John and Mary were going to have to look for something that would be more in keeping with their experience.

However, Mary had responded to a magazine ad for a restaurant franchise opportunity. The information they received described a complete franchise program for opening and operating a McDonald's restaurant. It promised continuous direction and support

from people who were experts in the field. With that kind of help, it looked more like the opportunity the Samples had been searching for. It answered their questions pertaining to running a business they had never been in and how to make a go of it. Best of all, they discovered the company had a franchise available in their hometown.

They did some research, checked with franchisees and a banker and a lawyer. After a great deal of soul searching they decided to take the plunge. So they invested in their McDonald's franchise, and with the help of some very capable food industry specialists and a lot of hard work, they now have a highly successful restaurant. John and Mary found a business of their own and they had a partner who had as much interest in their success as they did. It turned out to be a winning combination.

Or take the case of Mark Silverstone, a man in his mid-fifties, whose job had been terminated when his employer of 25 years sold the company. Mark and his wife, Emily, decided that it was time they considered a business of their own. They looked into a number of opportunities, but didn't find anything right away that fit in with their experience, money situation or interests.

Then one day they heard about a printing franchise that was available. Mark had always been an amateur photographer and Emily had an interest in the graphic arts. It sounded like a possibility. They contacted the Minuteman Press company and discovered that the franchise agreement being offered included help in finding a location, outfitting the store, advertising, getting supplies and helping the franchisee establish and operate a print shop.

Without any experience in the printing trade, the Silverstone's would have had a hard time making a success of the business. Through the franchise agreement they had all the help they needed to launch and maintain a successful instant print operation. After two years, they're now considering opening a second franchise location.

These are only two examples of the way some people, who have wanted to establish small businesses, have taken advantage of the franchising idea. Franchises enabled the Sample's and the Silverstone's to set up ventures that wouldn't have made sense for them any other way. It's the course many people have used to get valuable professional help in avoiding the countless traps that are always present in starting and running a business.

This chapter is devoted to explaining the concept of franchising, how it works, what it can do for you, what you should look for in establishing a franchising relationship, how to get financing and where you can find and check out good franchising opportunities.

FRANCHISING--A BIG BUSINESS

There are franchise opportunities in almost every industry: fast foods, motels, automobiles and parts, maid service, business services, dry cleaning, home repair, health clubs, industrial supplies, building products, schools, vending operations -- the list is growing every year. Franchising is a business method used by companies that are active in more than 60 different types of business enterprises.

The idea of franchising businesses is not new but its growth in recent years has been outstanding. Government statistics show a tremendous increase in activity in every segment of the franchise economy.

According to a report of the House Government Operations Committee, "The concept of modern franchising, particularly in its evolution since the late 1960s, has opened a remarkable door of opportunity for many of our country's small businessmen and women."

The Commerce Department calls franchising a, "significant part of the U. S. economy", and reports that franchising, "continues to prove its validity as a marketing method adaptable to an ever-widening array of industries and professions while providing immediate identity and recognition for prospective entrepreneurs joining the system."

FRANCHISING TODAY

As of 2007 there are about 1,500 different franchisors and about 750,000 franchised companies in the United States. In 2004, analysts estimate sales of goods and services through franchise companies and their franchisees were $1.5 trillion in annual U. S. retail sales. Analysts also estimate that franchising employs more than 18 million people.

The leading association in the field, the International Franchise Association (IFA), was founded by Dunkin Donuts entrepreneur William Rosenberg and other franchise pioneers. And they're only part of the growing franchising universe.

On an average, a new franchise outlet opens in the United States once every 8 minutes around the clock.

The **Top 10 Franchises for 2009** from Entrepreneur Magazine are:
1.   Subway
2.   McDonalds
3.   Liberty Tax Service
4.   Sonic Drive In Restaurants
5.   InterContinential Hotels
6.   Ace Hardware Stores
7.   Pizza Hut

8.   UPS Stores, The Mail Boxes Etc.
9.   Circle K
10.   Papa John's Int'l

WHAT IS FRANCHISING?

A franchise or a franchising operation is a legal agreement between the owner (franchisor) of a trademark, service mark, trade name, or advertising symbol and an individual or group (franchisee) wishing to use the trademark, etc in a business. The franchise controls the relationship for conducting business between the two parties.

As a franchisee you use a franchisor's name, special supplies and method of running the business. You pay for the opportunity and operate the way the franchisor tells you. It's your business, but the franchisor controls what you do. The basis of the franchise is an agreement which spells out both the rights and the obligations of you and your franchisor.

The franchisor owns all the trademarks, business methods and supplies that it allows others to use under their contract. The difference between a franchisor and a corporation operating a chain of stores is that the chain store has store managers who are company employees, whereas the franchise operation is owned and managed by self-employed business people.

The franchisor offers the use of a trade name, a store design, standardized operating methods and a protected territory. In addition the franchisor generally accepts the responsibility of keeping a continuing interest in the business of the franchisee.

The franchisor will usually help in such areas as site location, management training, financing, marketing, promotion, and record keeping. The franchisee, in return, agrees to operate under the conditions specified by the franchisor and pays a royalty fee.

For the help and services provided, the franchisee is usually expected to make a capital investment in the business and to pay fees and royalties to the franchisor. In some cases the franchisee agrees to buy all of his products from the franchisor.

A Practical Partnership

The appeal of franchising for the independent business man or woman is that it is a practical and economic means of fulfilling the franchisee's desire for independence with a minimum of risk and investment and maximum opportunities for success through the use of a proven product or service and a proven marketing method. Franchising is a way to be in business for yourself, not by yourself.

A franchising company depends upon the successful operation of franchise outlets to stay in business and build its profits. It needs individuals who are determined to succeed, are willing to learn the business, and have the energy for hard work. A good franchisor can supply the other basics for successful operation of the business.

KINDS OF FRANCHISES

There are two types of franchise systems:

1. **Product or trade name franchising** is the sales relationship between a supplier and dealer in which the dealer has been given some of the identity of the supplier. Automobile dealerships, gasoline service stations and soft drink bottlers

---

are some examples. As you would guess, they require large amounts of financial investment, frequently in the millions of dollars.

2. The field we're most interested in is called **business format franchising** because it deals with opportunities which are within the reach of millions of Americans. Some business format franchise opportunities require investments as small as a few thousand dollars, and there are many proven franchise businesses that can be started with an initial capital outlay of less than $100,000. Business format franchising accounts for more than 90 percent of the franchise operations in business today.

Business format franchising involves a continuing relationship between the franchisor and its franchisees. That relationship generally involves:

- A product or service
- A trademark
- A marketing system
- Location search and assistance in selecting a business site
- Lease negotiation
- Store design, store development aid and equipment purchasing
- Signage
- Financial assistance in the establishment of the business
- Operating manuals and procedures for standardized procedures and operations
- Initial employee and management training, and continuing management counseling training programs
- Centralized purchasing with the benefit of cost savings
- Advertising and merchandising support.
- Advertising counsel and assistance.
- Access to other franchisees for help or ideas.
- Ongoing assistance and guidance from the franchisor.

The greatest attraction of franchising is that it is one opportunity no one has to miss.   Even with its impressive growth over the past decade, franchising is a young system of marketing.   Thousands of great opportunities still exist for new franchisees.

In addition to types of franchises, there are many different industries including:

- Food
- Convenience Stores
- General Merchandise
- Diet and Services
- Fitness Services
- Business Services
- Real Estate Services
- Employment Services
- Printing/Photocopying Services
- Automobile/Truck Rental Services
- Construction/Home Improvement Services
- Laundry/Dry Cleaning Services
- Educational Services
- Hair Care Services
- Leisure and Travel
- Automotive

With so many choices it can be hard to figure out which one may be right for you.   There are many franchise consultants who can help you make a decision about industry and find one that matches you personal and business goals.   Search for one in your local area.

HOW A FRANCHISE WORKS

In addition to the original idea for the business, the franchisor provides the

---

135

identity and in many cases, the product which may have taken years and a good deal of money to establish. The franchisor offers a refined and tested operating system developed through years of experience of headquarters specialists and earlier franchisees.

The franchisee is an independent business owner who pays the franchisor for the right to put this recipe for success to use. As a franchisee you provide all or nearly all the working capital to establish and develop the outlet. There is a continuous financial relationship, usually including a fee paid in advance, plus a continuing royalty based on an established percentage of gross revenues.

Ideally, when you purchase a franchise, you are also purchasing a pre-packaged business. Although you own every part of it, you have a partner, your franchisor, who can insist or sometimes merely suggest how you run your business.

As you start searching for the exact franchise business that would meet your requirements, you will notice the large differences among them; the differences in quality of image, polish and approach. Some franchisors will seem aggressive, organized and professional. Others will seem thorough, plodding and simple. Still others may come across as slick, rigid and too anxious to close the deal.

A Respected Identity

The most important thing a franchisor has to offer is a good name in the industry. The worth of a franchise identity is also the result of the recognition, reputation and goodwill of the franchise organization. People who invest in franchises are looking for a successful image. When you take on a franchise, your franchisor's

---

character, in effect, becomes your identity.

The day you open up for business you cease being just an individual and become someone with something special to offer the public; you'll suddenly become Mr. Burger King...Ms. Nutri/System...or Mr. and Mrs. Dollar Rental.

A Successful Operating System

When you buy a franchise, you are purchasing more than just a trade name; you are also counting on a proven formula for success. So, one of the most important elements of franchising is the simplicity with which the organization's systems and procedures can be transferred to a franchisee.

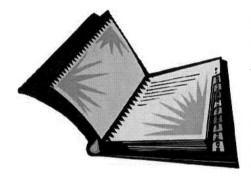 Some franchisors will offer you a complete "turn-key" outlet; when you are finished with franchise school, you receive the keys to a business in which everything has been set up for a ready-to-run operation. More commonly, a franchisor will provide you with blueprints, manuals, specifications, and training; then it's your responsibility to use your own drive to get the business established.

The franchisor's "how-to" bible is the franchise operating manual. The manual covers everything from accounting procedures to employee supervision. It also spells out standards and policies that all franchisees are expected to follow.

The manual is lent to you for the term of the franchise agreement. When the agreement is ended, you must return the complete manual to the franchisor. This requirement is intended to maintain the condition of secrecy about the franchise system and the know-how it takes to run it. After all, if the formula wasn't a valuable and special secret, why would you pay good money to purchase it?

At the same time, there will be questions that come up as you learn the business and even at times when new situations arise. That's when you'll need continuing help from the franchisee.

Here's what one franchisee has to say:

For Kay Lange, a former data processing consultant, McMaid (a maid service franchise) proved to be the right decision, bringing her more than $750,000 in annual sales. McMaid appealed to Lange because of its training and franchise services. "Ongoing service support is as important as training. The home office has helped me with everything from bulk purchases of equipment and supplies, to a marketing program. Help is just a phone call away."

THE FINANCIAL RELATIONSHIP

How does the franchisor receive payment for the franchisee's use of its identity and operating system? It collects a fee from the franchisee. The most usual franchise fee arrangement consists of three parts:

- The initial payment due on signing of the franchise agreement.
- A continuous royalty, usually charged on the gross revenues of the outlet.
- Royalty or contribution to a co-operative advertising fund.

Usually, a new or small franchise will charge a comparatively small fee. On the other hand, the larger the franchise organization, the more you can expect to pay for the privilege of joining.

THE VALUE OF EXPERIENCE

Investment in a franchise gains for the new business owner access to important specialized information, developed and organized by people who have already been successful in the business. The franchisor is a source of detailed working information that a new franchisee would find difficult to acquire without spending thousands of dollars and years of effort to acquire.

Franchising sets up a common economic interest between the franchisor and the franchisee, who share risk as well as profit. The franchisor has a built-in interest in helping its franchisee partner.

IS FRANCHISING RIGHT FOR YOU?

Now that you know what a franchise is all about, the big questions are; is franchising right for you, are you right for franchising? Despite all the tempting true success stories about franchising performance in creating successful small business owners; a franchise is not the ideal method of entrepreneurship for everybody.

Before you spend your money to make the big move, it's especially important to spend some serious thought and time on self-analysis.

Think about it, do the reasons for considering franchising outweigh the advantages of simply making a go of it on your own? You might well come to the conclusion that your personality, abilities and skills place you among the twenty percent of independent business owners who succeed on their own without becoming a franchise owner.

Consider that in a number of ways, the franchisee is not

his or her own boss. The franchisor's main interest is to maintain the special conditions and the uniformity of the franchised service he is selling, and to insure that the operations of each outlet will reflect successfully on the organization as a whole.

The franchisor wants to protect and build its good will. So the franchisor generally insists on a large degree of continuing control over the operations of franchisees and requires them to meet the franchisor's special standards. In some cases, franchisees are required to conduct every part of their operation strictly by the book, following every instruction in the franchisor's manual. Desirable or not, to your way of thinking, most franchisees are prepared to follow the franchisor's directions all the way.

What all this means is that the owner of a franchised business must give up some options and freedom of action in business decisions that would be open to the owner of a non-franchised business. When you buy a franchise, you will have to sacrifice some part of your business freedom. The big question is, can you live with the requirements and restrictions of a franchise agreement?

With all of this, as a franchisee, you are still an independent business owner, with the final responsibility for your business' success or failure. Are you willing to accept all the limits to your independence in return for all the benefits you'll receive from a successful franchisor?

FACTORS TO CONSIDER

As you think about whether or not to become a franchisee, you are faced with the necessity of taking on not one, but three types of responsibilities:

1.   **Financial**
     The first, of course, is the financial obligation to pay the initial fee, proceed with the cost of

building and running the business, and giving up a share of the gross revenues.

2.   Logical

You must be prepared to accept the responsibilities of starting, developing and managing a business with your franchisor. You must be prepared to accept the long hours, the extra effort, the operational headaches, and the burdens of a heavy paper work load.

You must be willing to accept the standards, restrictions, requirements and operating guidelines of your franchisor. You must be prepared to sacrifice some measure of freedom in exchange for the franchisor's ready-to-go business format.

3.   Emotional

The emotional commitment is just as important as the financial. Entrepreneurs often have a genuine love/hate relationship with their businesses. It always starts with love. They are enthusiastic about the industry they're in; the product, the image and identity the business provides for them. Eventually that love may turn to hate when the franchisee realizes the relationship is not working out exactly as planned, and may even turn sour.

As a prospective franchisee, you need to analyze your emotional investment in the business. Think of yourself in the franchise environment. How do you feel about spending a great many of your waking hours there? Will you be proud to call yourself the owner of the business? Does it stimulate pride, enthusiasm, self-esteem? How do you feel about the franchisor and his staff? Do they inspire loyalty, motivation, confidence? Will you feel comfortable working with your franchisor for the entire term of the agreement?

HOW TO RATE A FRANCHISE BEFORE YOU BUY

Once you've decided that a franchise is the best way for you to go, it's time to answer the question that will determine your success or failure in business and may likely have a critical influence on your life for years to come. How can you can tell whether a franchise is worth buying? Since there are thousands of franchises available, there is certainly no quick or easy way to make a decision.

The first thing to decide is the category of business you'll be most interested in, and then to get the necessary information for five to ten franchises in that category.

Most franchisors will send you a package of brochures that contain the information you will need to make an initial decision on which franchises you want to seriously consider. Much of the business data you need for this first step is available from a representative of the franchise through the Uniform Franchise Offering Circular, or UFOC.

Here are some of the factors you'll definitely want to keep in mind:

Background
Consider the history of the franchise; how it was started, who are the people who began it, who have operated it and what kind of results have they experienced in the past. Obtain additional facts and statistics about the particular industry that include the franchise you're interested in. Your local library can probably supply a great deal of the materials for the information you'll need.

People in your area, who are acquainted with a particular business, can provide another good source. Professional organizations, universities and the local chapter of the American Association of Retired Persons are also good likely sources of background information.

Demand for the Product

In any business you need to determine if there is demand in your community for the type of product or service the franchise has to offer. In some instances, the demand is there, but there are too many other businesses supplying that service. Another business in that industry will take away from all the rest. Is the demand seasonal? Is the demand increasing or decreasing? Is it a fad or does it encourage repeat customers?

Competition

What is the level of competition for your product or service in your community? What are the restrictions for the franchisor to put in another store across the street from yours? Are the competitors well known, with better name recognition? Do they offer similar goods and services at lower prices?

Business Background

Length of experience is one good indicator of the kind of success that can be expected. Consider how many years a company has been in business. How many years has the company been offering franchises? For example, McDonald's has been in business and offering franchises since 1955. No commercial enterprise can stay in business unless it is profitable, so if it has passed the test of time, it's a pretty good bet that it knows how to weather the ups and downs of business conditions.

Look carefully at the franchisor's financial condition. Examine financial documents especially for indications of the company's solidity and credit worthiness. Sometimes franchisors go out of business. Do you need the franchisor to be successful? Will you have access to suppliers?

Number of Franchises

Obviously the more outlets a franchisor has the more acceptance its business program has gained with entrepreneurs and the public. The total size of the business is another indication of how likely it is to be an ongoing operation with the greatest expectation of success.

Minimum Franchise Fee

As always, financial considerations are critical. If you can afford the price of admission, a more expensive franchise fee is less likely to be a consideration. If your funds are limited, for all practical purposes, you will have to limit your choices to those franchises that will accept a lower entry fee.

Minimum Capital Requirements

The franchise fee is one thing, the next most important financial consideration is the minimum capital required. This item includes your estimated or the franchisor's required minimum amount of cash and financing needed to begin the franchise operation. For the small investor the less expensive an operation is the more realistic prospect it becomes.

Company-Owned Stores

Many franchisors also have company-owned franchises. Certainly the fewer of these there are, the better from the franchisee's point of view. If a franchisor's profits are coming mostly from actual franchise operations, it will tend to pay more attention to its franchisees.

Growth Patterns

Consider how many franchises the company has opened in past years. Notice if the trend is up, or if the franchisor has reduced the number of franchises it has. Naturally, older firms may show a pattern of fewer new franchises as they mature, while newer companies may show greater activity shortly after they enter the market.

Total Royalty Fees

This item includes all monthly royalties and payments, advertising royalties and any other payment required from the franchisee by the franchising firm. To get a true picture of the value offered, it will be necessary to compare total royalties to the kind and quantity of services offered.

Financing Provided

Some franchisors will supply financial assistance to the franchisee to pay the initial and ongoing costs of conducting the business. Although an attractive extra, financial assistance should not be considered as a major decision factor; or a substitute for very careful, thorough investigation into all the facts in your choice of any franchise. It is simply another element that can be put into the mix.

How to Get Information

The majority of information you need to start evaluating a franchise is the company's Uniform Financial Offering Circular (UFOC). You can find many of the most popular franchises at www.ufocs.com.

Call or visit local current and past owners of the kind of franchises that you're interested in. Ask them what they think of the franchise company, its operations and the kind of help the franchisor has given them. Another good idea is to call or write some franchisees in other parts of the country. They may be experiencing better or worse economic situations in their areas and could give you an idea of how the particular business reacts to changed economic conditions.

Talk with your banker. He or she should have access to solid facts that will give you another view of the franchise's economic situation. Your banker may have inside details on the franchises you are considering and a good idea of the problems or opportunities you will have in gaining financing for your franchise venture.

Talk with an accountant. Have him or her check over the pro forma figures provided by the franchisor. These can include projected profit and loss statements, balance sheets, cash flow statements and projections for your location based on a similar demographic location. Have your accountant determine if they make financial sense.

Finally, talk with your lawyer and get a professional analysis of the franchise and the terms you are being offered. It is very important that your lawyer go over the franchise contract with extreme care. Remember, an agreement is just that; a bargain between two or more parties, and it can be changed or modified.

A contract that satisfies the needs of both parties at the beginning of the relationship can spare you grief and financial problems in the future, when it could be too late to change the arrangement.

Most important, avoid financial commitments before the agreement is completely worked out. Some franchisors may push for decisions before you have all the facts by offering special considerations. Avoid these situations at all costs, the final cost may be too high.

WHAT TO EXPECT FROM YOUR FRANCHISOR

CO-OP ADVERTISING
Your franchise must be promoted before, during, and after opening. You must sell yourself and your business however and wherever you can. It is rare for even the best product or service to succeed within a reasonable length of time without an active and intelligent advertising and promotion program.

146

Besides the initial fee and monthly royalty, most franchisors also require franchisees to pay a monthly ad royalty, usually a small percentage of their gross income, into a co-op fund. Monies gathered in an advertising fund are pooled to finance national and regional advertising campaigns for the benefit of all franchisees.

The franchisor benefits from increased promotion of the trade name and business, which in turn increases the value of your franchise and the amount of royalty dollars you will contribute.

 **Business Locations**

Not all franchisors have a co-op advertising fund. Many franchise systems have no central advertising program but require franchisees to manage and pay for their own advertising. The problem with this arrangement is that it can lead to a loss of control over the franchise image you paid for. Helter skelter promotions by various franchisees can lead to lowering the value of the franchise for all franchisees.

NETWORKING WITH OTHER FRANCHISEES

Being a part of a franchise system has some incredible benefits. One benefit is the access to other people that are running the same business as you, but in different areas of the country. Really good franchise companies are setting up methods for franchisees to communicate with each other. Some suggestions to look for are Intranet site, protected chat rooms, email addresses, and on-going conference calls and communications. These methods help all franchisee exchange data and ideas to each other.

SITE SELECTION HELP

The best franchise companies have established systems that can help you find a good location and acquire it on the best available terms. Actually, working with a franchisee in site selection, helping in the construction of a store or fixing up a storefront, are such important activities in the business mix that franchisors have become more active in these areas over the years.

A favorable site for one type of business will not necessarily be good for another. Each different business requires certain qualities that you will be seeking in a good location: a quality site for a Jiffy Lube shop will definitely be wrong for a Karmelkorn Shoppe or a Mr. Donut. Each business appeals to particular kinds of individuals with different tastes, needs and habits.

Many franchise companies have developed exact and scientifically selected requirements for locations in which experience shows their particular franchise operations will do best. Some companies have staffs that include marketing specialists who study census, population distribution and trend information about the best potential areas for franchises. This is valuable information for any entrepreneur who wants to have every possible advantage on his or her side.

The franchisor may have real-estate specialists who constantly seek out and update lists of available sites - vacant land, shopping centers under construction, empty storefronts, and so on, within the targeted areas. In some cases, a franchisor may already have made arrangements for ready-to-rent or purchase locations within your territory.

Some franchisors help negotiate the purchase or lease of your land or building. They may help arrange for a contractor to build the facility or, with an owner/developer, to lease it to you. If you are locating in an existing center or mall, the franchise company may lease a storefront and sublet it to you on as good or better terms than you could obtain for yourself.

If you have to build a structure, the franchisor may even provide plans that are already approved by local government agencies. In the case of most fast-food and some other franchises you will be required to build a store according to their set plans; put up required signage, and install the required equipment in a certain way.

Then again, there are franchisors who don't do any of these things. In that case you will have the whole burden of doing market research, finding a suitable location, leasing or buying the space, laying out the interior, fixing up the exterior, even buying a new structure. So, it's important to determine what the franchisor will do to help you find the best location and then make sure these steps are put into the agreement in writing.

TRAINING

Most men and women who buy franchises have no experience in the business they're entering. That's natural because a majority of the people who buy franchises are changing careers. But, in order to succeed, new franchisees must learn a great deal about what's involved in their new career before opening for business.

The best way to do this is to make the most out of the franchisor's training program.

The franchisor may offer training at a headquarters "college". These are usually well planned to provide the background you need to get the business off to a good start and to use all the know-how the franchisor has to offer. Formal training sessions are one of the most helpful supports a franchisor can provide to a franchisee and you should take advantage of as much as you can get.

But you should take one step more - get training at an actual store or franchise location. As part of your franchise arrangement, or if necessary, on your own seek out the opportunity to work for a week or two in a functioning store. Make hamburgers, clean carpets, sell mufflers, sweep floors - learn whatever you can that a seasoned operator knows is needed to make that franchise work.

Added to your classroom training, in-the-field practical experience will give you a first hand understanding of what you have to do to make your new business work.

Some franchisors will send a field representative to help train you and your new employees before the grand opening. If your franchisor doesn't offer this service you're on your own, so it's important to find out early how much on-site training is included in the franchise package and where you can locate the help you'll need.

Most franchisors offer some type of on-going training, even if it's only newsletters or regularly scheduled seminars. You'll want to find out about where your franchisor stands on such valuable services as advanced training on accounting and computer systems, new products and supplying a steady stream of marketing ideas.

It's a good idea to check with existing franchisees to find out just how effective the franchisor's training program is. If it looks like you won't be getting all the training support you'll need, the best source of help again is other franchisees who have faced the problem before you. They're usually very willing to help new people in the business and have often set up franchisee committees to provide mutual support.

OPERATING PRACTICES

The operations manual and the franchise contract will require you to meet the company's standards of quality and uniformity of appearance in these areas among others:

- ❖ Product, equipment, fixtures and furniture
- ❖ Number, quality, quantity, type, size and shape of products
- ❖ Product availability
- ❖ Advertising and marketing controls
- ❖ Internal security
- ❖ Auditing procedures
- ❖ Employee conduct

Several court decisions have held that a franchisor cannot require you to buy products or services only from them. Most however, can and do, enforce quality standards and specifications. Violations of these can lead to the termination of your contract. There have been cases in which franchisees have been found in breach of contract for such seemingly minor violations as having smudges on a men's room mirror. Franchisors can get very picky when they think you might be tampering with their image and business. That's why franchisors maintain staffs of company inspectors.

The contract may also dictate the days and business hours you must be open; set any sales quota and penalties for not meeting them and explain any wholesale or discount purchasing plans available through the franchisor

ONGOING MANAGEMENT ASSISTANCE

Continuing help for franchisees can range anywhere from advice over the phone to having a company representative visit you whenever you feel the need for guidance and advice. In dealing with some franchisors you may have to pay an hourly rate or flat fee every time you ask the company to help you solve a problem.

One franchisee may be so unsure of himself/herself that he demands a helping hand every time something doesn't go according to the manual. Others may be so confident of their own abilities that they feel no need to ever see the field rep and want no help or interference at all.

Here's how one outstanding franchisor, Midas Muffler supports its franchisees:

A field force of division and district representatives meet on a regular basis with franchisees.

Midas' real-estate, marketing, advertising and sales promotion executives work directly with all franchisees.

There is an open-door policy by which franchisees can go right to the top and get in direct touch with the president of the company.

The company goes to the dealers and asks their advice before any new programs are put into effect. Midas understands that the franchisees must believe in and support new programs to make them work.

The franchisor encourages its franchisees to expand. To support such a move Midas provides high quality market research.

Midas has a policy of giving current franchisees first crack at expanding and opening new outlets in their area.

That's how one first-class franchisor deals with its franchisees, builds a happy family of franchisors and a highly successful business.

THINGS TO LOOK OUT FOR

We've spent most of this chapter discussing the benefits of operating a franchise operation - and there are plenty of them. There have been  success stories enough to fill a raft of magazines and books. But, be warned; as in most things that look too good to be true, there are serious downside considerations as well.

As we've mentioned before, and it bears repeating, as a franchisee you are locked into a single company, and are required by contract to accept the company's rules, regulations and methods of doing business. There's always small print in the contract that defines your relationship to the franchise company for better or worse. In some ways a franchise relationship is like a marriage in which each side counts on the other party to provide help and support.

Sometimes this means that you, as an entrepreneur, are stuck in a situation where you cannot move quickly to meet your business' particular local needs - to take quick action against a competitor or meet changing financial or market conditions. As a franchisee you may have to wait for word from headquarters before you take steps to solve the problem.

Franchise fees are forever, or at least for the duration of the contract. When you sign that contract you are tied to a relationship that requires you to pay for the privilege of franchising and the advantages you get every month, every year.

Finally, if the franchise firm has business reverses, through no fault of yours, you have to live with the results of their actions. Everything they do reflects on you and your operation.

IT'S NOT ALL ROSES

Articles in business publications and franchisors who are anxious to sell you, indicate that buying a franchise is a guarantee of good fortune. Amazing success rates of 95 percent to 99 percent have been reported. Even the government seems to support these figures. Although franchising may be the most foolproof way of getting a business going, there are still failures; nothing like the rate of failure for independent small businesses but enough to keep potential franchisees on their toes.

You know what they say about liars figuring and figures lying. The statistics don't tell you about the franchisee in Des Moines who invested $100,000 in a business and eventually had to sell it to someone else for $15,000 because that was all he could get. The business is still in operation and it's included in the success statistics - the $85,000 loss however, is not shown anywhere.

Franchisors are not very anxious to report failures within their system. Some buy back failed franchises either at the original cost or at a loss to the franchisee. Others attempt to sell their distressed operations. A few hope their failures will simply go away and still others carry a franchise on their records even though it's been closed for months. When a franchisor states they have 250 operating units, there may only be 200 actually open for business. Fifty have been closed and are up for sale.

One man, anxious to get in on the franchise bonanza was contacted by a company that offered him not only a franchise but three existing company-owned locations. To complete the deal he was required to pay, in addition to the royalty fees, for the buildings and the equipment.

It wasn't until after he had signed the contracts and had been in business for months that he discovered the restaurants he had purchased were sold by the owners because they had not made a profit in over three years – while they were being operated by the franchisor. What's more he found that the used equipment he had purchased could have been bought new, on the open market, for less. It can not be emphasized too much - as in any venture, it is best to beware of who you are doing business with.

By and large franchising is the safest form of independent business ownership, but you should never think franchising is a sure thing. You can't give a franchisor a check and automatically expect instant success. Consider franchising with the same thorough eye you would any other investment.

If you look on a franchise as a guardian angel that won't let you fail, no matter what, you are unlikely to succeed for two reasons: A good franchisor who gets the idea that you're not likely to work hard at make it a success probably won't let you buy in.

Second, even the best franchise in the business cannot prevent lack of ability from causing failure. A franchisor may finally help to save an unsuccessful operation to preserve the franchisor's reputation and keep a store open, but you still carry the burden of success or failure. At worst you could lose your franchise and your investment – and your store may go on to another franchisee that could make a success of it without you.

> *In this chapter you have learned:*
> 1. *Franchising is a form of business partnership with a franchisor.*
> 2. *Franchises come in many different forms and industries.*
> 3. *Franchising has serious commitments, just like any other small business.*
> 4. *As a franchisee there are certain things you should expect from your franchisor.*
> 5. *Choosing a franchise takes as much research and time (may be more) as starting your own small business. Each opportunity its own positive and negative issues.*

 Websites & Books You May Find Useful

International Franchise Association – www.franchise.org
Uniform Franchise Offering Circular Directory – www.ufocs.com

 **Step To Success
One Action a Day Will Move You Forward**

It is time to move forward. Complete the **Step to Success** Action and feel your progress. No matter where you are going, you can get there one step at a time.

If franchising is for you, start making a list of the franchises that interest you. Then contact one of the current franchisees to see if you can interview them about the franchise. Make a list of questions and tell us how it went at Mentors@aisb.biz.

You can do it, so start NOW!

Chapter 10

Faster Success – Buy a Business???

"He who is not courageous enough to take risks will accomplish nothing in life." --Muhammad Ali (1942 -) American boxer

BUY A BUSINESS OR START FROM SCRATCH?

This is the $64,000 question! Should I start my business from scratch or, do I find just such a business that is available for sale? Each one has its advantages as well as its disadvantages. For those individuals who have a business idea that is new to the market or where their experience is unique should strongly consider starting a business from scratch. Transforming a current business into a new business process is difficult.

But what about the person who wants to go into a business in which the product or service is not new. That is, where competition is plentiful and the type of business has been around for some time. This is the scenario for most businesses. Many experts agree that the safest and most effective way into business is to buy someone else's business.

In this chapter you will discover the advantages and disadvantages of buying an existing business. In the next chapter, you will discover the benefits and challenges of starting from scratch. So let's get started.

BUYING A BUSINESS

When one thinks about buying business that is already set up and running, the first thing that comes to mind is: "Wow, all I have to do is to open the doors and let in the customers!" There are many advantages to buying a business rather starting one up from ground floor. The main reason to buy a business is the incredible reduction in start-up costs of time, money and energy.

Let us look at these advantages. They all do not apply to every business that is purchased, but, in many situations, several of these advantages do apply.

ADVANTAGES TO BUYING A BUSINESS

1. Name Recognition. A going business has a name. It is recognized by both customers and suppliers. In some instances, one cannot put a value on a name. Large franchises are a good example of name recognition. Take for example **"McDonalds"**-what comes to mind immediately? If you answered Hamburgers, you are correct! Or take the name of **Roto-Rooter**. What first comes to your mind? If you thought of: "Clogged plumbing or sewer lines", you would be correct.

2. History. History is defined as an "account of what has happened." This is equally true when applied to a business. It is reflected in every aspect of a business over a period of time including such important areas as start-up, sales, profits, product lines, and relationships to customers, employees and suppliers. It has often been said that history repeats itself. Thus one can learn much from studying a company that has been purchased and learn from it's past experiences and operations.

3. Customer base. One of the major advantages in the purchase of an ongoing business is that it has established customers. For without customers there can be no business. One can have the greatest product, or it may offer the greatest service, but without customers the business would be unable to survive.

Likewise one can have adequate financing and can have top management. Again, without customers, the cash register does not ring.

4. Distributor Base. If your business works through distributors, many of the agreements and contracts have already been negotiated for you. This may be good or bad for your company. So make sure you check out the agreements before you finalize the purchase.

5. Employees.   Elmer Smith, the father and pioneer of the oxygen acetylene welding and cutting equipment industry in this country was once asked by a business reporter from the **Wall Street Journal:** "What do you attribute your success to?" He responded by saying: "I surrounded myself in each area of my business with employees who were smarter then me!" Often when purchasing a business, a key element may be that it comes with good employees.

For example employees who understand the business and the industry. Those employees who are conscientious loyal and faithful. Or those who have good rapport with customers and have solid product knowledge.

6. Known product line. There is nothing like getting up in the morning and looking into your pantry closet and having a choice of your favorite cereals for breakfast. The same can be true for a company that has been in business selling a product or service that has name recognition within the community. In some instances, it may have taken years to establish this recognition. Regardless of the time length, having a product line that both customers and prospects are familiar with, has considerable value.

7. Company assets. The assets of an ongoing business fall into two main groups. They are tangible assets and those which are intangible. Examples of tangible assets include such items as inventory, cash, accounts receivables, equipment, supplies, and real estate. Examples of intangible assets include goodwill, business name, logos, company history, and employees. All assets have value. Thus when one purchases a business, he or she is able to see a value to part of their cost of buying the business. Some assets take not only money, but lots of time to create. A logo can be very valuable but take a long time to create.

8. Banking history. One of the more difficult problems for a person going into business, and particularly for one not having been in business, is to establish a banking relationship with a banker. This problem is greatly alleviated especially when one purchases an ongoing business. Whoever has been the seller's banker, is quite familiar with the history of the business and especially the financial history. Such familiarity facilitates the buyer in continuing on with the banking relationship.

9. Supplier relationships. We have already seen where one of the advantages to purchasing a business is that of the "known product line." Tied in with this is: who are the suppliers to this product line?" For it usually will insure that there will be an ongoing source of supply for the products being sold. It also means that the suppliers have confidence in the business and have an opportunity to open up a new relationship with their new customer. Considerable time and energy can be used up locating new sources of supply for a new business and in establishing a relationship.

10. Location familiarity. There is an old saying: "There is no place like home." That is because one is familiar with it and it's surroundings. Likewise, when a business has been in a specific location for a period of time, customers and prospects automatically know where to come. If the business is a store, they know where to go to find certain merchandise. Knowing the location comes from using the business which in many instances leads to familiarity with employees and even owners.

11. Equipment in place. Most businesses require the need for certain types of equipment. If it is a manufacturing firm, depending upon what is being produced will determine the type of machinery needed to produce what is being made. If it is a service company, then tools are usually the important equipment to run the business. A major advantage to buying a business is the fact that the necessary machinery, equipment and tools are in place.

12. Office furniture and supplies. When one thinks about starting a business the emphasis on cost is placed on inventory, if products are being sold, the location and leasehold improvements, employee salaries, and if it is a manufacturing firm, necessary equipment. Office furniture and supplies are generally last on the list unless the business deals with "walk-in customers." Obviously, when one purchases an operating business, most likely any needed office furniture and supplies will be in place.

13. Inventory. Imagine being able to open the doors to one's new business, such as a sporting goods store, for the very first time, and not having to order a single item that is going to be sold. Imagine having a customer enter your store, walk down the aisles putting tennis balls, athletic shoes, shorts, a tennis racket and shirts into a shopping cart. The customer then come directly to your cash register. What thought would be going through your mind?

Better still, what do you think you will feel when the customer puts his or her charge card or cash in your hand to pay for the purchase? This is what comes when you purchase an ongoing business such as the sporting goods store. Simply put, you open the doors and are ready to go.

14. Relationship with community. Often the success of a business rests with having a good relationship with the community. This includes the local government, such as the city council, licensing departments within the city, and possibly the city purchasing department. Likewise, certain groups of customers within the community may be important such as contractors, schools, or fraternal organizations. These relationships are already in place by an existing business which makes them a valuable asset to the next owners.

15. Historical image-advertising. What comes to mind when you hear the name of a business? **Walmart?**-Discount Store. **Home Depot?**-Hardware store. **IBM?** Computers. **Allstate?** Insurance. These names are all on the national scene. But in each and every community, small or large, certain business names in each and every field or industry stand out over and above all others. Likewise, when one purchases a business, he or she is purchasing a name which hopefully has high recognition in the community where it is located.

---

16. Consultants and advisors in place. One of the advantages of purchasing a business, is that it may come with invaluable advisors who may have assisted the business over a long period of time. Examples of these include consultants in advertising, insurance, banking and finance. Or if the business has an uncommon mission, such as a publisher of software, then having the right copyright attorney and software developers in place could prove to be invaluable.

17. Business policies. Business policies come in all forms. They cover a broad range of the operations of the business. Policies may include how to handle return goods to when to charge for delivery or gift wrapping. Other policies on employee personnel policies such as sick leave, vacation, overtime, working hours, dress code and review procedures are already written. It is easier to update current policies than to create new ones.

Another type of business policies are in the area of products and services such as warranties and guarantees. Business policies are usually in

written form in order to be meaningful both to consumers and employees. Considerable time and effort is saved in this area when purchasing a business. In purchasing a business, be sure to ask for all the written policies.

18. Using the business to buy the business. One of the leading advantages to purchasing a business over that of "starting from scratch" is the possibility of using the assets of the business as collateral in the actual purchase of the business. Assets of an existing business can be in the account receivables, real estate, machinery and equipment, inventory, even good will (business name or logos).

For example, let us assume that you are giving consideration to the purchase of a sporting goods store. The seller's price is $150,000. You have only $25,000 in cash. If the store has $75,000 in good clean inventory, one can use this inventory and pledge it as collateral to the bank for a loan. Or, if the store has $25,000 in account receivables, such as from schools and athletic teams, this too can be used as collateral in obtaining the loan.

In finance language, this is called "assigning the asset" to the bank or organization that is making the loan." In most instances, banks will require collateral or something which has corresponding value or importance, to cover the amount of the loan. This is protection that the bank requires in the event that one is unable to repay the loan.

19. Cash flow. To the owner of a business, there is no better music to one's ears then hearing the cash register ring. The "feel" of money is like instant gratification. Therefore, when purchasing an ongoing business, the buyer can experience this instant gratification as the cash register rings over and over again.

This is important since it is a direct reflection of what is considered positive "cash flow" for a business. Unlike opening a new business from starting at it's very beginning, one that is already operating produces cash from day one.

20. Availability of owner's knowledge and advice. One advantage of buying a business is the opportunity to learn from the experiences of the past owner. The owner can represent a wealth of knowledge particularly if he or she started the business or has been operating it over a relatively long period of time. The buyer can learn from both mistakes that the previous owner has made as well as the successes of the business.

Probably the most important areas that any new owner can learn from the seller, is what mistakes were made in the past. What advertising and marketing programs should be avoided? What are the important sources of supply? What products sold better than others? In plain and simple words, what works and what does not work?

21. Reduced Time. Many of the tasks associated with starting a business from scratch are time consuming. Constant decisions need to be made on products, policies, hiring, site selection, tax filings, banking relationships and supplier negotiations.  When buying a business so many of these items have already been done for you. You always can update them over time, but at least they are set up in the beginning. Creation always takes longer than modification. One more advantage would be the time saved in creating financial projections. It is much easier to create projections if you have past figures to use. This reduces the amount of time you need to spend on your projections.

WHAT TO LOOK FOR IN BUYING A BUSINESS

It is important to make a good decision in buying your own business. Remember this can be one of the safest and most effective ways to have your own business. Here is what to look for:

1. Look for something you enjoy – Fit with your business is incredibly important. It doesn't make sense to purchase a profitable business if you hate what you are doing. Every day will be harder and harder to get out of bed. It is also difficult to keep up with changes in the industry and helping customers is stressful.
2. Seasoned small business – This is a business that has 3-5 years of financial records and tax filings that coincide with the financial statements. Failure rate of businesses that have been around for 5 or more years is lower than start ups.

3. Growth pattern – These businesses are keeping up with the trends and moving in the right direction.

4. Trained employees – Monitor the employees and the number of years they have been with the business. The longer they have been employed, the more they can teach you about the business.

5. Good customer base – Review the customer database and determine how often customers are contacted. A current database of customers is much more valuable that an out-of-date database. Also make sure the customer data is an electronic format.

6. Proper Equipment – Check with other businesses in this field and make sure you have equipment that is current. For example, in buying a restaurant, you need to know how old the refrigerators are, because they only last a few years.

7. Established Inventory – Having inventory already purchased and in stock makes selling easier. As you get more knowledgeable about your new business you can add products as they become available.

8. Written policies and procedures – Not only have the systems in place, but documentation around the processes will help you succeed faster. The documentation helps you from making the same mistakes the previous owner made.

WHERE TO FIND BUSINESSES FOR SALE

There are approximately 6 million businesses in the United States that have under 20 employees. Most of these businesses would be perfect to purchase, if they meet the criteria above. The majority of businesses for sale are found in five different areas:

1. Local newspaper in the Classified section.
Look under "Business Opportunities" or "Business Opportunities for Sale". Some local communities also have a section in local business magazines.

2. Search the Internet at www.bizbuysell.com, www.businessesforsale.com, the Wall Street Journal site or other

business for sale sites.

3. Find an experience business broker. You can find a listing of brokers in your local yellow pages or contact the International Business Brokers Association for a referral. See following section on how to chose a broker.

4. Call local Certified Public Accountants. These individuals prepare the taxes for many small businesses. They may know of a client that is interested in selling their business.

5. Call the owners of businesses that you frequent or look like you would enjoy owning. Ask the owner if they would like to sell. Be careful in this approach, because you may pay too much for the business if you look too eager.

FINDING A GOOD BUSINESS BROKER

A business broker is much like a real estate agent. Brokers match buyers with sellers and receive a commission for setting up the transaction.

When selecting a business broker it is important to find one that you like and trust. Start by setting up meetings with a couple of different brokers. Interview them just like you would interview any other potential partner. Ask questions like:

- How many years have you been a broker?
- What professional organizations do you belong to? The International Business Brokers Association (IBBA) is a non-profit trade association for business brokers. It has over 1,300 members and provides a professional certification process.
- Ask for previous customers as referrals and follow up to find out their experience.
- Ask your lawyer, accountant and peers for some referrals for good brokers.
- Ask about lawsuits or complaints against the broker. Follow up with the Better Business Bureau in your area.
- Have they purchased or sold businesses in the industry you are interested in?

- Avoid large up-front fees. Most brokers will receive 10-15% of the transaction in commission. Avoid brokers who ask for money up front to start looking for a business for you.
- Avoid brokers who put too much pressure on you to buy. Buying a company is a complex transaction and should be considered carefully.
- How accessible is your broker? When you call the office can you get a hold of him/her or do they return calls in a timely manner?
- Active database of businesses for sale. Each broker will have access to their own listings and connections into other brokers with additional businesses.
- Is the broker licensed? Although it is not required in all states, it is important to check it out.

The decision to hire one broker over another is an important decision. You want to make sure you make the best decision available to you.

VALUING A BUSINESS FOR SALE

 Coming to agreement with the owner on the price for the business is one of the most difficult negotiations. The main part of the price is based on the value of the business. Typically an owner will value the business far more than it may be worth because the business has been such an integral part of their lives. Ultimately, the value of any business is based on what someone is willing to pay for the business. Many times the financial statements will need to be recast to come up with a value. Business owners are motivated to pay the least amount of business taxes, so specific items may need to be adjusted to calculate an accurate value for a new owner.

Be sure to consult an attorney and an accountant before you make a bid for a company. Both the attorney and accountant can make sure you have covered all the financial bases before making a decision. Paying too much for a business is one of the leading causes of business failure after businesses change owners.

DISADVANTAGES TO BUYING A BUSINESS

As with any business situation, there are disadvantages. The following is a list of disadvantages of buying a business.

1. **Reduced Reward**. Because you normally will have a debt payment to the previous owner or a financing source, for purchasing the business. This will limit your cash flow for a certain length of time.

2. **Possible Problems.** No business is without problems. Normally you only want the "Good" problems, but in buying a business that is not always the case. Later in this chapter, we will discuss some due diligence questions that should help you reduce the unknown problems. However, it will not take away all the problems in a business.

3. **Ownership Transfer Issues.** Different issues pop up after all the documents have been signed. Selling a business is sometimes an emotional issue for the original owner, which makes it hard for them to let the new owner take control. In addition, it is difficult to document all  of the assets in the sale of a business. For this reason, it is important to work with an advisor/attorney that has experience in buying and selling businesses. They can help you identify the most important items that you will need to put in the agreements.

4. **Purchase Financing may be difficult to find.** Most of the decision to lend on a purchase of a business will be on the historical financials of that business. If the business is not doing well with the current owner, you will have to prove what you will do differently to

improve the sales of the business.

5. **Difficult to find the RIGHT Opportunity.** Sometimes you want to open a retail dress shop, but finding the one that will work can be difficult. This becomes increasingly difficult if you as the new owner want to install significant changes. Customers and employees are used to the "way things were".

6. **Unknown issues** with the business or the previous owner. One issue may be the pay history of the previous owner to the suppliers. Suppliers can not run an efficient business when their customers do not pay on time. If an owner has a history of late payments, it may reflect on your relationship with the supplier. One issue that is very important if you are purchasing property is the unknown environmental issue. You as a new owner can be held responsible for environmental clean up if you do not have adequate protection in the documents from buying the business. When the current owner of 1-800-Flowers decided to purchase that business he wanted to save money on due diligence. In the end he ended up with $4 million of liabilities that he didn't realize he had agreed to. It can not be stressed enough that you need a good attorney and accountant when purchasing a business.

7. **Large Initial Investment** – You may need to invest a lot more money into the business because the business has been neglected. This may include new equipment, professionals, or more marketing dollars.

8. **Employee Issues** – Depending on the previous owner, the employees may be upset that they will report to a new owner. Employee morale may be very low and it will take a while to get them productive again.

Whether you decide to buy a business or start from scratch, it is important to understand all the advantages and disadvantages. With the population aging and many business owners also aging, there are some great businesses for sale and will continue to be for sale for the next few years.

In this Chapter you have learned:

1. *When starting or buying a business you need good advisors to reduce the disadvantages associated with each scenario.*
2. *Buying a business has many advantages that can help you get up and running faster, including:*
   a. *Name recognition and company logos*
   b. *Customer base*
   c. *Employees*
   d. *Location familiarity*
   e. *Business Policies*
3. *On the other hand, buying a business has disadvantages including:*
   a. *Ownership transfer issues*
   b. *Difficult finding purchase financing*
   c. *Unknown issues from previous owner*

Websites You May Find Useful

The Internet's Largest Business for Sale Marketplace – www.bizbuysell.com

Small Business Administration - http://www.sba.gov/smallbusinessplanner/start/buyabusiness/index.html

Step To Success
One Action a Day Will Move You Forward

It is time to move forward. Complete the **Step to Success** Action and feel your progress. No matter where you are going, you can get there one step at a time.

Go to www.bizbuysell.com. Select a **Business Category** or **Business Location** on the left side of the page. Send us an email mentors@aisb.biz with the most fascinating or out-of-the-ordinary businesses you find.

Chapter 11

Starting Your Dream Business From the Ground Up

"There is only one valid definition of business purpose: to create a customer."
    --Peter Drucker (1909-2005) Austrian-born management consultant and writer

In this chapter you will learn:
    1. Advantages of starting a business from scratch
    2. Top 5 Disadvantages of starting a business from scratch.
    3. How to create a profitable list.
    4. How to manage the information on your customer list.
    5. What information to keep about your customers.

ADVANTAGES TO STARTING A BUSINESS FROM SCRATCH

1. Your own thing. One of the great joys in life is the fulfillment of a dream especially if the dream is that of having one's own business. How often does one have this childhood dream of having a business of their own and actually seeing fulfillment of the dream during their adulthood? Or, if having one's own business is not a childhood dream, how often does one work for someone else and feel he or she is not appreciated?

Regardless of why one wants to go into their own business the end result is that it satisfies the dream of "doing one's own thing." When this relates to one's own business, it is usually done with enjoyment and the desire to be successful.

2. Enthusiastic exuberance. Have you ever seen a child with a new toy? Can you describe the reaction on the child's face? If you can, imagine your own feelings and reaction, when you open the doors to your new business for the first time. You have boundless energy. Your chest swells with pride. Your feelings are one of excitement, anticipation and satisfaction. It is a culmination and fulfillment of one's dreams and aspiration. All of this leads to what one calls "enthusiastic exuberance." Such a feeling is much stronger when starting a business from scratch rather then purchasing an existing business.

The Small Business Administration has found the following on success factors of small business: "Major factors in a firm's remaining open include an ample supply of capital, being large enough to have employees, the owner's education level, and the ***owner's reason for starting the firm in the first place***, such as freedom for family life or wanting to be one's own boss."

3. New kid on the block. There is nothing like something that is new. Whether it be an automobile, new dress or suit of clothes, piece of jewelry, or for kids, a new bicycle, pair of skates or a sound system. They all attract the attention of friends and neighbors. Likewise, the same can be said about a new business especially if it the "new kid on the block." If it is a retail store or offering a potential consumer service, everyone who may possibly be a prospect or customer of the new kid wants to see what the premises look like, what products and services are offered and who are the owners.

Should the new business offer products and services that one has an interest now, or, in the future, then curiosity will prevail. One will want to see what products are being offered? What does the establishment look like? Who are the owners and employees? How are items priced? Even if it is a business that may not offer merchandise that one has an interest, the curiosity factor still prevails.

Take for example a restaurant that features an ethnic or nationality type food. Most people do not have a taste for every type of ethnic food whether it is Chinese, Indian, Mexican, French, Italian, New England early American, or Cajun style. Yet, most people are curious enough to see how is the restaurant decorated? What is on the menu?

4. Location. One major advantage of starting a business from scratch is the opportunity to choose where to locate the business. The only restriction is availability, zoning and cost. Aside from these, one has the opportunity to study the market and market conditions, and determine where their customers are concentrated.

When starting a business from scratch, you can select a location where you feel you can maximize sales and profits. A site or location can be chosen where there will be no restraints with regards to parking, hours of operation, traffic flow, and access.

5. New surroundings-leasehold improvements. Whether one opens their business in a new building or leases space which formerly housed a business, the owner has the opportunity to do all phases of the interior decorating to their wishes. One is not strapped with past facility restrictions. Like the "new kid on the block" one can have the lease hold improvements which best suits their clientele and in the new business owner's opinion best meets their needs and likes.

6. All new inventory. When one purchases a business, the entire existing inventory normally is included. If it is a manufacturing firm, the raw materials, goods in process and finished goods make up the inventory. If it is a retail or wholesale establishment, then the inventory includes all of the items available for resale. Or, if it is a service company, then the inventory is made up of the parts and supplies used for resale.

One disadvantage to purchasing a business is the fact that a portion of the inventory is outdated, damaged or obsolete. For example, should one purchase a gift store, most likely twenty five per cent (25%) is outdated. When one opens a new gift store, all of the inventory is current and will include all current and new giftware items hitting the market. This is especially true for a business in which the seasons of the year are of major importance.

Examples of seasonal businesses include gift stores, lawn and garden centers, and clothing stores such as women, men's and children's ware.

7. New suppliers, co-op advertising and assistance. As with a new inventory, starting a business "from scratch" enables the owner to work with new suppliers. Continuing to work with existing suppliers, may present several wonderful opportunities. For example, suppliers often like to present special incentives to their new customer such as introductory discounts, cooperative advertising dollars for grand opening advertisements, free goods included in first time orders, special assistance whether it be technical, marketing or service.

8. New image and advertising. Opening a new business presents marvelous opportunities to the owner to present oneself as the exciting "new kid on the block." How often does one see a grand opening newspaper advertisement full of special discounts, free merchandise, door prizes, free drawings and free factory personnel assistance and say: "gee, I am anxious to see this new store or. . . .try this new restaurant?" In addition, one can paint an entirely new image, possibly one in which high prospect and customer appeal will prevail.

9. Publicity opportunities. Just like the advantage of "new image and advertising" has, the opportunity for "publicity" abounds. Unlike advertising, publicity usually comes with no cost. Instead, it relies heavily on the news worthiness of the subject. With a new business, there are endless publicity subjects such as the:

-A unique name for the business
-The business itself-what it does-Who it is!
-Uniqueness of the product lines
-Who is the owner-Experience-Known in the community
-Why the business-Fill an existing void
-New location-Servicing the community
-Grand opening specials-Sales-Give-always
-Meet factory representatives

10. New equipment and supplies. The word "new" appears in almost

every area of this "Advantages Of Starting a Business From Scratch" section of the chapter. As in new inventory, the business will have new equipment and supplies. This is so very important especially if it be a manufacturing firm where production machinery is so vital. Here one does not have to worry about breakdowns or repairs since most new equipment is covered by a warranty. The same is true for a retail or service business where computers, office equipment and delivery vehicles are used.

11. Training employees to your mold. There is an old saying which says: "You can lead a horse to water, but you can't make it drink." This usually applies to employees who have worked under one set of conditions for a long period of time. Thus, when a new business opens its doors for the very first time, the owner has the opportunity to set forth the working conditions and business policies that the business will operate under.

This may include such areas as working hours, dress code, return policies, credit policies, gift wrapping, and all of the many employee fringe benefits including sick leave, insurance, bonus and commission schedules, over-time, and vacation and holiday time.

12. Fresh banking arrangements. The opportunity for a new business owner to work with suppliers for the very first time yields several potential benefits. The same opportunities exist to the new business owner relative to his or her "banker" relationship. One of the principal sources of income to any bank are the business loans that they make. A new business start-up affords the bank several interesting opportunities which, when turned about, offer several advantages to the borrower.

First every banker is looking for new business opportunities, which have the potential for future growth. A $25,000 loan today may turn out to be a $250,000 loan tomorrow. For the business owner, having one's banker on one's side can yield many benefits. These include:

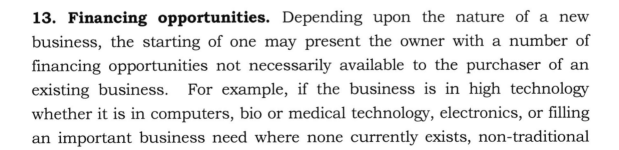

-Opening a line of credit
-Credit reference to suppliers and vendors
-New business prospect and customer referrals
-Potential source for business advice

13. Financing opportunities. Depending upon the nature of a new business, the starting of one may present the owner with a number of financing opportunities not necessarily available to the purchaser of an existing business. For example, if the business is in high technology whether it is in computers, bio or medical technology, electronics, or filling an important business need where none currently exists, non-traditional

---

177

financiers are ready at hand to provide capital.

These include venture capitalists, silent partners, and private investors who are unlike banks, do not rely upon collateral to make a loan. Often the loan is available without interest and without a payback requirement.

14. No bad history. A business that "starts from scratch" comes into the market place without any history: good or bad! The latter is particularly important since it does not open with so called bad baggage or be looked upon unfavorably due to past actions. For example, some businesses which are purchased and opened under new ownership may be strapped with having had faulty products, bad service or treated its customers rudely.

It is often difficult to remove this stain or past bad image. On the other hand, a new business starts with a clean slate in all aspects of the business be it products, customer service, customer relationships, employees, location and image.

15. Knowing your competition. No one should ever go into a business without first knowing one's competition. It has often been said that if one starts a new business, then in order to guarantee its success is to at least be equal to what competition does, if not exceeding what it does. When purchasing a business, one often relies upon the seller to have all of the intimate knowledge of competition.

Who it is? How it operates? What product lines does it carry? What is their pricing policy? What are their hours? Who are their key employees? What makes them successful? What are they missing that would make them more successful?

However, the owner or owners may not be that knowledgeable. When one starts a business, a business plan not only should be prepared, but **MUST** be prepared. One of the most important parts of any business plan is to know everything there is to know about competition such as the answers to the questions mentioned above. Knowing your competition is like having an insurance policy.

One would not think about purchasing a home without having adequate insurance. Likewise, one should not start a new business without knowing one's competition.

16. Filling market wants and needs. One never starts a new business unless he or she has a strong feeling as to what consumers want in products and services. This is especially true if starting a business from the ground floor. That is opening the doors for the very first time. Unlike purchasing a business in which the buyer may be strapped with outdated merchandise or not offering the most up-to-date services, the owner of a new business has obviously studied consumer wants and needs. This is usually the first prerequisites in starting a new business.

Consumer needs and wants vary within each community and from one community to another. History has shown that new businesses generally do not fail as a result of not filling consumer needs and wants. Rather, from under financing and poor management.

DISADVANTAGES OF STARTING A BUSINESS FROM SCRATCH

Every business scenario has its advantages and its disadvantages. Starting a business is no exception. The following are some of the disadvantages of starting a business from scratch:

1. **Financing.** Finding money for a non-existent business is much more difficult than finding money for a currently running business. This is true even if the business was not making money. Financing sources understand the market better with company history.

2. **Uncertain Idea.** Even if you are creating a duplicate of another business, but in a different area, the idea is still unproven. Nobody really knows for certain if a business is going to "make it". In this case the formula has not been proven.

3. **Most Difficult for Inexperienced Entrepreneur.** New businesses have lots of decisions that need to be made. With an inexperienced entrepreneur, the decisions take longer and more money to research the answers. This normally takes up the small business owner's time from more important activities like selling.

Whether you chose to buy a franchise, buy an existing business or start from scratch, you will need a variety of skill sets to be successful. Running a business takes dedication and passion to your industry and company. All options for starting a business have advantages and disadvantages. It is best to evaluate your own personality, business idea and geographic options to make a wise choice.

In this Chapter you have learned:

1. *When starting or buying a business you need good advisors to reduce the disadvantages associated with each scenario.*
2. *When starting a business from scratch, the new owner has control of all the different aspects of the new business, from choosing the building, the inventory, and the image of the new company.*
3. *Starting a business from scratch may give you more control, it will also take up more time. Disadvantages also include difficultly in finding financing and the uncertainty of the future of the business.*

Websites You May Find Useful

International Franchise Association – www.franchise.org
Uniform Franchise Offering Circular Directory – www.ufocs.com

Step To Success
One Action a Day Will Move You Forward

It is time to move forward. Complete the **Step to Success** Action and feel your progress. No matter where you are going, you can get there one step at a time.

If you are starting from scratch, the best thing you can do right now is to go buy a 3-ring or spiral notebook to start keeping all your ideas in one place. On one sheet of paper write, "Questions" and start writing questions about the market or about profit margins or any other question that you think you should know the answer to, but don't at this time. Then when you get to a library or talking with a business associate it is a lot easier to remember your questions and get them answered.

You can do it, so start NOW!

Chapter 12

Finding Your Most Profitable Client – Market Research Basics

"I don't know the key to success, but the key to failure is trying to please everybody."
   --Bill Cosby (1937 -) American comedian, actor, producer and father of five

Asking the Right Questions - Everything depends on it

In this chapter you will learn:

   1. *What is market research?*
   2. *How can you use market research before you go into business?*
   3. *What are the ways of conducting market research?*
   4. *How do you prepare a questionnaire?*
   5. *How do you interpret and use the results of the survey?*
   6. *What are some sources of information for market research?*

Several years ago, two Japanese car manufacturers, Toyota and Datsun, decided to survey American car owners on both their likes and dislikes about the automobiles they were driving.

The American owners' major complaint was that their cars were not "energy efficient". In other words, they felt they were not getting as many miles to the gallon as they would have liked.

The Japanese quickly realized that if they introduced their energy efficient cars into the American market, the cars would sell.

At the time of this research, the energy crisis had tripled the price which consumers were paying at the pumps. The Japanese brought their energy efficient cars to America and took advantage of the tremendous sales demand for them. These two cars are still very popular with consumers.

Another company, a leading food producer of margarine, conducted its market research for a different reason. In 1981 and 1982, one of its leading products, a special blend of margarine, enjoyed a sixty percent market share.

Then in October 1982, two competitors entered the market and the company immediately noticed a sharp decline in market share. Sales continued to decline in early 1983. To find out what the problem was, they did a consumer market research survey. It showed that the two competitors introduced their margarine blend with much stronger packaging which had far greater eye appeal.

As a direct result of these findings, the margarine producer redesigned its packaging and immediately began to recover some of its lost market share.

In both these examples, market research helped two big corporations make important decisions about their products. You've seen hundreds of examples of market research at work including the current "taste tests" of soft drinks, beer, cake mixes and peanut butter.

All these manufacturers realize, as you do, that it is the public who ultimately decides the fate of their companies.

But market research is by no means limited to big business. Indeed, smaller companies usually have more to gain from finding out what consumers want.

For example, a local car wash business felt that they weren't getting enough mileage out of their advertising dollars. The owner was spending his advertising budget on newspaper, direct mailing, and yellow pages advertising. Although the business was profitable, the owner felt it could be doing better.

He decided to set aside an entire week to conduct a market research survey and during that time, he asked every one of his customers how they had heard about his car wash. Much to his surprise, he found that the majority of customers had either seen his sign outside the car wash or received one of his advertising flyers in the mail. Only 5% of his customers had come to the car wash as a result of seeing advertising in either the newspaper or the yellow pages.

Since the owner was spending 80% of his advertising dollars on newspaper advertising, he quickly switched his concentration of advertising to direct mail and built a larger sign outside his car wash. Not surprisingly, his business doubled over the next year.

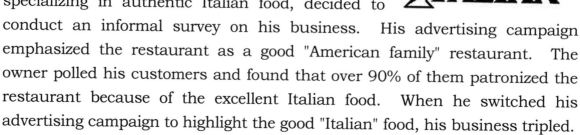

Likewise, the owner of a small restaurant specializing in authentic Italian food, decided to conduct an informal survey on his business. His advertising campaign emphasized the restaurant as a good "American family" restaurant. The owner polled his customers and found that over 90% of them patronized the restaurant because of the excellent Italian food. When he switched his advertising campaign to highlight the good "Italian" food, his business tripled.

In both cases, a market research survey brought direct, positive results in the form of increased sales and profits. Such a survey can help you in the same way. Market research may not always tell you what you should do, but it should always tell you what you should not do.

WHAT IS MARKET RESEARCH?

Market Research is, very simply, a way to get particular information from certain consumers and available resources. The main purpose of market research is to provide data that will help a small business's marketing efforts be more effective. Market research is absolutely necessary when you are starting a business from scratch.

Market Research tells you about the market and its preferences, opinions, habits, trends and plans. It also tells where the market is, its geography, its demographics (statistical characteristics) and information about the psychology of the market and the marketplace. The information you get from such research can help you make very important decisions affecting your business.

It is essential for a small business to have accurate, current consumer information. A small business owner does not usually have large amounts of money to gamble on making a wrong move or wrong decisions regarding his business. For example, when Nabisco decided to introduce Oreo Cookie ice cream to the public, they chose three cities in which to test market their product.

Whether or not the ice cream made it to the national market depended on the public reaction from those three cities. This method of testing the market is probably the best way to determine if there is a public demand for products and services.

Unfortunately, a small business simply cannot afford to make a large investment in something that might not work. Of course, you want your business to be a success; but how can that be guaranteed? Well, it can't be. But using a market research survey can reduce some of the risks which you'll take.

One of the greatest thrills for the entrepreneur is to learn something new about his market that gives him a competitive edge. Imagine what you will be able to do if you can discover an unmet need in the marketplace - why, you could be the only one with the missing product or service, which means you

---

can have **ALL** of the market share.

So -- in the process of learning about your market through your research, you will be able to attach definite numbers to your plans and verify your marketing strategy. And, if you're lucky, you will even be able to uncover unfilled needs that you can take advantage of!

TYPES OF MARKET RESEARCH

Market research is very important to the success of a small company. There are generally two types of market research, primary and secondary.

Primary Market Research

Primary market research is conducted by yourself or someone in your company. This type of research will can be exploratory or specific. The goal of **exploratory** research is to get to the heart of a customer problem. Typically you will use open-ended questions with long detailed answers. These interviews are longer in nature with fewer participants and require a more skilled interviewer. **Specific** research is used with larger groups and is used to find specific solutions to problems identified in the exploratory research. These interviews are fairly structured and scripted. In conducting specific research you can use direct mail, telemarketing or personal interviews. Specific research is more costly to perform.

Secondary Market Research

Secondary market research is research and data that have been collected and assembled by other parties. Examples may be a database of names you purchased, city property records or other government agencies. Secondary market research saves time and money in collecting the data on your own because you don't have to find people and conduct the surveys. Secondary sources of market research are located in libraries, government agencies, commercial businesses (Dun & Bradstreet) or education locations like colleges, universities and technical colleges. Business collections in public libraries carry a wealth of information for market research. Ask you librarian today!

Market research can be done by anyone who is able to ask questions, is able to record the information, and takes the time to learn what it says. It can be done by you or someone you hire. And there are several ways you can accomplish this. If you are about to go into business, here are some things you might want to know about:

MARKET DEMAND
- How much of your product is currently being purchased?
- Who is buying what you want to sell (individuals, companies)?
- Where are they buying the product now (Internet, Walmart etc)
- When do they buy this type of product? Bicycles, for example, are sold during summer.
- Are the current customers satisfied with the quality, price and convenience?

COMPETITION
- Who are the competitors currently selling this product/service?
- What exact products or services do they sell?
- What type of quality do they offer?
- What is their pricing?
- How are products packaged?
- Where can customers get your competitor's product?

TRENDS
- What are the long-term trends that will affect my business?
- What do buyers want to see changed about the product?
- How are your target customers changing? Are they aging, eating better, spending more?
- Can you see other groups starting to use the product?

MARKETING STRATEGIES
- How to factors like aging, gender, family income, the economy, brand loyalty or lifestyle affect your business?

- How have prices for your product changed in the last year and 3 years?
- What is the main factor that determines the price you can charge for your product (quality, size, demand, convenience)?
- What are the benefits of my product?

If you are already in business, use the information you have before you go anywhere. You have a gold mine of information at your fingertips that is unavailable to the person not yet in business -- your own business records. If you record your customers' addresses on sales receipts or credit applications, you will be able to get a sense of what your market area is. Where do your customers come from? Your customers' phone numbers will provide you with the same information -- just check with the phone company to find out the areas of your community to which the prefixes (the first three digits) are assigned. Take a local map and mark an star everywhere you have a customer; then look at where they are concentrated. Is there a pattern? If there is, you may be able to concentrate your advertising dollar.

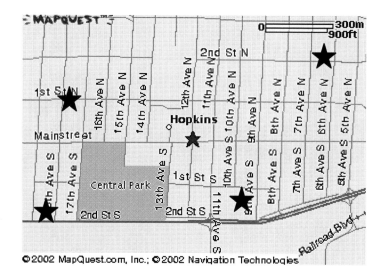

In some states, car license plate numbers are assigned by county. Send an employee out to your parking lot once in the morning, afternoon and evening to take a tally. In a couple of weeks, you will have a rough idea of how many of your customers live outside your county area.

After you are in business -- even for a short time -- your own employees will be an excellent source of information about customer characteristics and attitudes. Ask them to talk more with the customers they are serving over a one- or two-week period. What can they tell about their occupations, interests, and buying habits from some first-hand observation? You both may be surprised! Ask them to pay attention to what customers' request that you don't have in stock. Have them ask if they've tried anywhere else. Your employees will also know at what times of day you're the busiest, and what type of customers you're getting at those peak times.

If you are an established business, your market research will have a slightly different slant. Here are some examples:

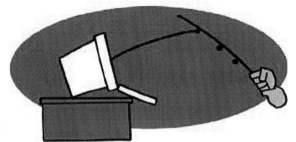

- To whom is my advertising directed and is it reaching them?
- Is there a change in my customers' spending habits?
- Have my competitors made any recent changes?
- What services should I offer my customers?
- Should I be offering more than I offer now?
- What hours should I be open?
- What changes have taken place in the market?

These are just a few examples of the questions you might want to ask. Of course, you can easily alter the list to meet your individual needs.

How Do You Conduct Market Research?

Since Market Research is primarily the gathering of information about your market, there are any number of resources and places of information to help you. These include:

A. **The Internet**. The internet is one of the best places to start conducting research even if you are a local business. You can research products, suppliers, competitors, demographic information and much more. The following is a beginning list of helpful websites, but you should also be using directories and search engines like www.google.com and www.yahoo.com. As for your competitor's information, go directly to their websites. Sometimes they even put their customer's names online and press releases that gives you good information about what they are doing.

Demographic Data Resources

Census 2000: http://www.Census.gov

- Results from the latest decentennial census, such as population totals, rankings, comparisons, summaries and reports, as well as redistricting and apportionment data.

Rating: ★★★★☆

Census Statistical Abstract http://www.census.gov/compendia/statab/

- As the National Data Book it contains a collection of statistics on social and economic conditions in the United States. Selected international data are also included. The Abstract is also your Guide to Sources of other data from the Census Bureau, other Federal agencies, and private organizations.

Rating: ★★★★★

DataPlace http://www.dataplace.org/

- Data Place is one of the most comprehensive sites for finding statistics on cities, counties, and states on the web. Pulling together data from the Census Bureau, the IRS, the Department of Housing and Urban Development, and other governmental departments and councils, this site conglomerates a complicated search into one simple interface.

Rating: ★★★★☆

Resources contributed by J.J. Hill Reference Library, find more FREE resources at www.jjhill.org

---

Research and Industry

HillSearch **http://www.hillsearch.org/membership.cfm**

Give yourself the power of the nation's top business research library. Use HillSearch to gather competitive information and perform business literature searches. HillSearch provides access to more than 8,000 newspapers, industry journals, magazines and newswires all through a simple to use, OneSearch interface. Members also receive one-click access to expert, live, business reference assistance. *HillSearch is a membership program and is only available to individual entrepreneurs.* **Request a free HillSearch trial by emailing** **membership@jjhill.org**

Rating: ✮✮✮✮✮

Economic Census **http://www.census.gov/econ/census02/**

Statistics from the Economic census, with links to more recent business data from the Federal government. Includes number of establishments in each NAICS code (US, state, county, or metro area/MSA), number of employees, revenue statistics, employer and non-employer firms, minority businesses, and more. This Census takes place every five years, with 1992, 1997, and 2002 data available online (2002 data will not be fully available until 2006).

Rating: ✮✮✮✮✮

Associations by Industry
http://www.businessresearchdatabase.com/html/associations.html

Associations are an invaluable resource when conducting industry research. Use the associations listed on this site, organized by industry heading, to find industry statistics, trends, and overviews.

Rating: ✮✮✮✮

American Society of Association Executives Gateway to Associations
http://www.asaecenter.org/Directories/AssociationSearch.cfm

Associations often track and report on key statistics and trends for their industries. Search for trade associations, industry associations and professional associations with a presence on the Internet. **TIP: conduct your search and then contact the association and request information.**

Rating: ✮✮✮✮

Statistics of US Business **http://www.census.gov/csd/susb/susb.htm**

Find data on the # of businesses--by state, MSA, county, etc--by # of employees and by sales. Also, business "births" and "deaths," expansions & contractions, more.

Rating: ✮✮✮✮

Resources contributed by J.J. Hill Reference Library, find more FREE resources at www.jjhill.org

B.   **The public library**. A trip to your public library is the best place to start.   Come armed with a list of materials and head straight for the reference librarian. They're more than willing to help! Here are some of the resource materials available in your library.

C.   **Any college in your area.** Marketing departments of local universities and colleges will know where to find information that can help your business. If you are thinking of doing any survey research, they will be especially helpful -- and lots less expensive than professional market research firms. Call the business school or management department and ask for the person who coordinates the internship program or the outreach program. You will also profit from a visit to the college library.

D.   **Observation**. You can learn a great deal by simply observing what takes place in a shopping mall or individual store. You can count the number of people who pass by a certain store and watch their reactions. Do some people go in just to browse? You might even note the average length of time a customer spends in the store. Observation is one of the best methods of conducting market research. It provides quick and reliable information and is easy to do.

E.   **Ask questions of potential consumers.** This is commonly known as conducting a survey. And because of the importance of asking the right questions we will concentrate heavily on this subject in the rest of the chapter.

F.   **Wholesalers and Manufacturers.** This is a good source of information about a particular market, its customers and competition. Wholesalers, manufacturers and retailers generally know the trends in their business and will be pleased to help you. After all, when you go into business, you'll be buying from them!

G.   **The Federal and State Government.** The U.S. Department of Commerce maintains field service offices throughout the country and each of these offices can provide you with pertinent information. The government also publishes reports on specific markets, industries and products, which may be of use to you. Likewise, you can obtain information from various state departments of commerce or business.

H.   **Trade Associations**. The trade associations which serve a particular industry are wonderful sources of information about your industry and market.

I.   **Business Publications.** Every industry has magazines, newsletters or pamphlets written exclusively for and about themselves. These can either be local or national.

J.   **Media Representatives.** The advertising space salesmen who represent magazines, newspapers, radio stations and television stations are usually an excellent source of market information. Many of their companies maintain extensive research departments for this express purpose. And the information which they have is free.

K.   **Competitors.** It is amazing what you can learn by going directly to your competition and asking for information, advice and help. If you feel uncomfortable about going to your direct competition, try contacting a business owner located 100 miles away or in the next state. Keep in mind, however, that information from a competitor, located even a short distance from you, may not necessarily apply to your business.

INTERNATIONAL MARKET RESEARCH

If you are looking at selling in the global economy, you need to expand your market research into the international arenas. Some specific resources for conducting international market research are:

Encyclopedia of Global Industries
> This publication contains background information with trends and key statistics on 125 different business sectors.

Global Data Locator
> By George Kurian
>
> This book contains descriptions of the major international statistical publications with a listing of the tables found in them.

Guide to Country Information in International Governmental Organizations Publications
> This guide will lead you to governmental sources of information on specific countries and topic areas. The book is organized by region and topic area.

International Business Information: How to Find It, How to Use It
> By Ruth Pagel
>
> The resource provides descriptive listings for sources of information that may be useful in researching company information, marketing data, industrial statistics or international transactions.

ASK THE RIGHT PEOPLE

If you can ask the right people the right questions, then interpret and apply the information to your best advantage, you'll be in Utopia. It's hard to find the "right" people, and it's difficult to formulate those perfect questions. But the time you invest at the front end will pay big rewards.

First, who are the "right" people? Naturally, they are the ones who are most like the people with whom you'll be doing business. At this point, you will have to do some "blue sky" thinking. If you know exactly what business you are going into, write down everything you know about the kinds of people who will buy from you. This could include factors such as:

Income level	Buying habits
Age	Special interests
Sex	Physical handicaps
Education	Own or rent a home
Location	Do-it-yourself type
Race	Eating habits
Religion	Spare time activities
Hobbies	Vacation activities
Skills	Age and type of car
Health	Household pets
Marital Status	Job and position
Number of children	Age of home

If you plan a business-to-business activity, develop a similar list from a business standpoint including:

Sales level	Titles of people you need to contact
# of employees	Duties
Geography	Buying power (authority to buy)
Industry	Specific needs
Category (doctors, lawyers, chiropractors)	
Qualifying criteria (what makes them a target)	
Charities supported	Company goals
Time frame for decisions	Dollar limits
Competitive products	Substitute products

When all the factors which apply to your potential customers are described completely, you have what is called a "customer profile":

```
┌─────────────────────────────────────────────────────────┐
│                    CUSTOMER PROFILE                       │
│                                                           │
│   Income:     $30,000 to $55,000                          │
│   Age:        21-35                                       │
│   Sex:        Male                                        │
│   Education:  Some College or graduated                   │
│   Location:   10 mile radius                              │
│   Hobbies:    Sports, especially hiking & biking          │
│   Health:     Excellent, very active                      │
│   Married:    Yes                                         │
│                                                           │
└─────────────────────────────────────────────────────────┘
```

It could be a very specific profile, as it would be if you were selling chair lifts to handicapped homeowners. Or it could be a broad profile as it would be if you were opening a photography studio.

Your next step is to locate the right people to match your profile. A large number of possibilities exist. Do you stand on a street corner, watching for the most obvious match-ups? Do you stand near a store (that might offer the same product you plan to offer) and interview customers? Do you buy a mailing list that seems to match your profile then conduct a mail survey? Or -- if your profile is particularly tough -- do you first conduct a general survey, then try to extract a smaller group that matches your profile? You'll have to decide.

When you identify the group of people who most closely match your customer profile, these people become your "sample". They are a sample of the general public who are the type of people you will most likely do business with. If they are a truly representative sample, their number could be quite small. (National polling organizations, such as the Gallup Poll and the Harris Poll, use such a scientifically selected sample that they can reach conclusions from a tiny fraction of 1% of the total audience.) Just remember that the smaller your sample, the greater will be your margin of error. A sample that's too small, or poorly selected, can give you false information.

Surveys are an essential part of market research. As we've stated before, the object of a survey is to gather information from a group of individuals or businesses on a specific subject. There are basically four types of survey interviews:

1. Personal interview
2. Telephone interview
3. Mail interview
4. Focus groups or group interview

Personal Interview

This is the most popular questioning technique. It's the one which produces the most accurate and complete information. It is also the most costly and time consuming.

Using this method, you deal with people on a one-to-one basis. You conduct the interview yourself or hire someone to do it for you.

The participants in your survey can either be chosen randomly (i.e., on a downtown street corner) or specifically (i.e., in front of a particular store or every house on a block).

It is the most accurate method because you are talking directly to the people involved in the survey. In fact, you will probably find that some individuals will tell you more than you want to know on the subject.

It is the most costly because it involves a large amount of your time, especially if you, or people you hire, interview people in a number of different locations.

There are some very important advantages in using the personal interview survey. They include:

➢ You can ask your questions in great detail.
➢ You can show pictures and diagrams.
➢ You can ask follow-up questions.

One thing to keep in mind when conducting the survey is to aim for a good cross-section of the population. Or more specifically, look for people who are **most like** the customers you will serve. For example, if you are thinking of starting a cooking school, you might assume you need to interview only women. Wrong! There are plenty of boys and men who enjoy cooking and would like to start taking lessons. And, if they don't, they have wives, girlfriends, mothers and sisters who might have some very definite opinions on the subject.

The same is true if you're planning to open a sporting goods repair shop. Don't assume that all of your customers will be men. You might be omitting a very valuable group of people who could give you some necessary insights into your business.

Telephone Interview

The second, and perhaps the easiest, type of survey can be done by phone. You can conduct this type of interview from your home and do as many or as few as your schedule allows. One disadvantage is that it is much harder to choose a select group of people to interview using this system. Instead, you will probably have a very random sampling of people. Your questionnaire should be brief. People can become very impatient when they are kept on the phone for a long period of time. It's important to remember that every person you talk to is doing you a favor and they know it. Be considerate of their time schedules.

Mail Interview

This type of survey requires much more organization than the first two. You will need a select list of people and their mailing addresses to send out your questionnaire. You may find that a mailing list is available (at a cost of $20-$40 per thousand names) that enables you to reach just the right people. You must include postage or a reply envelope for the return mail.

It is ideal for reaching people living out-of-town or businessmen who are hard to reach by phone or in person.

The disadvantage is that you have no control over who will respond. The people to whom you send the questionnaire will see no advantage in helping you. Some will probably decide they do not wish to spend the time answering your questionnaire, some will immediately throw it away, and some will lose either the questionnaire or return envelope in the pile of mail on their desk. Those who do respond may scribble in unreadable answers, may answer some questions and not others, or may return the questionnaire **months** after you mail it to them. You will be lucky to get as high as a 5% return (that is 5 surveys returned for every 100 mailed out).

By comparison, the telephone survey should give you a 60% response; and the personal interview should give a response as high as 90%. With both of these, you will be better able to judge the accuracy of individual comments.

Focus Group or Group Interview

An interesting variation of the personal interview is the "focus group" or group interview. This technique enables you to get the reactions or opinions of several people at one time. It offers the advantages of a personal interview and adds the spontaneity and depth of a group.

Many companies use this technique when developing new products, new marketing strategies or new business procedures. It gives them quick feedback in a private atmosphere. Each member of the group has the opportunity to see, hear, taste or whatever is required, and offer opinions. Often one opinion or idea will spark another. And, if the group is encouraged to speak freely, a highly productive brainstorming session develops.

You can organize your own focus group from among your friends, provided they are carefully chosen. Or you may find a local church, school or civic organization that may provide a group for a modest charge. Try to make sure, however, that the group bears some resemblance to that customer profile you developed.

To get maximum value from a group interview, here are a few rules to follow:

1. Use a strong leader. If that's not you, ask someone to take that important role. Every group needs a leader to keep steering in the right direction, to prevent someone else from dominating, and to ask the right questions.

2. Encourage the group to provide honest, accurate opinions and to express them openly.

3. Each individual, however negative he might be, represents a segment of your market. If he is silent or withdrawn, he must be encouraged to speak.

4. Do not feed opinions of your own or show your prejudices in any way to the group. This will lead to false feedback.

5. Use a blackboard or flip-chart to record opinions. The visual impact usually sparks helpful conversation.

6. Appoint someone to take notes for you.

7. Don't trust the results of one such group interview. Verify your findings through another group, or even a third one.

How to Design a Questionnaire

One of the keys to successful market research is to have a clear purpose in mind before you begin. This means you need to know which marketing questions will help you to conduct your business successfully. Having this purpose in mind will prevent you from wandering off the track into information that will not pay off for you. To determine the value of a question before you start your research, judge **how you would use the results.** Doing this exercise before you have the results usually will point out useless or inadequate questions. Make each of your questions worthwhile.

Since you have decided to go to the trouble and expense of conducting a market research survey, it's important that you develop questions which suit your needs. Basically, there are several rules to follow when designing a survey. They are:

1.   Keep your questions brief and clear. For example, asking: "When you purchase milk, what is the usual size you buy?" is much better than asking: "When you go to the store to make your grocery purchase and you stop in the dairy department after making other grocery purchases, when you select the milk you wish to purchase, what size or how large a purchase is it?" Vague questions lead to vague answers.

2.   Ask direct questions about your subject. In one survey conducted by a store manager, this question was asked:

"What brought you here today?" The manager wanted to know **why** the customers had chosen to shop at his store. Unfortunately, some people misunderstood the question and put down such answers as "a car", "the bus", and "a friend brought me". The answers weren't wrong, but they didn't help the store manager find out what he wanted to know.

3.   Ask questions which can be answered easily, but remember to follow up most YES and NO questions with a "WHY" question or one that asks for more information.

4.	Ask questions which can be interpreted easily. You are going to be interviewing anywhere from 10 to 200 people and you need to get information from them that can help you make decisions about your business. When questions become too long and involved, so do the answers. And you will spend more time trying to figure out what people meant than is necessary.

5.	Make sure the questions are understandable to a wide range of people. You don't want to waste time explaining the same question again and again.

6.	Make sure your questions do not offend anyone. A recent merchandising survey done by a national magazine included the question: "Are you the head of the household?" The magazine was trying to find out if the person whom they were interviewing made the majority of the purchasing decisions. Many women (and men), however, found the question outdated and offensive. On a revised survey, the question was left out. Questions about family income, occupations and age should all be handled delicately, and included in your survey only if relevant.

7.	Be honest with the intent of the questionnaire. If you're thinking of opening a hardware store in the shopping mall, say that. Don't tell people that you're asking these questions to see how newspaper advertising affects the hardware business. It isn't fair to them and you could be cheating  yourself as well. You may get a long speech on what's wrong with newspapers and advertising, and learn nothing about the potential customer's feelings about a hardware store in the shopping mall.

8.	Don't answer the questions for them. The reason you are interviewing consumers is to find out what they know, not what you know.

Recently, a computer company decided to do a survey on how their brand of computer was viewed by the public. They conducted the survey nationally, but cautioned the interviewers not to mention the name of the computer when asking various questions. Their reasoning was simple: If the results of the survey showed that a majority of people had not heard of their product, there was something wrong with their advertising campaign. The same is true for your questionnaires. Do not prompt people into saying something they don't mean.

9.   Give the person you are interviewing enough time to answer the questions. In point one we advised you to keep the questions brief. But this does not mean the answers have to be brief. The hardest obstacle you will encounter in doing a market research survey is getting someone to take the time to talk to you. Once they have agreed to do the survey, everything should go smoothly. So don't set a time limit of, say, 5 minutes per person, or you are going to miss out on some helpful comments. Don't cut someone off while they are responding. That isn't to say you should listen to the entire story of their last gall bladder operation or admire 17 pictures of grandchildren either. A good rule to follow is to treat the people interviewed the way you would like to be treated. Ask for their advice" and emphasize how much they are "helping" you.

10.   Be sure you understand all the answers you receive. Don't be afraid to read back what was just said to make sure it's accurate.

11.   Do not be alarmed or upset by any of the answers you receive. And if you are, don't show it. Don't argue about an answer to any of your questions. If the person says they've never heard of your product or service, they haven't. If they say they wouldn't want a health food restaurant in the shopping mall, take them at their word. Try to remember that you are doing this survey to find out what should be changed, and you need people to be as honest as possible.

12.   Be courteous when asking people to participate in your survey. Some people simply will not have the time or the inclination to help you. Do not press them or act insulted when they refuse. In one case, a young

woman told the interviewer she was in a hurry to get her shopping done. About an hour later, the same woman came back and said she had finished her shopping early and now had the time to fill out the questionnaire. This probably won't happen often, but it doesn't cost you anything to be courteous to everyone you deal with.

A good way to double check your questions is to test them with another question: CAN THE ANSWER BE MEASURED? If the answers can't be counted or categorized in some way, be careful. Questions which ask for subjective answers should probably be changed.

> *Now you can easily conduct surveys online. If you have an email list of clients you can purchase a survey tool at www.surveymonkey.com. It is an inexpensive tool that helps to tabulate your information for you.*

It is a good idea to "test" your questionnaire on a few friends before you actually use it. That way, you can determine if your questions are clear and will give you the answers you need.

Questionnaire Examples

The following are four types of questionnaires which were designed by the owners of small businesses. In the first (the car wash survey mentioned earlier in the chapter), each customer was handed a clipboard and asked to fill out a questionnaire while their car was being washed.

This was not a random sampling because each person used was a customer of the Rose Car Wash. It was designed to be completed in the length of time it took to wash a car. And it was done over a week's time to reach the customers who washed their cars during the week as well as the weekend.

You'll note that the owner was primarily interested in how each customer had heard about his business. However, he also included questions on what he could do to improve his business such as changing the hours the car wash was open. As a result of his findings, he decided to keep his car wash open an additional 2 hours on Sunday.

The next survey, dealing with commercial warehouse space, was done by a businessman who was interested in building a warehouse. Before he made the commitment of time and money, however, he needed to know if there was a demand for such a service. He sent his survey to all business establishments within a two-mile radius of the proposed site.

He found that not only was there a demand, but several businesses wanted to reserve space before it was even built! He built a warehouse with space for 50,000 square feet of storage room, and before it was completed, 30,000 square feet had already been leased.

This same businessman developed the third questionnaire on warehouse space, but sent the survey to home and apartment dwellers. The results revealed that these people would represent a very small portion of his business. Therefore, he decided to emphasize business use in his advertising campaign.

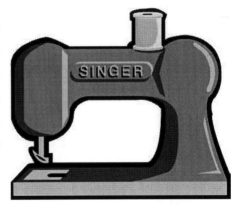

The fourth questionnaire was designed by a man who wanted to know if there would be a demand for giftware from India and Pakistan in the small town where he lived. He found that the majority of people would be interested in such a store, particularly since there was nothing of that type in the surrounding area.

The last questionnaire was developed by a woman who was interested in opening a fabric store and offering sewing lessons. From the women she interviewed, she discovered that there was a real need for both a fabric store and sewing lessons. She opened the shop which did extremely well.

In each of these cases, the small business owners learned enough from a market research survey to make intelligent, responsible decisions. But what happens when the results of the survey aren't so positive? Does this mean you discard the idea and go into another business?

Not necessarily. To a certain extent you must use your own judgment. The market research survey should be used as a guide, not the final answer. If, for example, the survey on giftware from India and Pakistan had revealed that the majority of people were not interested in seeing a gift shop of this type in their town, you need to analyze why they responded that way.

It could be that the people were unfamiliar with this type of giftware. Maybe they assumed the items would be too expensive because they were imported. Whatever the case, the way they answered the questionnaire might not necessarily reflect the way they would react if the store were actually there.

In any case, the market research survey can give you some valuable information about your customers and potential business location. What you choose to do with the results is up to you.

Other Types of Market Research

There are other types of research you can do yourself that may be easier than a survey -- and more creative too!

You can learn a lot from **your competitors**. Pretend you're a customer and visit them at different times of the day. When you're back in your car, fill out a competitor analysis form. (See chapter on Site Location.) Your answers will give you lots to think about for improving your own operation.

Try a license plate analysis of your competitors. Where do they come from? How many of these people would find it more convenient to shop at your establishment?

Another great way to get information is to **make your advertising** dollar do double duty.

When you look into the advertising chapter, you will learn about tracking for advertising. What this means is that when you advertise, there are a number of ways for you to find out who responded to your ad.

For example, whenever you run a coupon in a publication, code it so that when your customer redeems it, you will know where it came from. For instance, code the coupon offer in the campus paper "A", and the ones in the neighborhood papers "B" and "C". Save all the coupons that are redeemed and when the offer is over, figure out which paper had more customer response. Or more important, figure the cost per inquiry for each publication. Also, when the coupons are redeemed, you can write the customers' phone numbers on the coupons (let them know you won't be calling them) and you can pinpoint the responses even better.

The same can be done with broadcast ads. Do a "Tell 'em Joe sent you" ad for one radio station and a different one for the second station. Try rock, country, classical, or easy listening format stations. Keep track of which station sent in the most customers. Then check with the station to find out who their average listener is -- age, occupation, income, etc. -- you'll find out about your clientele for the same money you're using to boost sales.

Another group that really knows your territory is the **sales reps** and **wholesalers**. These hardworking men and women make it their business to know what is happening in your business community. Take one out for coffee and pick his or her brain.

One final word: Don't fall blindly in love with your research findings. There might have been flaws in your survey or the people you questioned. But if you ask the right people the right questions, you can use the results to draw up a blueprint for the future.

But don't stop there. You'll need more surveys later to tell you about the trends, preferences and attitudes of your customers.

In this chapter you have learned:

1. *If you are considering going into a small business, market research can be very valuable in helping you answer certain questions you may have.*
2. *If you are already in a small business, market research can be a valuable tool for you in solving problems.*
3. *Market research is a tool by which you can gather information from people like your future customers.*
4. *There are four basic methods you may use when conducting a market research survey: 1. personal interview; 2. telephone interview; 3. mail interview; and 4. focus group or group interview.*

 Websites You May Find Useful

There are many listed in this chapter, but more are available at:

Biz Info Library - http://www.bizinfolibrary.org/ (click on Market Research)

Business Statistics – www.bizstats.com

Hoover's Company Research – www.hoovers.com

 Step To Success
One Action a Day Will Move You Forward

It is time to move forward. Complete the **Step to Success** Action and feel your progress. No matter where you are going, you can get there one step at a time.

Start right now and make a short list of questions you want to ask potential customers. Call two friends and ask them to take the survey before you send it to customers. Use the samples on the pages that follow.

You can do it, so start NOW!

ROSE CAR WASH SAMPLE SURVEY

We are interested in knowing what you think about our service. Accordingly, we have prepared a brief questionnaire which we would appreciate your answering while your car is being washed. Your candid criticisms, comments and suggestions are important to us.

Thank you, ROSE CAR WASH

1. Do you live/work in the area? (Circle one or both)

2. Why did you choose to come to ROSE CAR WASH today? (Circle all that apply.)
   - Close to home
   - Close to work
   - Convenience
   - Good Service
   - Full Service Car Wash
   - Other

3. How did you learn about us?
   (Circle one)
   - Newspaper
   - Mailing
   - Drove by and stopped
   - Recommended by someone
   - Received coupon at work
   - Other

4. How frequently do you have your car washed during the winter? (From November 1 to April 30) Please try to estimate.
   ____ times per month
   ____ Other

5. How frequently do you have your car washed during spring and summer? (May 1 to October 31)
   ____ times per month
   ____ Other

6. Which aspect of our car wash do you think needs improvement?
   _____
   _____
   _____
   _____

7. Our operating hours are from 8:30 a.m. to 6 p.m. weekdays and Saturdays and from 9 a.m. to 2 p.m. on Sunday. We are closed on legal holidays. What changes in our operating hours would be better for you?

Weekdays	Saturday		Sunday
Open 8 a.m.	Open 8 a.m.		Close 3 p.m.
Close 7 p.m.	Close 7 p.m.	Close 4 p.m.	
Close 8 p.m.	Close 8 p.m.	Close 5 p.m.	
Close 9 p.m.	Close 9 p.m.	No change	
No change	No change		

8. Approximate age: Circle one
   Under 25   26-39   40-59   Over 60

Comments: (Favorable and Unfavorable)
_____
_____
_____

IMPORTED HANDMADE GIFTWARES SAMPLE QUESTIONNAIRE

1. Have you ever purchased or received as gifts any imported handmade giftware?

    Yes _____ No _____

2. Have you ever purchased or received as gifts any handmade giftware from India or Pakistan?

    Yes _____ No _____

    If Yes, what type of giftware?

    Wooden _____ Marble _____ Brass _____

    Copper _____ Cotton _____ Other _____

    Please specify:

3. Would you be interested in purchasing the above mentioned handmade gifts from Pakistan or India?

    Yes _____ No _____

    If Yes, would the item be used:
    a. In your home for you or your family's enjoyment _____
    b. As a gift _____
    c. Other _____ Please specify:

4. Do you know where to shop for such giftware?

    Yes_____ No_____

5. When buying foreign handmade giftware, what do you value the most? On a scale of 1 through 4, list in order according to preference beginning with number 1 as your most valued choice:

    Craftsmanship _____ Cost _____ Uniqueness _____

    Other _____ Please specify

FABRIC STORE SAMPLE QUESTIONNAIRE

1.   Do you do home sewing? _____ Yes _____ No
       If NO, please answer questions to Part A.
       If YES, please answer questions to Part B.

A.   Please check reasons for not doing home sewing.
       Lack of interest _____
       Lack of knowledge _____
       Poor availability of fabric selection _____
       Other

B.   Check type of sewing you do.
       Children's wear _____
       Ladies wear _____
       Home decorating _____
       Other

       Which patterns do you use?

       _____ McCall's _____ Simplicity _____ Kwik Sew

       _____ Butterick _____ Vogue

       Check your age group
       10 - 18 _____
       19 - 29 _____
       30 & Over _____

       Where do you buy your material?

       In town _____ Out of town _____

       How far do you live from our town?

       In town _____ 10-15 miles _____ Out of town _____

       Do you think our town needs a fabric shop?

       Would you be interested in sewing classes? Yes_____ No _____

       What classes would interest you?

       Basic sewing _____   Lingerie   _____
       T-shirt   _____   Infant wear   _____
       Pants   _____   Men's wear   _____
       Tailoring   _____   Other   _____

Please note any suggestions or comments you might have.

Chapter 13

Writing Simple Business Plans That Get Money

"The will to win is important, but the will to prepare is vital."
--Joe Paterno (1926 -) American college football coach.

Perhaps the most important document to your small business

As a potential entrepreneur, you are part of a gigantic wave that's growing in size and sweeping across America. We are slowly reverting back to pioneer times when cottage industry and small businesses were the backbone of our nation. Indeed, many business experts predict that in the future 95% of all new innovations and changes will come from people like you and me in the small business arena. Small business continues to grow because of the following factors:

- Increase in Entrepreneurship Education
- Movement to a Service economy
- Increase in businesses on the Internet
- Technology advancements allowing people to work from home

While the corporate giants continue to grow, merging and swallowing each other, thousands of energetic, talented people are spun off. Thousands more, who have never been part of the anonymous, faceless existence within a big corporation stand on the sidelines with heads full of ideas, wondering if NOW is the time to start up their own businesses.

Is this you? Well, take heart! You have plenty of company. Last year there were more than 600,000 new businesses in the United States.

But sadly, about 80% of those start-ups will unnecessarily fall by the wayside within a few years.

YOU DO NOT HAVE TO BE ONE OF THEM!

What can you do to keep your bubble from bursting? Perhaps the best preventive medicine is expressed in a single word...PLANNING.

In this chapter you will learn:

1.   *Why do I need to create a business plan?*
2.   *What is included on a 1-page business plan?*
3.   *What parts of a business plan are more important than others?*
4.   *The different parts of a business plan*
5.   *What is an Operational Plan?*

THE BUSINESS PLAN

The Financing Chapter guided you through the procedure for a loan proposal. While this procedure may or may not be all you need to get a loan from a bank, but it will not be adequate when trying to raise money from other sources. On the other hand, a complete business plan which includes a loan proposal is a document which will not only be a powerful money-raising tool, but it will serve as a road map during the first vital years of your new venture.

A properly developed business plan provides more than mere numbers on paper. It serves these main functions:

1.   To provide you with the ROAD MAP that you need in order to run your business. It allows you to make detours, change directions, and alter the pace that you set in starting or running the business.

2.   To assist you in financing. Whether one is starting up a small business or is an entrepreneur, banks and financial institutions want to see that you know where you are, where you are going, and how you are going to get there.

3. The plan will tell you how much money you need, when you will need it, and how you are going to get it. In other words, how you will do your financing?

4. To help you clearly think through what type of business you are starting, and allows you to consider every aspect of that business.

5. To raise the questions that you need to have answered in order to succeed in your business.

6. To establish a system of checks and balances for your business so that you avoid mistakes.

7. To set up bench marks to keep your business under control.

8. To help you develop the COMPETITIVE SPIRIT to make you keenly prepared and ready to operate.

9. To make you think through the entire business process so that you do not open the business blindly or lack vital information in opening and maintaining your business.

10. To force you to analyze competition.

11. It will give you a "GO" or "NO GO" ANSWER about starting the business.

If these functions don't convince you that you need a business plan, we have a suggestion: Ask any business person who has failed whether or not they had prepared a business plan ahead of time.

Sure, it takes time, effort and maybe even money to prepare a document like this. But if it can make the difference between success and failure, it's worth it. So, let's get started.

HOW TO PREPARE YOUR BUSINESS PLAN

First, decide right now that your business plan will be neat and well-written. Its final appearance will have a significant effect on others who read it. Therefore, if you are weak in the areas of writing, hire someone to help with the final preparation.

Your plan is a reflection of you and your ability to organize, to think, to manage and to communicate. In the eyes of a financing source -- one who may invest his or her money in your new enterprise -- it demonstrates on paper your potential ability to compete in the business arena. If your plan is sloppy, with spelling and grammatical errors, the financing source may determine that if you write that way, you may not run your business well.

No two business plans will be alike. The one thing to keep in mind as you write you business plan is: Would you give money to the owners of this business? How do you show that your hair salon is going to be more profitable than the one down the street?

If raising money is the primary purpose of your plan, you can readily understand its importance to you. Treat it accordingly. It **must** be well organized, easy to read, sound, logical and factual. Investors must see the direct relationship between **future growth** and past **knowledge** and **experience**. The "blossoms" of tomorrow will be the natural fulfillment of the "seeds" you plant today.

Your business plan is not written in stone. You will probably discover its need for fine-tuning at brief intervals at first. And, certainly, if your initial requests for capital are rejected, you should take another look at it. The idea is to make this document serve **your** needs.

If you have done your homework and the result is an idea that has merit, there is a good chance that someone or some group will want to support you financially. Most good plans can find funding with the right financing source. Once you sell your idea, it will be up to you to implement the plan and continue planning for growth.

ONE-PAGE BUSINESS PLANS

One page business plans are used to evaluate an idea or to get initial thoughts down on paper. These beginning plans are great to get your feet wet and get going. In a one-page business plan, you want to get a good picture of what the business will look like and areas where you may need to focus. Here is a sample one-page business plan:

AISB Quickie Business Plan

Introduction
Company Name: _____
Vision: _____
Main Goal: _____

Evaluating Ideas and Concepts
Does our friends & family like our idea? _____
Why do they like it? _____
How many would buy it? _____
What will they pay for it? _____
Why would they buy ours vs. competition?_____
What need do we fill? _____

Researching Your Idea
Market Size: _____
Industry opportunities/challenges _____
Competition strengths:_____
Possible Site Location_____

Preliminary Plans
Marketing Plan
Product: _____
Price: _____
Promotion: _____
_____
Place: _____
Selling Plan: _____
Financial Plan
Start Up Costs: _____
Sales: Yr 1 _____   Yr 2 _____
Expenses: Yr 1 _____   Yr 2 _____
Profits: Yr 1 _____   Yr 2 _____

Money
Amount Needed: _____
Loans: _____
Cash on Hand: _____
Cash for Equity of Company: _____ Equity given up: _____%

Setting Up The Business
Team: _____
Who does What: _____
Technology Needed: _____

Advisors: _____   _____
_____   _____
Suppliers: _____   _____
_____   _____

MORE COMPLETE BUSINESS PLAN OUTLINE

There are many different forms of business plans. Each industry and business has its own type and format, but the following outline is used by many, many financing sources and banks around the country. It is very important to have your business plan in a format the bankers are familiar with. It shows that you have thought through all the pieces of your business.

I.   Cover Sheet and Table of Contents
II.   Executive Summary
III.   Company Information
IV.   Industry, Market and Competition
V.   Products and Services
VI.   Suppliers and Operations
VII.   Marketing Plan
VIII.   Management Team and Key Personnel
IX.   Financial Plan
X.   Appendices

EXECUTIVE SUMMARY

The executive summary is your first place to make a good impression on the reader, but normally this is the last section written. Some financing sources will only read the Executive Summary to see if they are interested in the business concept. The page should start with your business name, your name and title, business address and phone number. It should also be no more than 2 pages. The Executive Summary should include the following topics which are summaries from the other parts of your plan:

A. Mission Statement – What is your purpose and goal for the business? What do you think the business will look like when you are finished building it. A Mission Statement should be no longer than 5 sentences long.

B. Summary of the Description of the Business

Will yours be a sole proprietorship? A partnership? Corporation? In this section, you should cover the nature of your business (i.e. restaurant, bakery, catering, or farming). In addition talk about the type of business you are thinking about (manufacturing, services, wholesale, retail or other). Briefly describe your products and/or services and who your customers will be and how you will sell to them (i.e. walk-in, stores, telephone sales, mail order). Discuss the quality of products and services and an estimate of prices.

If your company is new, state it. If it is an existing business or you are purchasing a business, briefly discuss the history of the business and your philosophy to expand it.

C. Industry, Market and Competition

Explain the big picture first. What is the total universe of your market? Is the industry growing or declining? Is anything happening now or expected to happen in the future that will impact your business? Who are your competitors? How successful are they, and why? Do they have any weaknesses? If so, will your business fill a need created by their weakness? Who will your customers be? Why will they buy your product or service?

E. Products and Services

You will need to provide a complete description of what you plan to sell or rent. Emphasize the basic product or service that will provide the bulk of your income. Explain advantages and benefits and anything about your products or services that will help "sell" your business concept to a complete stranger. If your product is still on the drawing board, explain when it will be available, including any test data you have.

Describe how your product or service will be sold. Include pricing strategy, estimated sales and market share for each of the first three years. Add your advertising and public relations plans, plus your service and warranty policies.

F. Supplier and Operations

Cover all the specifics, such as how, where and by whom your product will be produced. What is the raw material? Is it readily available? What is the manufacturing process? What is your anticipated rate of production? Will you use union or non-union labor? Who are your major suppliers?

G. Marketing Plan

Your marketing plan is going to cover the specifics of Product, Price, Place, Promotion and Persuasion. Also included will be your advertising, public relations and publicity strategy and goals. In this section, talk about the different types of media your will use and why.

H. Management Team

How many people are involved, and what are their skills? How well are they qualified? At what points in time will you add personnel? If you're running a one-man show, explain convincingly how you have the necessary skills and talent to achieve your goals.

I. Financial Considerations

If yours is a new business, you won't have the benefit of past history. As a bare minimum, you will need a personal financial statement. If your business is already established, include a financial statement for the business. Demonstrate how you plan to elevate existing figures from point A to point B. Ideally, you will be totally familiar with all of the financial details of your business, and will be able to answer -- line-by-line -- how you arrived at each figure.

Include summary Profit and loss projections for 3 years and an expected balance sheet at the end of each year.

Be careful not to make you executive summary too long. It should stick to 1-3 pages. Focus on the opportunity in this part of the plan. The rest of the items will be discussed in further detail later in the plan.

COMPANY AND LOCATION

The Company part of your business plan should talk about the past and the future of your business. If you are an existing business or you are purchasing a company discuss how the company did historically and how you intend to improve. Include when the company was founded, what financing has been used, what does the organization look like, and if buying a company, why the current owners want to sell the business.

After discussing the history, describe the current status of the organization. What are the strengths and weaknesses? Many owners can talk freely about their company's strengths. Many of the same owners will not discuss the potential weaknesses in their concept. It is important for you and your financial sources to understand the weaknesses and determine how to minimize them. Most people who will read your plan realize that ALL businesses have weaknesses.

Finally talk about the future. Describe your goals for the future. Try to quantify your goals. What will your sales be 1 year from now? 3 years? 5 years? How about profits? Can you match any of your projections to outside trends? Are clothing retailers increasing business because the population continues to grow where you live? Is the Census Bureau seeing the same trends continue? The objectives are more believable if you have an experienced management team with a history of setting and achieving their objectives.

Location

When writing about your location, describe the location and why you chose it. Refer back to the chapter in this book on Site Selection. Describe items like:

- Your trade area – where are your customers compared to where you are?

- Traffic patterns – Can customers get to your place easily?
- Complimentary businesses
- Competition location – Where are they compared to your location?
- Parking spaces for clients - Is it enough?
- Zoning restrictions – check with local city/town hall to make sure you can do business in this location
- Permits and Licenses – check with local city/town hall to make sure what permits you will need. For example, most cities will limit the size of the sign you can have in front of your business.
- Expansion room – Is there room if you need it?
- Blueprint of your store or office – How will everything look once you have it set up?

Be sure to mention if you plan to rent or lease or purchase your site. If you rent or lease, what are the terms of the lease. For example, how long is the lease, how much notice can you give to get out of the lease, what penalties, payment, and when can payment be increased.

In writing this part of your business plan, make sure it doesn't just repeat the information in the executive summary, but adds more detail to it.

INDUSTRY, MARKET & COMPETITION

Industry

Understanding your industry is very important. You would not want to start a business in making and selling personal computers with 486 computer chips. This would not be a business that would last very long. Even in the restaurant industry there are certain types of restaurants that are increasing in business while others are decreasing or closing. You need to focus on the how the industry is performing now and how it will continue to perform in the future. In the industry section you should include research on:

Industry Size – How big is the pie? To determine the industry size talk to different people that are connected with the industry. These can be current business owners or trade associations. Estimate the industry size in annual dollars or units sold for the past few years. It is growing or shrinking? Although you may know a lot about the industry size and characteristics, the reader of your business plan may not know. Explain the industry at a national level and then try to bring the information to a local level.

Growth Rate – From the industry size you can determine at what rate it is growing and determine if the trend is to continue to grow or to become steady. Compare your company's growth rate with what you calculated for the industry. Are they alike?

Key Growth Factors – These are factors that are up and beyond the control of the industry or any company within the industry. There are factors that affect the industry's market size and level of demand. For example, the tragedy of September 11, 2001 strongly affected the travel and hotel industry. Both of these industries had decline factors that were beyond their control. It is important in this section, for your benefit, that you describe both positive and negative growth factors that may affect your business. It will help you develop a strategy for the different factors. Growth factors will include situations like the economic condition of the United States, trade relations between your suppliers and the countries where your products are produced or specific economic conditions of the city or town where you live.

Cyclical Features – Some industries have a pattern that happens every few years. For instance, the mortgage industry is very cyclical. Every few years the rates go up and then in a few years the rates go down. During the period where rates are down, more people can start businesses in the mortgage industry. Whereas if you try to start a mortgage company when the rates are up, it is much harder to do. Understand your industry to know when it may be a better time to start a business in that industry.

Seasonality – Many businesses may be seasonal, which means they have better sales in different parts of the year. For example, in Minnesota, boat sales do not do as well in the months of November to March. On the other hand, snowmobile sales are way up during this time of year. Both businesses depend on the season for their sales. Garden Centers, bike shops, and outdoor restaurants are also seasonal businesses. Use this information to your advantage and start a business at the right time of year for the earliest success.

To find some of this information you can check with your local library and look for industry publications in the Business Periodicals Index. Other places to find information would be in general business publications like Forbes, Fortune or Business Week. Some of the information may be difficult to interpret as a small business. Therefore industry size and growth will need to be estimated.

Market

How big of a slice of pie are you targeting? Once you understand that the industry has total sales of $10 million, what percentage of that do you want for your business? You want to make sure there are enough customers to support your business. Start by looking at market or customer characteristics like: age, sex, ethnic group, education, family size, income, business type, and geographic location. You are trying to determine the most important characteristics that relate to your customers.

Competition

The goal of the competition portion of your business plan is to convince the reader that you know what you are up against. Refer back to the chapter on Site Selection for your research. Review your notes on the competitive analysis survey that you did on the competitors in your area and the map of the locations of your competitors. This will help you more easily describe who the competition is and what are their strengths and weaknesses. Be sure to include answers for the following points:

❖ Annual sales   ❖ Location

- ❖ Strengths
- ❖ Weaknesses
- ❖ Product line depth & breath
- ❖ Pricing compared to yours
- ❖ Marketing activities
- ❖ Supply sources
- ❖ Expanding or declining
- ❖ Skilled employees

PRODUCTS AND SERVICES

The next parts of the plan will go into more detail about your products in your business. A sample outline would be:

A. Initial Products and Services
B. Proprietary Features
    1. Patents
    2. Copyrights
    3. Unique or different features
C. Future Products and Services
    1. New products and services
    2. Research and development
    3. Expansion plans

Before you start writing for this section take a few minutes to think about your objectives. What level of quality are your products going to be, high, average or low quality? What price level are they going to sell at? At this point start to make a list of products or services that you would initially like to offer. Refer back to the Market Research chapter to see the answers you received on your questionnaires and surveys. Target products that customers were looking for and see if the pricing allows you to make a profit when selling it.

Secondly, almost all businesses have unique features for their products. Even in a standard flower shop, unique or secret features may include a special distributor for a specific flower or a new way creating special occasion flowers. It may even be a location that is convenient or added benefits when customers shop there.

Unique features can include things specific to your products, your store or office or your customer services. All these items together will make up your unique business. Think about Disney World. When someone goes to Disney World it is a destination. It is all about the experience. Can you make your place of business or the way you conduct business with your customers a better experience? Are you easy to do business with?

Next list the products you want to add in the future. These may be products that are in research and development. They may be products that you want add to your product line that you currently do not have funding to carry. In expanding your product line are you going to add more products to the same market or are you going to increase your customers for your same products? Remember it is much easier and less expensive to sell to current customers than to find new ones.

Keeping your product line current and up-to-date is important to keep sales coming in the door. Make sure you continue to understand your customer's changing needs for products.

SUPPLIERS AND OPERATIONS

Suppliers.
Having reliable and cost effective suppliers is very important to a small business. You should include suppliers for the initial equipment and for ongoing supplies and raw materials. In this section, you can list major suppliers and backups if the major supplier can not deliver. You can discuss payment and delivery terms for each supplier. Buying on price may not always be a wise decision. Some suppliers may allow you to buy on credit or with extended payment terms.

Operations.
Production processes should be discussed in detail in this section. Include facility requirements, equipment requirements, and labor requirements. Explain how customer service will handle questions and problems from customers, how your networks and telephone will be maintained, how your software and hardware will be updated or how your shipping department will be managed. If you are manufacturing a product be sure to include flow of materials through your plant and other necessary processes.

You will also want to discuss briefly if you plan to buy your equipment or lease your equipment and from whom.

MARKETING PLAN

You should start this section with the goals for your marketing plan. These would include your marketing objectives and the measurements you plan to use to see if your advertising and promotional events are working up to your expectations. Refer to the Advertising and Publicity and Promotions chapters for more information.

The marketing part of your business plan should be a detailed plan of your promotion mix. Promotion Mix should include a breakdown of your advertising, sales promotions, personal selling, publicity and public relations events. Which one of these you choose depends on many factors on how much money you have to spend, what your competition uses, and how each one will meet your marketing goals. Your strategy should be a result from weighing the different options and your different goals.

It should include what type of media, the number of times you plan to use that media form, cost of media types, and who you are targeting with the media you chose. Make sure to include the reasons you chose the different media types and why you think they are going to be most effective.

A calendar is the best way to show when the different events or media publications will be used. You can also include the deadlines for submission to the different promotions. Try to schedule at least some event for each month. Also be sure to track results you are receiving from your different marketing programs.

Marketing Calendar

Activity	Jan	Feb	Mar	Apr	May	Jun	Jul	Aug	Sep	Oct
Grand Opening Publicity	X									
Grand Opening Event		X								
Special Offer Publicity		X								
Sponsor Block Party - Publicity					X					
Open House						X				
July 4 Sale - Publicity										
Photo Contest								X		
Winning Photos to Newspapers									X	

It is important in this section to focus on how you will get the edge on your competition and how you will win customers. This should be an action plan for your business. Continually refer back to your target market to make sure you are targeting the promotion to fulfill a customer's need.

Remember the most valuable asset in any business is its client list. It is therefore important to show how you will add customers to your list and how you plan to communicate and sell to them on an on-going basis.

The best way to add clients to your list is to have a process within your company to ask customers for their information. If you have customer who are reluctant to give out their information, offer them an incentive to become part of your mailing list, maybe a free gift or special introductory offer.

MANAGEMENT TEAM AND KEY PERSONEL

The management team is very important to the success of your business. It has been said that financing sources will "fund" a business with an "A" management team and a "B" idea before they will fund a "B" management team with an "A" idea. Keep in mind that not everyone on your management team will be receiving a paycheck. The management team can consist of advisors and other business professionals that you work with, including your banker, accountant, consultants and lawyer. This section should answer the following: "What qualifies the management team to run this type of business?" If you have one, include an organizational chart.

Next include a short paragraph on each person with management responsibilities. The write up should include information that directly relates to the current business you are starting or buying. For example, your Senior Marketing person should have not only experience in marketing for a small company, but also for your specific industry or a closely related industry.

Business advisors, consultants and other professionals should be included next. These individuals tend to bring experience and knowledge that other members of your management team may not posses. Business advisors can include a formal board of directors or an informal advisory board. Either should include someone with expertise in banking, law, accounting and marketing. It is incredibly helpful to have input from outside parties. Sometimes small business owners get caught up in the day to day activities and lose sight of the big picture. Outside advisors can help make sure this does not happen.

In addition to management, a short paragraph should be included for key personnel. For example, you were starting a home remodeling business and your mother has agreed to help you get started. You should include in this section that your mother has over 8 years working with Habitat for Humanity as a carpenter. Although she will not be active in the management of the business, her experience is invaluable.

Finally talk about the on-going personnel needs of your business. What do you see as the next employees that you will have to hire? Will it be easy to find those individuals with the experience you are looking for? What is your final plan for number of employees? 5 employees? Or 100 employees? Does the future personnel needs match the other growth projections? Do you have access to a qualified pool of employees around your place of business?

FINANCIAL PLAN

The financial plan should be the last piece you create before the Executive Summary. Review the chapters on Finding Money and Beginning

Bookkeeping. These will help you to create the plan for your specific business. The financial plan should include the following plans:

Summary of Financials
Sources and Uses of initial funding
Balance Sheets for 3 years
Income Statements for 3 years
Cash Flow Statements for 3 years

All of the financial plans should be in the common form known to financing sources. Most of these people look at dozens of financial statements a day, so making them look different will only make you look like you do not know what you are doing in the financial area.

If you have an existing business, cover the past financial performance of the business. You should use those numbers to calculate the future. You can not make the assumption that you will grow by 100% over the next three years, when in the past you have grown by only 5%, without some reasons.

Explain your assumptions. The reader may not be familiar with your industry. If you are estimating expenses, explain how you can to that number.

Summary of Financials

The summary of financials should include the profit or loss projections for the next three years, when positive cash flow is expected, net worth summary from the balance sheet for the next three years and any assumptions made in the financial statements.

Income Statement Summary

	Year 1	Year 2	Year 3
Sales	$100,000	$150,000	$200,000
Expenses	75,000	100,000	150,000
Profit	25,000	50,000	50,000

Cash flow is expected to turn to positive cash flow in 15 months from start date.

Balance Sheet Summary

	Year 1	Year 2	Year 3
Owner's Equity	$125,000	$150,000	$200,000

Sources and Uses Statement

This spreadsheet should contain where the monies are coming from and what are they being spent on. The following is an example:

SOURCES AND USES OF FUNDS

SOURCES

Anywhere State Bank

Commercial Loan, Anywhere State Bank	$50,000
Cash from the Ashford's Savings and	
sale of some of their common stock	$25,000
Total Sources	$75,000

USES

Equipment Suppliers, Inc.	$20,000
Initial Food Inventory	$10,000
Working Capital	$45,000
Total Uses	$75,000

Balance Sheet Example

ED ENTREPRENEUR

BALANCE SHEET AS OF OCTOBER 31, 200X

ASSETS		LIABILITIES	
Cash in Bank	7,470	Accts Payable	
Accts Rec	1,000	Commission Payable	250
Inventory	350	**Total Liabilities**	250
		Capital Paid In	350
		May Earnings	900
		June Earnings	1,770
		July Earnings	500
		August Earnings	1,000
		September Earnings	1,775
		October Earnings	2,275
		Total Equity	8,570
Total Assets	**8,820**	**Total Liabilities & Owner's Equity**	**8,820**

Income Statement Example

ED ENTREPRENEUR
INCOME STATEMENT
OCTOBER 31, 200X

REVENUES:		
Sales of 50 widgets	5,000	
Less: Returns	0	
		$5,000
EXPENSES:		
Sales Commissions	500	
Cost of Goods Sold	600	
Tools	25	
Depreciation	400	
Building Rent	375	
Interest Expense	240	
Accounting Services	100	
Total Expense		2,240
Net Income		**2,760**

Cash Flow Statement Example

Projected Cash Flow Statement
For the Twelve Months Ended December 31, 20XX

	Apr	May	June	Jul	Aug	Sep
Sources of Cash:						
Sales	**2,500**	**3,000**	**3,500**	**500**	**500**	**1,000**
Uses of Cash:						
Cost of Sales	1,175	1,350	1,575	275	275	450
Operating Expenses	1,443	1,555	1,668	893	893	1,055
Total Uses:	**2,618**	**2,905**	**3,243**	**1,168**	**1,168**	**1,505**
Increase (Decrease)	**(118)**	**95**	**257**	**(668)**	**(668)**	**(505)**
Cumulative Cash Flow	**(118)**	**(23)**	**234**	**(434)**	**(1,102)**	**(1,607)**

	Oct	Nov	Dec	Jan	Feb	Mar
Sources of Cash:						
Sales	**1,000**	**6,000**	**6,000**	**12,000**	**6,000**	**6,000**
Uses of Cash:						
Cost of Sales	450	900	900	1,800	900	900
Operating Expenses	1,455	2,380	2,380	3,530	2,180	2,330
Total Uses:	**1,905**	**3,280**	**3,280**	**5,330**	**3,080**	**3,230**
Increase (Decrease)	**(905)**	**2,720**	**2,770**	**6,670**	**2,920**	**2,770**
Cumulative Cash Flow	**(2,512)**	**208**	**2,928**	**9,598**	**12,518**	**15,288**

APPENDICIES TO THE BUSINESS PLAN

The Appendix should include any other information that you feel is important that does not fit in another area of the business plan. This may include:

1. Resumes of the management team
2. Business policies regarding return policies, personnel policies or employee handbook
3. Estimate on equipment that you would need to run your business
4. Initial marketing campaign
5. Potential lease agreement
6. Partnership agreement
7. Signed contracts for product
8. Letters of recommendation from industry experts or potential clients

---

In this chapter, you should have learned:
1. *The important reasons for creating a business plan.*
2. *How to create an effective Executive Summary to entice the reader*
3. *That talking about the weaknesses of your company can reassure investors that you have thought about how to overcome the weaknesses.*
4. *The industry section is a valuable tool to help educate potential investors about your product and the industry.*
5. *The marketing plan is important to show how you are going to reach your sales goals.*
6. *Finally the financials are what investors will compare against your plan and decide if this business is "do-able".*

Websites You May Find Useful

Bplans – www.bplans.com
Business Plans - http://www.businessplans.org/
My Own Business – www.myownbusiness.org

Step To Success
One Action a Day Will Move You Forward

It is time to move forward. Complete the **Step to Success** Action and feel your progress.   No matter where you are going, you can get there one step at a time.

Grab your notebook and start working on your one-page business plan. Use the sample in this chapter as a template. This is your opportunity to start pulling your ideas together into something concrete. Send us your 1-page business plan to Mentors@aisb.biz for feedback and comments.

You can do it – so let's get going!

Chapter 14

Bookkeeping Made Easy

"There's no business like show business, but there are several businesses like accounting."
David Letterman – late night host

More mental than fun

Depending on whom you ask, the subject of accounting is likely to produce one of three responses: Great! or Huh? or Yuk!

Too many entrepreneurs are less than enthusiastic about accounting, and that's unfortunate. They view it as a necessary evil -- to satisfy tax reporting requirements. And we all have varying views of taxes, don't we -- most of them unfavorable!

Accounting is nothing more than a process of organizing and recording financial activities in a **disciplined** manner. "Disciplined" is emphasized to stress the need for a thoughtful, deliberate approach.

Back to attitudes about accounting; why do so many view it negatively? In most cases, it's probably because they haven't recognized the full value of knowing where they are and where they've been (financially). You see, good accounting is a little like good navigation of ships and airplanes -- financial "fixes" are just as important to the entrepreneur as good navigational "fixes" are to the ship captain or the aircraft commander. If you know where you've been, and where you are now, you have a much better chance of arriving at your chosen destination. This chapter will focus on ideas which can help you establish financial "fixes" as you "navigate" to economic security.

Many bookkeeping and accounting courses offered in high schools and colleges emphasize the technical aspects while appearing to ignore the practical side. To overcome this problem, we will concentrate on converting the technical to the practical.

In this chapter you will learn:

1. *Understand basic accounting terms and procedures and why they're so important;*
2. *Organize your financial activities into an understandable form;*
3. *Calculate the value of your business; and*
4. *Determine whether or not you're making money.*

When we're finished, while you may not be qualified to hang out your public accountant's shingle, you will have a reasonable understanding of the fundamentals of accounting, and an appreciation of their value.

So much for the preamble -- let's get to the meat of accounting fundamentals! We'll start off with some of the more obvious items so we can build a foundation.

First of all, why even start a business? Usually, it's: a) to make money (increase wealth); b) to satisfy an ego drive; or c) some combination of the two. Please understand; there is nothing wrong with giving in to a healthy ego -- it's what makes us all tick deep down inside. At the same time, unless a person is blessed with an unending supply of funds, chances are that he or she will want to make a reasonable profit from the venture at the same time as feeding the ego.

What happens all too frequently is that

some business people (perhaps you've known one or two) overlook the little details of keeping good business records in their enthusiasm to satisfy the ego. In fact, they might have made a better income if they had merely put their funds in a passbook savings account! Others may be operating at a loss and don't even know it, much less know what to do about correcting the situation.

The function of accounting could be defined as the creation and organization of records about a business's financial activities and transactions. We can subdivide this rather broad definition into four components:

1. **Documenting** -- The individual documents pertaining to each activity, sometimes called Source Documents.

2. **Recording** -- Listing each activity (transaction) in an orderly manner (usually chronologically) on individual pages or in books commonly called journals.

3. **Organizing** -- Placing these transactions into workable categories in order to provide meaningful summaries, usually in a book called a ledger.

4. **Development of reports** which provide the overall pictures of a company's financial activities and health.

The owner/manager needs reliable information about the company's financial activities in order to guide its growth and development. While a shoebox full of receipts and bills may be considered to be reliable **data** it certainly will not qualify as **information** for the effective management of the firm.

Another definition is necessary -- something called the Accounting Equation: Assets = Liabilities + Owner's Equity -- or:

A = L + OE

Assets (the value of the things owned by the company) equal Liabilities (the amounts owed to others) plus Owner's Equity (the net value or worth of the company). From this it becomes obvious that if we know two of the values, we can solve for the third. For example, given Assets and Liabilities, we can compute Owner's Equity merely by turning the equation around to:

OE = A - L

Assets, Liabilities, and Owner's Equity are commonly combined into a report called a Balance Sheet which reflects the financial position of the company at a given point in time.

Another equation deals with day-to-day activities and has no specific name: Revenues (the monies we've collected or are scheduled to collect) = Expenses (the amounts we've paid or are obligated to pay) + Net Income (whatever is left over). It, too, can be turned around to:

NI = R - E

These three components are usually combined into a report called the Income Statement and reflect the profitability of a company during the period for which the report was prepared.

These two reports -- Balance Sheet and Income Statement -- are intimately tied together because at the end of each accounting period (a month, quarter, year -- whatever is desired) the Net Income is added to Owner's Equity. It becomes obvious, then, that Owner's Equity goes up and down with the fortunes of Net Income!

Now that we have established some basic definitions,

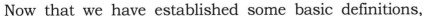

let's look at the situation facing Ed Entrepreneur.

Ed has been a machinist for most of his life and takes a great deal of pride in his work. The pay is satisfactory, and the company for which he works has been good to him over the years.

At the same time, he is a tinkerer -- the kind of individual who has a good imagination and who enjoys putting ideas to work. He has developed some miscellaneous devices for use around the home which have been quite useful and, most recently may have discovered the pot of gold at the end of the rainbow! It seems that Ed has invented a new household gadget (he calls it a "Widget") which performs just about any function desired by the householder. Further, Ed has discovered a special technique which makes it easy and simple to shape and assemble the Widget, cutting manufacturing time to about 15 minutes.

When Ken, his neighbor, saw and tried the Widget, he asked Ed to make one for him, insisting on paying $5 for it since it was so useful. Ed didn't mind doing it for a couple of reasons. First, he enjoyed the work. Second, Ken was a highly respected doctor and Ed enjoyed the compliment. Third, he had the necessary materials in his scrap drawer. And, fourth, he could always find some good use for the $5! It wasn't until a couple of weeks later that Ed discovered his new device should have been called the "Tiger" (as in 'by the tail').

At a neighborhood barbecue, Ken told Ed that he had shown the Widget to some of his medical friends who instantly saw great value in it not only as a household device but also as a medical instrument if he could make it out of stainless steel. And, to top it off, the other doctors would be willing to pay $100 for one of stainless steel because it was extremely useful and they had never before seen anything like it for any price! Could he deliver 20 in the next two weeks?

That evening, Ed started doing some serious thinking. The cost of stainless steel would be several dollars compared to a dollar or so for the cold rolled steel he had been using. Machining would be more time consuming; so it might take a half-hour to make this new version.

The biggest problem was that his lathe was old and rather worn. It was good enough to do his home jobs, but when it came to handling stainless steel, it wouldn't be able to provide the precision he needed. The machine shop had the equipment, but Ed didn't want the boss to know he was moonlighting because others had gotten into trouble before.

Then he remembered that his brother-in-law George had a first class shop in the garage. While George wasn't much of a machinist, he had been smart enough to buy top-of-the-line equipment.

He called George, explained the situation, and asked if he could use the shop.

"Sure," said George, "for $50 per hour."

Ed thought briefly about George's offer, and said he would call him back.

Giving himself time to cool off, Ed did some more figuring. First, he knew how to do the work and do it well. Second, he could probably make two Widgets per hour; so the cost of George's equipment would be only $25 per unit. Third, if he were going to collect $100 per Widget, he could still make about $65 per unit after subtracting another $10 for the costs of the materials. Fourth, in spite of George's outrageous charge, Ed was still excited about the possibilities.

20 widgets at $100 each	A	$2,000
Garage charges 2 widgets per hour @ $50/hour	B	500
Cost of materials at $10 each widget	C	200
Net Income for 20 widgets (A-B-C)	D	$1,300
Revenue per widget (D/20)		$35

He called Ken to see if his doctor friends were really serious.

"Absolutely," said Ken.

Ed took a deep breath and told Ken he would do it.

Then Ed called George, agreed to the $50 hourly charge, and set up a schedule to use the equipment.

On Friday he took a day's vacation and went to several suppliers, buying raw materials, rivets, nuts and bolts, along with the special cutters he would need for the lathe and bits for the drill press. Altogether, he spent nearly $350, musing that it was a mere pittance compared to the $2,000 he would make in this venture. Over the weekend he completed 15 of the stainless steel Widgets (SSW). He could have done all of them, but decided to put some extra care into them since Ken's reputation was also at stake. By the end of the next week, he had finished the lot and called Ken. When Ken arrived and looked at the finished SSW's, he was genuinely excited. Since he was meeting with his doctor friends on Monday, he said he would take them along and deliver them.

On Tuesday Ken called Ed and said his associates were really pleased with the SSW's and would promptly send their checks as soon as Ed sent invoices for their records.

Ed had an old beater of a typewriter at home, so he bought some packaged forms at the local stationery store and laboriously pecked out the 20 invoices. When he was done, he mused to himself that it seemed to take nearly as long to prepare the invoices as it had to manufacture the SSW's.

By the end of the month, he had received checks from 12 of the doctors and deposited them in the bank, feeling rather smug. The $1,200 would help him make the down payment on the new Olds 98 he wanted, and the $800 coming later would pay for his summer vacation.

Then, he remembered George -- and winced as he gave him a check for $750 for the 15 hours spent using George's shop.

Now he was faced with another problem. His phone was ringing every evening when he arrived home from work -- other doctors had learned about SSW's and wanted to order them. Before he knew it, he had agreed to make another 35 units.

He called George again and arranged a new schedule.

Over the next couple of weeks (or weekends), Ed worked diligently on SSW's -- producing and delivering all 35 finished units. There was a little more scrap than he had expected, and it took a little longer for each one than he had planned. Still, Ed thought to himself that he was making money -- in fact, more than he had ever made!

He began to resurrect an old dream of having his own machine shop where he could turn out first-class goods at a fair profit instead of the boring activities he did at his current job. The only problem was his concern over continuing to make a reasonable living -- he realized there were a lot of things he didn't know about running a business.

At the next neighborhood barbecue, he found himself chatting with Alice Accountant and he discussed his dilemma with her. She asked him some rather serious questions, such as how much did a finished SSW really cost and how many could he produce in a given time, and was he really making a profit.

Ed commented that things seemed to be going quite well but admitted that he didn't really have the precise answers. He asked Alice if she could help him over the weekend, offering to pay her $25 per hour to get the financial records straightened out.

By Saturday, Ed had found all the sales slips from his purchases, along with the duplicates of the invoices sent to the doctors. He and Alice began organizing things.

"The first thing to remember," Alice emphasized, "is to keep all of your original sales slips and invoices, the source documents. From them we organize and record the financial activities in a logical manner. Let's begin with purchases -- we will create a Purchases Journal."

She took the sales slips from the first purchases, broke the items into categories, and posted them to the journal using Ed's check numbers as a reference. Then she added the cost of renting George's equipment as another item. When she was done, it looked like this:

PURCHASES JOURNAL

Date	Purchased From	Description Ref.	Materials	Tools	Rental
5/10	Jones Steel Co.	Steel 3012	$250		
5/10	Jones Steel Co.	Bolts, Rivets	50		
5/10	Smith Mach Tool	Cutters, Bits		50	
5/30	George	Shop Rental			750
5/31	Monthly Totals		$300	$50	$750

Then she took the duplicate invoices from the first order and, assigning a number to each as a reference, posted them -- this time to another sheet she called a Sales Journal:

SALES JOURNAL

Date	Sold To	Description	Ref	Dr. Amt.	Cr. Amt
5/20	Doc #1	Widget	101		$100
5/20	Doc #2	Widget	102		100
5/20	Doc #3	Widget	103		100
5/20	Doc #20	Widget	120		100
5/31	Total Month				$2,000

Alice stressed that each transaction should be posted separately to minimize the chance of missing something. She also urged that the items be posted chronologically, in date order.

Then, since Ed was selling Widgets on credit, she set up a journal to reflect the amounts owed to him by others, and also to record the payments received from these same people. She placed the ones for which Ed had been paid in a **closed** file and the remainder in an **open** invoices file.

ACCOUNTS RECEIVABLE JOURNAL

Date	In Acct With	Description	Ref	Dr. Amt	Cr Amt
5/20	Doc #1	Sale on Acct	101	$100	
5/20	Doc #2	Sale on Acct	102	100	
5/20	Doc #3	Sale on Acct	103	100	
5/20	Doc #20	Sale on Acct	120	100	
5/20	Doc #6	Recd on Acct	106		$100
5/20	Doc #7	Recd on Acct	107		100
5/20	Doc #8	Recd on Acct	108		100
5/20	Doc #12	Recd on Acct	112		100
5/31	Month Totals			$2,000	$1,200

Another journal was set up to record the cash transactions.

CASH JOURNAL

Date	Name	Description	Ref	Dr. Amt	Cr. Amt
5/10	Jones Steel	Materials	3012		$300
5/10	Smith Mach Tool	Tools	3013		50
5/22	Doc #1	Recd on Acct	101	$100	
5/24	Doc #2	Recd on Acct	102	100	
5/24	Doc #3	Recd on Acct	103	100	
5/29	Doc #11	Recd on Acct	111	100	
5/31	George	Shop Rental	3025		750
5/31	Doc #12	Recd on Acct	112	100	
5/31	**Month Totals**			**$1,200**	**$1,100**

As she went along with the various journals, Alice explained that each item was of significant importance if Ed wanted to know how his business was really doing. She stressed that credits of $100 in one journal required complementing total debits of $100 in another journal (or journals) -- she called it **double entry bookkeeping.**

Alice pointed out that as Ed recorded a sale (she called it a **Credit**) in the Sales Journal, he either was or was not paid for it at the time the sale was made. If he received payment on the spot, it would be directly recorded (as a **Debit**) in the Cash Journal; if not, then it must be recorded as a debit in the Accounts Receivable Journal.

Similarly, as Ed purchased materials, they must be recorded as Debits in the Purchases Journal and as Credits in the Cash Journal (if he paid for them at the time of purchase), otherwise, in an Accounts Payable Journal. In this way, Ed would always know the balance of outstanding accounts as well as his cash position.

"Great Scott!" Ed exclaimed. "I didn't know that you had to do all these things just to run a small operation like mine. Is it all really necessary?"

Alice smiled. "Well," she replied, "I've already taken a few shortcuts in order to keep things as simple as possible. For example, if you had lots of cash transactions, such as a retail store, we would set up separate journals for cash receipts and cash disbursements. I just didn't feel that was necessary at this time.

"However," she went on, "your purchases tend to fall into different categories; so I decided to spread them out to allow you to see more accurately just how you're spending your money.

"Now that we've summarized your activities for May, we need to prepare a couple of reports which will really put things in perspective. First, though, we'll do a worksheet which will help us.

ED ENTREPRENEUR
TRIAL BALANCE WORKSHEET ENDING MAY 31

Account Title	Opening		Adjustments		Closing	
	Debit	Credit	Debit	Credit	Debit	Credit
Sales				2,000		
Materials			300			
Tools			50			
Shop Rental			750			
Net Income			**1,100**	**2,000**		
Cash			1,200	1,100	100	
Accts Rec			2,000	1,200	800	
Accts Pay						
Owner's Equity			1,100	2,000		900
Totals			**4,300**	**4,300**	**900**	**900**

"Here, too," Alice explained, "I've taken a few shortcuts. If your activities were more complicated, I would have to enter more detail -- but the result would be the same.

"The idea here is to transcribe the activity from each journal and, when we balance, we can be pretty sure that we've covered all the details. You will note that once we determined the Net Income, we then posted it to the Owner's Equity account -- that's the one which tells you how much your business is worth at the end of each accounting period."

"You mean my business is already worth something?" asked Ed.

"Sure, by an amount equal to the Net Income. If you had opened a separate checking account at the very beginning and put the same $350 into it that you used to buy the materials and tools, the Balance Sheet would have been a little different. You merely would have posted a $350 debit to Cash and a corresponding credit of $350 to Owner's Equity; and the value of your business would now be $1,250. Our situation here is the same as if you had then taken the $350 back out of the business account and returned it to your personal account. Now, let's prepare the Income Statement."

ED ENTREPRENEUR -- INCOME STATEMENT FOR MAY

REVENUES:		
Sales of 20 widgets	$2,000	
		$2,000
EXPENSES:		
Raw Materials/Cost of Goods Sold	300	
Tools	50	
Shop Rental	750	
Total Expense		$1,100
NET INCOME		**$900**

"Let's see," said Ed rather thoughtfully, "if I sold 20 Widgets for a $900 profit, that's $45 per Widget. Not too bad!"

"Looks pretty good," responded Alice. "Just how much time did it take you to earn the $900?"

"Well, I spent more time than I had expected -- about 15 hours, I guess."

"Yes," she acknowledged, "but how about the time you spent getting the materials and preparing the invoices?"

"Oh! I forgot about that. There's probably another 15 hours tied up there, too. Still, $900 for 30 hours isn't bad, is it?"

"Not at all," she agreed. "Let's finish up the first month by preparing one more report -- something we call a Balance Sheet. It will give you a bird's eye view of where you stand as of the close of each monthly period. Once again, all we have to do to prepare this report is to pick the numbers right off the worksheets."

ED ENTREPRENEUR -- BALANCE SHEET AS OF MAY 31

ASSETS		LIABILITIES	
Cash in Bank	100	Accts Payable	0
Accts Rec	800		
		Total Liabilities	0
		Capital Paid In	0
		May Earnings	900
		Total Equity	900
Total Assets	**900**	**Total Liabilities & Owner's Equity**	**900**

"Well," said Ed, "I can see one thing for sure -- my Cash is low and my Receivables are high! In fact, most of my value is sitting in someone else's pocket. I'll call Ken and see if he can push on his doctor friends a little."

"Before we do that," advised Alice, "let's go to work on June's activities." She glanced at the source documents. "You go ahead and post these transactions as I watch over your shoulder."

Ed took the first one, the sales slip for the materials to make the second group of Widgets, and began to post the details, following that with the postings of cash received and the 35 new sales he had made, along with the Widget returned by Doctor #18. Oh, yes, and $1,000 of the $1,200 he owed to George for the month's use of the machine shop.

PURCHASES JOURNAL

Date	Purchased From	Description Ref.	Materials	Tools	Rental
5/31	Month Totals		$300	$50	$750
6/3	Jones Steel Co.	Steel 3033	500		
6/3	Jones Steel	Bolt/Rivets	100		
6/30	George	Shop Rental			1,200
6/30	Month Totals		$600		$1,200

CASH JOURNAL

Date	Name	Description	Ref	Dr. Amt	Cr. Amt
5/31	Month Totals			$1,200	$1,100
6/3	Jones Steel	Materials	3033		600
6/4	Doc #13	Recd on Acct	113	$100	
6/5	Doc #15	Recd on Acct	115	100	
6/7	Doc #16	Recd on Acct	116	100	
6/8	Doc #17	Recd on Acct	117	100	
6/28	Doc #44	Recd on Acct	144	100	
6/28	Doc #48	Recd on Acct	148	100	
6/30	George	Shop Rental	3057		1,000
6/30	Doc #53	Recd on Acct	153	100	
6/30	Month Totals			2,000	1,600

SALES JOURNAL

Date	Sold To	Description	Ref	Dr. Amt.	Cr. Amt
5/31	Total Month				$2,000
6/17	Doc #21	Widget	121		$100
6/17	Doc #22	Widget	122		100
6/17	Doc #23	Widget	123		100
6/26	Doc #55	Widget	155		100
6/27	Doc #18	Return	118	100	
6/30	Total Month			$100	$3,500

ACCOUNTS RECEIVABLE JOURNAL

Date	In Acct With	Description	Ref	Dr. Amt	Cr Amt
5/31	**Month Totals**			**$2,000**	**$1,200**
6/3	Doc #13	Recd on Acct	113		100
6/4	Doc #15	Recd on Acct	115		100
6/5	Doc #16	Recd on Acct	116		100
6/7	Doc #17	Recd on Acct	117		100
6/17	Doc #21	Sale on Acct	121	100	
6/17	Doc #22	Sale on Acct	122	100	
6/17	Doc #23	Sale on Acct	123	100	
6/26	Doc #55	Sale on Acct	155	100	
6/27	Doc #18	Return	118		100
6/28	Doc #44	Recd on Acct	144		100
6/28	Doc #48	Recd on Acct	148		100
6/30	Doc #53	Recd on Acct	153		100
6/30	**Month Totals**			**$3,500**	**$2,100**

Oh yes, Ed had to set up a new journal, Accounts Payable, to handle the amount which he still owed George for the June shop rent.

ACCOUNTS PAYABLE JOURNAL

Date	Acct With	Description	Ref	Dr. Amt	Cr Amt
6/30	George	Balance of Rent	3057	$200	
6/30	Month Total			$200	

It took them the better part of another hour to pull all of June's figures together and get them properly posted.

"Whew," Ed sighed, "isn't there an easier way to do all this?"

"Sure," laughed Alice, "hire someone else to do it! The point remains, however, that it does need to be done."

"But aren't there more shortcuts I could take? How about that Accounts Receivable Journal -- of the 35 sales I recorded, I received payment for 16 of them during the month. Do I really have to go through all that effort?"

"If you're especially careful, you can probably put all of June's invoices in a separate file and pull them out as you receive the checks. Those which remain in the file at the end of the month will still have to be posted to Receivables if you're going to keep track of things."

"Oh, by the way," Ed suddenly remembered, "what happens if I don't use all the raw materials I bought? I'm getting better as I do each Widget, and I've got about $120 in unused materials left over."

"Then we'd better set up another journal -- we'll call it Inventory.

"We'll handle this one a little differently because we have to 'back' into the figure we need for the Operating Statement. At the same time, we will include the approximate value of the Widget returned by Doctor #18 because at the end of the month it's unsold. Let's assume its worth is $50."

INVENTORY

Date	Description	Begin	+ Purch	- End	=Used
6/30	Stainless Steel		500	100	400
6/3	Bolts, Rivets		100	20	80
6/27	Widget (finished)			50	-50
6/30	Cost of Goods		600	170	430

"You see," Alice commented after preparing the journal, "what we need is the Cost of the Goods which you sold during the month. We determine that figure by taking the balance of the Inventory at the beginning of the month -- in this case zero -- adding to it the amounts you purchased during the month, and then subtracting the value which remains at the end of the month.

"Now, let's do the worksheet for June. Note that we ignore the Opening and Closing columns when we transcribe the Revenues and Expenses. But, for the Balance Sheet accounts, we first transcribe the Closing figures from the previous month into the Opening column. This way, we assure ourselves of staying in balance. Remember, Net Income is the remainder after we subtract Total Expenses from Total Revenues."

ED ENTREPRENEUR
TRIAL BALANCE WORKSHEET
ENDING JUNE 30

Account Title	Opening		Adjustments		Closing	
	Debit	Credit	Debit	Credit	Debit	Credit
Sales			100	3,500		
Materials			430			
Tools			0			
Shop Rental			1,200			
Net Income			1,730	3,500		
Cash	100		2,000	1,600	500	
Accts Rec	800		3,500	2,100	2,200	
Inventory			600	430	170	
Accts Pay				200		200
Owner's Equity		900	1,730	3,500		2,670
Totals	900	900	7,830	7,830	2,870	2,870

"Oh, I see!" exclaimed Ed. "We use the worksheet to verify the month's transactions. We took the $100 Cash from last month's closing, added the $2,000 received this month, then subtracted the $1,600 paid this month, to arrive at a closing Cash balance of $500."

"Good! I think you've got the idea! Now, let's prepare the month's Income Statement and Balance Sheet."

ED ENTREPRENEUR -- INCOME STATEMENT FOR JUNE

REVENUES:		
Sales of 35 widgets	3,500	
Less: Return of 1 widget	100	
		$3,400
EXPENSES:		
Cost of Goods Sold	430	
Tools	0	
Shop Rental	1,200	
Total Expense		1,630
NET INCOME		**1,770**

ED ENTREPRENEUR -- BALANCE SHEET AS OF JUNE 30

ASSETS		LIABILITIES	
Cash in Bank	500	Accts Payable	200
Accts Rec	2,200		
Inventory	170	**Total Liabilities**	200
		Capital Paid In	0
		May Earnings	900
		June Earning	1,770
		Total Equity	2,670
Total Assets	**$2,870**	**Total Liabilities & Owner's Equity**	**$2,870**

"Whew," sighed Ed, "that's a lot of work, but I do have to admit that it gives me a good view of the activity in June and where I am now. The only problem is, what happens when I get a big bunch of these reports? It seems to me that I can get buried in numbers and paper, and still not know which way I'm heading."

"For example, I've had this idea about leaving my present company and going into the Widget business full-time. How can I do a better job of determining whether or not this business can support me?"

"An excellent observation and a worthwhile question," Alice replied. "While there's probably nothing which will answer all your questions, there are **some** things you could do to help reduce the uncertainty."

"For example, you should probably get some more knowledge about the industry in which you're selling your products -- perhaps some kind of market research to determine the need for Widgets, the competition you're likely to encounter, and the price you'll be able to charge over the long run. Unfortunately, the things we've done here won't help you with this part of the decision making process."

"There are some ways, however, to use the results of your accounting efforts to help you in your decisions. One good approach is to develop ratios which, in turn, can help you figure out the trends. In other words, the idea is to establish comparisons to see if things are improving, staying pretty much the same, or getting worse.

"For example, let's compare Expenses as a percentage of Revenues. Using the May and June figures, we can set up a little chart -- something like this:

ED ENTREPRENEUR -- EXPENSES VS. REVENUES

Account Title	Month of May		Month of June		Year-to-date	
	$	%	$	%	$	%
Net Sales	2,000	100	3,400	100	5,400	100
Cost of Goods	300	15	430	12.65	730	13.52
Tools	50	2.50	0	0	50	.93
Shop Rent	750	37.50	1,200	35.29	1,950	36.11
Net Income	900	45	1,770	52.06	2,670	49.44

"Now," Alice invited, "what can you see from this?"

"Hey, that's easy! My Cost of Goods Sold is going down -- I'm getting more done with less scrap. Likewise, my costs of Shop Rent are declining -- it's not taking me as long to make a Widget. Now, I can see not only that my profit is improving, but I can also see which factors are affecting the improvement."

"Right!" she acknowledged. "And, one of the reasons we took the effort to add that returned Widget to Inventory was to avoid distorting the Cost of Goods Sold. Oh, sure, CGS would have still improved, but the results of your work wouldn't have been as obvious."

"But," Alice continued, "We've got one more step which will further help us to see how things are going. Remember, you commented earlier that you could get buried in the numbers? Well, here's a method which can help turn the numbers, the data, into truly useful information. I'll add a few hypothetical values for purposes of illustration," she said graphically, as she took out a piece of paper and began to plot some data points.

"Keep in mind, Ed, while this graph reflects Cost of Goods Sold as a percentage of Sales, it could have shown CGS in dollars per unit."

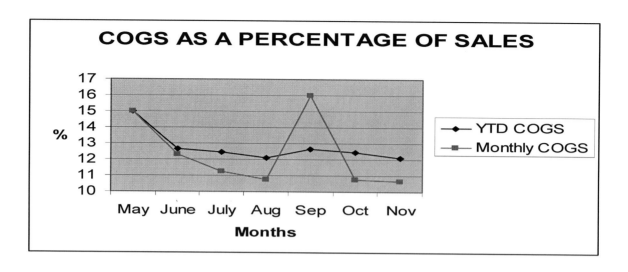

COGS AS A PERCENTAGE OF SALES

As Alice finished her efforts she asked, "What would this chart tell you, Ed?"

"Holy cow!" Ed exclaimed. "Everything looks great except for that big jump in September."

"If this were your company and you saw this chart, what would you do?" Alice asked.

"I'd be looking very seriously to see what happened -- could be an increase in the price of materials or, more likely, an increase in scrap. If I had a number of people working for me, I'd also check into labor costs. As long as I'm fairly small, though, I'll probably know about these things as they occur."

"Still, it makes sense to put things in this form so I can focus on the important items without being overwhelmed by all the data. Now I understand why the boss at the shop has all those charts on his wall.""

"Ed, my friend and neighbor," Alice smiled as she stood up and stretched, "you've just graduated with flying colors from Alice's beginning school of accounting and financial management!"

"I'm truly pleased with what you've taught me this afternoon. And, looking at the clock, I think I owe you about $125 for the education."

"I'll tell you what, Ed. Make it $100 even, and a steak on the grill, and I'll call it even."

"Done!" And Ed started the grill.

As they relaxed on the patio after dinner, Alice decided to give Ed some additional food for thought.

"Earlier, Ed, you mentioned that you had made about $30 per hour in May. What do you feel your hourly earnings were in June?"

"Let's see," he said thoughtfully, "I spent about 24 hours in manufacturing, an hour getting raw materials, about six hours preparing the invoices, and another hour delivering the Widgets -- say, 32 hours altogether." He punched his calculator quickly. "That's a little over $55 per hour!"

"Now," challenged Alice, "if I correctly understand what you've said, you have an interesting problem facing you." Taking another worksheet from her pad, she put down some more figures.

ED ENTREPRENEUR -- HOURLY LABOR EXPENSES

Account Title	Month of June Hours	$/Hr	Month of June Hours	$/Hr	Year-to-Date Hours	$/Hr
Manufacturing	15	30	24	55	39	45.38
Pickup/Delivery	5	30	2	55	7	37.14
Administration	10	30	6	55	16	39.38
Totals	**30**	**30**	**32**	**55**	**62**	**43.06**

"Now, Ed, as a businessman, what does this set of figures tell you?"

"If I owned a company and saw figures such as these, I'd blow my stack! Fifty-five dollars an hour for these jobs is just as outrageous as $50 per hour for George's shop!"

"And," Alice continued, "your labor costs for this month are going to have to include another four hours of bookkeeping."

"What I hear you saying is that I should allocate an appropriate value to these jobs, and then decide which ones I'm going to do, and which ones are better done by someone else." Ed paused, then said, "A good machinist should earn about $15 per hour. Jones Steel will deliver my materials for $15 per load. What should I expect to pay a good assistant to handle the paperwork?"

"Probably about $10 to $12 per hour for, say, three hours per month," she responded. "Add another one-third for fringe benefits and payroll taxes if the person is an employee, or pay him or her the same additional amount if the work is done as an independent contractor."

Ed worked furiously with his calculator for a few minutes.

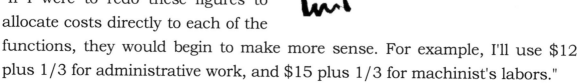

"If I were to redo these figures to allocate costs directly to each of the functions, they would begin to make more sense. For example, I'll use $12 plus 1/3 for administrative work, and $15 plus 1/3 for machinist's labors."

ED ENTREPRENEUR
REVISED HOURLY LABOR EXPENSES

	Month of May			Month of June		
Account Title	Hours	$/Hr	Total	Hours	$/Hr	Total
Manufacturing	15	20	300	24	20	480
Pickup/Delivery			15			15
Administration	3	16	48	3	16	48
Management- Ed			537			1,227
Totals			**900**			**1,770**

"Now I can see what my profit line is, or at least what the value of my management efforts are -- because I separated them from the other jobs."

"If I were to keep track of my hours spent in management tasks, such as planning, and allocate an hourly value to that work, I'd get a much better idea of whether or not my business is really making any money," he concluded.

Ed was quiet for several minutes. When he finally spoke, there was a gleam in his eye. "I've been planning on taking off for a couple weeks of vacation. It's time for my annual fishing trip. Orders are down for the moment -- guess all the doctors are on vacation, too.

"This time it's going to be a working vacation. I hear that the fish aren't biting too well right now anyway; so I'll have plenty of time to do some thinking.

"What I really need now is a business plan. But, I need another bit of information before I can put one together. If I were to purchase my own equipment, how would I handle the bookkeeping?"

"Quite simply," Alice responded. "Equipment, such as the kind used in a machine shop, should have a useful life of at least five years and is considered a capital investment, rather than an expense. One way to handle it is to expense a fraction, say 1/60 of the equipment's value, each month. This would be similar to a charge for rent, but it's called depreciation. It's a method of writing off the equipment's value over a period of time to compensate the owner for wear and tear."

"But," she cautioned, "There are several different ways of handling depreciation -- I've only mentioned one. When you come to the point of making a decision about a purchase of this magnitude, I suggest that we get together first to discuss it. In that way, you will be more informed and can pick the one most appropriate for you."

"That really makes some sense," agreed Ed. "I'm going to work on my business plan while I'm waiting for the big ones to bite. This should be a fascinating fishing trip."

When Ed returned from his vacation, he had his plan fairly well organized. He went over it with Alice, who helped him smooth out a few wrinkles.

Realizing that he could keep better track of his business cash if he separated it from his household finances, he opened a business checking account, depositing the current business cash balance. He also added the original $350 as capital paid in.

He retained Alice's accounting firm to handle his firm's books and prepare invoices. The charges would be $100 per month which included not only the bookkeeping services and preparation of invoices, but also periodic consultation with Alice to help him as questions arose.

On Ken's recommendations, he also contracted with Mike to promote the sales of SSW's. Mike was a seasoned medical supplies salesman who represented several manufacturers, and who had earned Ken's respect. The understanding was that Mike would receive a 10% commission only when the payments for SSW's were received by Ed.

Over the next couple months, Accounts Receivable dropped to about $1,000 and Sales increased to about 50 units per month. Ed was able to concentrate his time on the manufacturing, a long time love, along with the new excitement of being a manager.

Ed's current financial statements were as follows:

ED ENTREPRENEUR
INCOME STATEMENT FOR OCTOBER

REVENUES:		
Sales of 50 widgets	5,000	
Less: Returns	0	
		$5,000
EXPENSES:		
Sales Commissions	500	
Cost of Goods Sold	600	
Tools	25	
Shop Rental	1,500	
Accounting Services	100	
Total Expense		2,725
Net Income		**2,275**

ED ENTREPRENEUR
BALANCE SHEET AS OF OCTOBER 31

ASSETS		LIABILITIES	
Cash in Bank	7,470	Accts Payable	
Accts Rec	1,000	Commission Payable	250
Inventory	350	**Total Liabilities**	250
		Capital Paid In	350
		May Earnings	900
		June Earnings	1,770
		July Earnings	500
		August Earnings	1,000
		September Earnings	1,775
		October Earnings	2,275
		Total Equity	8,570
Total Assets	**8,820**	**Total Liabilities & Owner's Equity**	**8,820**

One problem remained -- that $50 per hour Ed had to pay George for the use of the shop.

By sheer luck, Ed found out that he could purchase some nearly new shop equipment from an estate for $24,000. Further, the estate would rent that portion of the building where the equipment was installed for $375 per month if he bought the equipment.

He went to see his favorite banker, Larry Lender, to find out what kind of financing they would suggest. Larry told Ed that based on the reputation Ed had established together with the financial reports Ed had the foresight to bring with him; the bank would be willing to lend 80% of the funds necessary to purchase the equipment. The loan would be amortized (paid off) over three years, with interest at a rate of 15% on the unpaid balance. Monthly payments would be $666.

Ed hurried over to Alice's office to get the benefit of her insight.

"What should I do?" he asked.

"I'm not in a position to tell you what to do, Ed," she responded, "but I can help by showing you how last month's financial statements would appear if you had owned the equipment at that time."

She took another worksheet and began to make some adjustments to last month's reports. "I'm going to include only those accounts from the Operating Statement which will change as a result of a purchase."

ADJUSTMENTS TO OCTOBER FOR NEW EQUIPMENT

Account Title	Actual Debit	Actual Credit	Adjustments Debit	Adjustments Credit	Projected Debit	Projected Credit
Shop Rental				A 1,500		
Depreciation			C 400			
Building Rent			D 375			
Interest Exp			E 240			
Net Income Adj			**1,015**	**1,500**		
Cash	7,470		A 1,500	B 4,800		
				D	3,129	
				375		
				E 666		
Accts Rec	1,000				1,000	
Inventory	350				350	
Machinery		B	24,000		24,000	
Depreciation			C (400)		(400)	
Comm Payable		250				250
Bank Loan			E 426	D 19,200		18,774
Owner's Equity		8,570	1,015	1,500		9,055
Totals	**8,820**	**8,820**	**26,541**	**26,541**	**28,079**	**28,079**

As Alice made the adjustments, she labeled each one and discussed it with Ed:

- A. represented not having to pay the $1,500 for shop rental;
- B. was the addition of the machinery as a capital asset and required corresponding credits to Cash of $4,800 (the down payment) and Bank Loans of $19,200;
- C. was the allowance for Depreciation for the month, treated uniquely as a negative Debit so that it makes more sense when printed on the Balance Sheet;
- D. was the monthly Rent for the new building; and

E.   was the monthly payment to the bank, split between the interest which would have been due on the loan, and the remainder of the payment which would have been applied to the reduction of the loan.

"Are you saying," Ed challenged, "that by buying the equipment my Net Income would have gone up by $485?"

"Yes," she confirmed, "as a result of decreasing costs. In addition, if we can set the down payment aside for a moment, your monthly cash flow would have improved by $451 -- the $1,500 saved on rent to George minus the new charges for the rent on the building and the payment on the loan."

"I think you can already see the results of this opportunity," she remarked. "We'll finish the financial statements anyway, just so there is no confusion."

ED ENTREPRENEUR
ADJUSTED INCOME STATEMENT FOR OCTOBER

REVENUES:		
Sales of 50 widgets	5,000	
Less: Returns	0	
		$5,000
EXPENSES:		
Sales Commissions	500	
Cost of Goods Sold	600	
Tools	25	
Depreciation	400	
Building Rent	375	
Interest Expense	240	
Accounting Services	100	
Total Expense		2,240
Net Income		**2,760**

ED ENTREPRENEUR

ADJUSTED BALANCE SHEET AS OF OCTOBER 31

ASSETS		LIABILITIES	
Cash in Bank	3,129	Accts Payable	
Accts Rec	1,000	Commission Payable	250
Inventory	350	Bank Loans	18,774
Machinery	24,000	**Total Liabilities**	19,024
Less: Depn	(400)		
		Capital Paid In	350
		May Earnings	900
		June Earnings	1,770
		July Earnings	500
		August Earnings	1,000
		September Earnings	1,775
		October Earnings	2,760
		Total Equity	9,055
Total Assets	**28,079**	**Total Liabilities & Owner's Equity**	**28,079**

"Remember, though, that the rent for George's shop has varied in the past depending on how many Widgets you were making. These new payments will be there even if you have no orders."

"Alice, I really want to go ahead with this change. How do you see my chances of success?

"There's no way I can forecast any company's success," she reminded him. "You still need to survey the marketplace and draw conclusions as to the likelihood of continuing increases in sales. Once you've done this, you can use your newly acquired skills in accounting to predict the results. "And, by the way, now that you have a sales rep, you can use him for valuable feedback from the marketplace. Ask him to keep his eyes open for information, especially regarding opportunities for new products or accessories.

"There will always be some uncertainty - that's what we call **business risk**. And, because of this risk, the entrepreneur deserves to make a profit."

There you are -- an overview of the world of bookkeeping and accounting. You should now have a reasonable understanding of the fundamentals and an appreciation of their value

We have covered the basics -- the Balance Sheet categories of Assets, Liabilities, and Owner's Equity, along with the Income Statement categories of Revenues, Expense and Net Income. And, we've shown how the periodic Net Income affects the Balance Sheet.

We have also demonstrated how diligence and thoroughness are keystones in the accounting process. We've discussed how each posting to one journal requires a corresponding entry in another journal (or journals) in order to keep things in balance. Discipline is an absolute **must**!

We've learned that Revenue accounts are those which reflect our earnings, whether we received the cash at the time of sale or merely the right to receive payment in the future. Revenues are considered **Credits** (abbreviated Cr.).

Expense accounts, we found, were those to which we posted the costs of day-to-day operations. Once again, this was true when we had made payment immediately, and also when we had incurred the obligation to pay later. Expenses are called **Debits** (abbreviated Dr.).

To keep things in balance, we discovered that Assets (the value of the things which we own) are normally Debits, and both Liabilities (the amounts we owe to others) and Owner's Equity (the remaining value) are Credits.

Further, we have explored some methods of using and interpreting the results of your accounting efforts as devices for management of a business. You see, the figures are not an end unto themselves. Instead, they are tools which are there for your use as you seek ways of establishing your business on a firm foundation and guiding it toward your goals.

In this chapter you have learned:

1. *The definitions for basic accounting terms including: assets, liabilities, owner's equity, net income, balance sheet.*
2. *The differences between the journals that you need to keep in running a profitable business. Even though accounting software packages keep these journals for you, you need to understand how they get created.*
3. *How to manage your cash flow and tell if you are making money and where you may be short on cash to pay bills.*
4. *How to use the financial information to make better decisions as you grow your business.*

 Websites You May Find Useful

Quickbooks - http://quickbooks.intuit.com/
Quickbooks training – www.aisb.biz

 Step To Success
One Action a Day Will Move You Forward

It is time to move forward. Complete the **Step to Success** Action and feel your progress. No matter where you are going, you can get there one step at a time.

If you are starting a very small business, you can create your own journals. If not, determine how you will manage your accounting and financial data.

You can do it, so start right NOW!

Chapter 15

Accurately Forecasting Sales

"I have never worked a day in my life without selling. If I believe in something, I sell it, and I sell it hard."
--Estée Lauder (1908-2004) American businesswoman

Dollars In, Dollars Out

By now you probably have some good ideas about what kinds of products and services will sell in your market. You are well along the way toward developing a plan for your business that will work as hard as you do. Good planning means success will soon follow.

Wouldn't it be helpful if you could estimate what your sales and expenses would be 6 or 12 months in the future? Just imagine: you would know how much inventory you would need to have on hand; you would know what your overhead expenses would be; you would even know how much money you were going to pay yourself!

With a little bit of imagination and a sharp pencil, you can do this kind of "fortune telling" for yourself.

Some people call it forecasting. Some call it budgeting. Your accountant probably calls it projecting or calculating a "pro forma". No matter what you call it, it means the same thing -- you are imagining what will happen in the future so that you can plan accordingly.

> *In this chapter you will learn:*
>
> 1. *Different types of forecasting methods; advantages and disadvantages of each*
> 2. *How to accurately forecast your sales*
> 3. *How to calculate your Fixed and Variable assets*
> 4. *How to project your cash flow*
> 5. *How to compare your forecasts to actual sales and expenses*

THE ART OF FORECASTING

Financial forecasting is an art, not a science. No matter how carefully you think you have planned, you will not hit your projection exactly.

You can, however come very close.

Forecasting sales is like forecasting the weather. A sales forecast is no more (and no less!) than an educated guess as to how many sales you expect to make over a specified period of time. There are several ways of doing this:

1. You can use the LET-THE-BOSS-DECIDE Method, also known as the "jury of executive opinion" method. If this method were used at General Motors, the heads of its major divisions would pool their knowledge of the market to arrive at a joint opinion of how many sales to expect.

2. You can use the GRASS-ROOTS Method. This method is directed at your sales people and other

employees who have the closest contact with the customer.

3.	But since you are not a major American automaker, and you probably do not yet have a payroll, you had better consider the USER-EXPECTATION Method. With this method, you go directly to the consumer -- with questionnaires, on-the-street-corner surveys, telephone polls and any other opinion gathering device that will give you the story on what product or service sells (and why) and what doesn't (and why not).

Whichever method is used, the sales forecaster must consider seven elements which are as important to the neighborhood auto mechanic as they are to General Motors. These are:

1.	The SALES PERFORMANCE OF YOUR COMPETITORS.
2.	The LEVEL AND TREND OF CONSUMER SPENDING, in general and or the specific products or services of your business.
3.	The GENERAL TRENDS OF YOUR INDUSTRY OR PRODUCT FIELD.
4.	Past, present and future ECONOMIC CONDITIONS.
5.	MARKET TESTS.
6.	KEY VARIABLES.
7.	Prior SALES and PERFORMANCE PATTERNS of your business, if available.

Do these look familiar? They should. These are among the questions you raised while doing market research. The answers to your earlier market research questions now play major roles in your sales forecast. To do this forecast accurately, you need to carefully analyze your research results. You need to put them all together, like the pieces of a puzzle. But you must do it in such a way that the picture of the future you get is the most accurate one possible. Don't let your hopes get in the way. Look at the facts long and hard; see how they relate to each other; and let your head (not your heart or your pride) make the decisions.

LOOKING AT THE BIG PICTURE

One of the easiest ways to develop a forecast for your business is to get a grasp of the industry big picture. Suppose you are considering a television dealership which sells to all of Jefferson County. You will sell television sets, video cassette recorders, stereos, microwave ovens, radios, tape recorders, and various supplies.

By talking to potential suppliers -- either distributors or factory direct salesmen -- you learn what the national sales are for each of these products and how much moves at what price.

In addition, the good salesmen have industry-supplied figures for Jefferson County sales for at least televisions and video cassette recorders. With their help, you estimate the retail sales for your product line for Jefferson County. You learn which months are best for sales and which are worst. For example, you are told that a large share of your sales will be between Thanksgiving and New Year's Eve.

Thus, by looking at the total sales potential for the county, you have a good starting point for your sales forecast. Because many of these salesmen formerly sold at retail or have sold other brands, they can tell you a lot about your market and the industry. With their help, you devise marketing plans and strategies and estimate your share of the Jefferson County market. Because these salesmen have seen many new dealers enter markets in their territory (and some drop out), they can review your strategy and estimate your early monthly sales quite accurately.

These same salesmen can help you estimate your budget. They know average pricing and markups, county sales trends, credit policies, delivery costs, warranty opportunities, advertising expenses, inventory costs, and rebates. In addition, they can help you pick the best location because they know the strengths and weaknesses of retailers. If the salesmen know their business, they will make it easy for you to see a profit down the road. Remember, they want your business in order to fill in their weak market share areas.

But don't make a commitment to anyone at this point. Remember that you are just getting information. So, keep in control and make your own decision. Next week, your trusted salesman may be helping another entrepreneur get into business or converting your competitor to his line of products.

Not all businesses have such good statistics or easy access to competitive information. The following is a practical story of doing a survey to determine your sales forecast and establish a budget.

A SIMPLE STORY OF SUCCESS

To make this process as clear as possible, let's imagine a simple success story with you as the main character. In the beginning, long before you even saw a need to research your market, you did a lot of soul searching. You asked yourself what it was that you really liked to do and -- of equal importance -- what it was that you did best.

You always loved tools and tinkering. Over the years, you found much satisfaction in working with bicycles and, eventually, became the informal bike repair shop for the neighborhood kids and their parents. Even though

your responsibilities at your regular job grew, you still spent your happiest hours putting bikes back together.

You never gave much thought to the idea of starting your own business though, much less a bike business, until the "get healthy" craze and gasoline prices both began to rise. You saw the trends before most: people once again were taking to the two wheelers. If you were going into a business of your own, you thought, it ought to be the bicycle business. When you caught wind of yet another layoff at the plant, you finally began to consider the idea seriously. Your head, however, told you that you had better think it through completely. Your heart beat faster at the thought of turning your hobby into a bona fide business.

Your head began to swim as you began to think about the details. Should you make your shop a repair shop, or should you sell new bikes at retail? What about used bikes -- you certainly could get your hands on a lot of them. Where is the best location, anyway? And how much could you really make in the bike business -- where was the money?

Now, imagine that you have a savings account of modest proportions (say $8,000) to start with, and you cannot afford to lose it by starting off on the wrong foot.

STARTING OFF ON THE RIGHT FOOT

Starting off on the right foot means getting the answers to those market research questions we discussed in the Market Research. And to do this, you know that you have to:

1.   Ask the RIGHT questions of the RIGHT people.
2.   Read the RIGHT material.
3.   Survey the RIGHT customers.
4.   Think clearly and cautiously.

So from your own home and on your own time, you set about researching your market.

First, ask the right questions of the right people who have at least part of the answers: You go to those already in the bike business, especially the retailers and wholesalers, and not surprisingly, find that bike sales are climbing and service jobs are up. Also, while there is not a noticeable increase in the number of bicycle shops, department store bike sections have clearly expanded.

Then, do the right reading: At your public library, you pour through back issues of "Bicycle Business News" and learn that today's big bike buyers are people over forty-five and people between the ages of eighteen and twenty-five. In the library's demographic and census materials, you discover that these people are found primarily in suburban areas; although a number of those in the lower age group also live near universities and colleges. You learn that this is true at the large state university a few miles from your home.

In the university's student newspaper, you read that an enrollment increase of nearly seven percent over the next five years is expected. Another article concerns programs aimed at attracting even more of the state's college-bound high school students.

In your city newspaper, you read that several schools that were once closed for lack of enrollment are being reopened. With more kids on the way, you correctly reason there will be the need for more bikes.

Next, survey the right consumers: Some clear thinking of your own tells you that the older folks want to steer clear of cardiac arrest.

Your oldest daughter, who has just begun her first year of college, also sheds some light on the buying habits of the second population group. With part-time employment and summer jobs as scarce as they are, she asks, how many college students have enough left to spend for a car? Not many. But for a good ten-speed? Quite a few. Besides, bicycle transportation for a college student makes good sense: no gasoline prices, no parking problems, no traffic jams, and you can take it almost anywhere -- even up four flights of dormitory stairs and into a room for one.

Add a dash of clear, cautious thinking: At this point, you begin to intensify your research. There is only one bike store in the university area, you discover; and this has been passed down from a father to a son. Casual chats with your daughter and her college chums, as well as a quick personal visit to the store, tell you that the father's out-dated and inefficient business practices have also been passed down. Customers wait weeks for simple repairs to be made; none of the more popular makes of bicycles are stocked; and apparently very little money is spent on advertising. People say the old man is hard to talk to, also -- a sure sign that people are not getting the attention they feel they deserve.

So far, the picture looks promising: there might just be room in the market for a bike shop with your strategy of featuring the latest models, the best repairs -- and QUICK delivery.

There is one dark cloud on the horizon, and it has snow in it. You live in an area where snow is on the ground at least three months of the year. This fact of life will hurt sales during this period of time, although it may be compensated for by more sales later on in the year.

There are several important conclusions that your research has led you to -- all of which seem to say: YOU CAN DO IT -- YOU CAN MAKE MONEY in the bicycle business.

After you are "reasonably sure" that there is a "reasonable chance" of success, you decide that it will be worth it to explore this business concept in more detail by putting some real numbers on paper.

Now you begin to construct your sales forecast for your imaginary bike shop. Basically, it is a process of elimination and decision-making; you need to answer the following questions in the following order:

- Are the trends right?
- Does the idea seem realistic?
- Would it all be worth it if you succeeded?
- Who is the customer?
- Where is the market?
- How big is the market?
- How many prospects will actually buy?
- How many of the buyers will buy from YOU?

Based on your research, here are the answers for your imaginary bike shop:

The time is right. By all indications, the present social and economic climate is favorable -- not the liveliest the country has ever known, but one well suited to the sale of bicycles. (Remember: a bad time for one industry, like the automobile industry, might just be a good one for another, like bikes.) People young and old want to stay fit, conserve fuel and save money -- and they are finding they can do it all with a bike.

The people are right. Based on a couple of conversations with the bike distributors you've bought parts from, you can conclude that the university area students and young professionals cannot get the prompt repair service that their fast lane lifestyle requires. What's more, they almost always go to those suburban competitors when they buy new bikes. One distributor told you, "The old guy doesn't seem to care about the new stuff. He only sells about six of our bikes per month." You know this distributor is tough to work with, and may just tell you what you want to hear so he can sell you some bikes, too. So, you take his comments with a grain of salt. But he confirms what you have been hearing. The customers could do well, it seems to you, with an alternative bike store close at hand.

Finally, the icing on the cake. What really makes this picture glow is the hard data you get from your own informal market survey. With the help of your daughter and a couple of her friends, you set up a table on the university's busiest mall for a few hours (with the University's permission, of course -- a marketing instructor was very helpful in setting it up as long as a few of his students could help out and get some experience).

You attract your potential customers with a display of three of the latest models from Peugeot, lent to you from a distributor eager to please you as a potential new retailer. After some "bike talk" around the display table, you make sure that every student leaves with a postage-paid questionnaire in his or her backpack.

About 1,000 people walked by, and 180 stopped to look at the bikes and talk. These, you figure, are the "serious prospects" who are at least thinking about owning a bike in the near future. Of the 180 questionnaires you passed out, 136 are completed and returned within 10 days. (Ten days to two weeks allows enough time for everyone who is going to send them to do it. If you need to, you can raise the response rate by offering a discount coupon for merchandise or service if they cooperate.)

As you began tallying up the questionnaires that came back, you began to "meet" your potential customers. It turns out that 100 of these prospective customers actually live on campus; the rest drive to school from the suburbs. Out of this group of 100, 35 own bikes now. Seventeen bought their bikes new during the last 12 months, but only 9 of those 17 bought their bikes from the crotchety old man and his son.

You are becoming convinced that with a good location, adequate advertising and hard work, you can corner more than half of the area's market -- in other words, 5 of those 9 university area bike buyers. That's your conservative estimate. You really believe that you can probably sell a lot of those kids who go to the suburbs to buy their bikes. And you can probably even convince some people to buy that otherwise wouldn't have just because you're on campus and they see you every day.

But you don't want to get swept away by your own enthusiasm. You settle on 5 as the conservative number of sales you could make out of that original 100 students who lived on campus.

WORKING FOR THE NUMBERS, AND MAKING THE NUMBERS WORK FOR YOU

Now you are ready to translate your research into a sales forecast. Out of 1,000 people who passed by, 180 or 18.0 percent identified themselves as prospective customers because they were interested enough to stop.

$$1,000 \times 18\% = 180$$

This agrees with what you read in "Bicycle Business News" which stated that about 15% of the general population is bikers. This "litmus test" of your market test gives you confidence in your research. Had the number been very different, say 7% or 70%, you would have had to rethink your assumptions and, probably, find another way to get to talk to your customers. You are a little suspicious of the low number of people that appeared to own bikes already -- 35 percent or 3.5 percent of the thousand who went by. But then you remember that many of your potential customers were pedaling by on their way to class and were just too pressed for time to stop. You decide to count this group as a "fudge factor" and stick with the group you have "hard" information on because of the questionnaires.

According to the housing office and the university handbook, three out of every five or 60% of all students enrolled at the university lived either on campus or in the immediate vicinity. There is a total enrollment of 25,000; so that gives you a non-commuter, on-campus student market of 15,000.

25,000 X 60% = 15,000

Add to this the 5,000 young professionals who are said to live nearby, and you have a general market population of prospects of 20,000 people.

15,000 students + 5,000 young professionals = 20,000 prospects

Your informal survey -- which you have good reason to believe in -- tells you that, theoretically, 18 percent of those 20,000 people like bikes and own or want to own one.

20,000 X 18% = 3,600 "serious prospects"

How many of these serious prospects will actually buy bikes in a year? And how many will actually buy from you? Based on your research, you calculate that about 17 percent of these 3,600 serious prospects buy new bikes in a 12-month period (17 buyers out of every 100 prospects).

17% X 3,600 = 612 bikes

You know you can't sell all of them, but you conservatively figured that you could sell 5 out of the 17, or 5 percent (you can also think of it as 5 buyers out of every 100 prospects).

3,600 prospects X 5% = 180 bikes sold per year

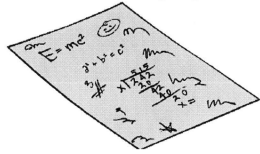

Let's now transfer this math into money. You are getting very close to your sales forecast! You are beginning to see what your business could look like!

You figure the average ten-speed bike sells for $350. But that's been marked up from the wholesale price of $200. So, for every bike sold, you'll realize a profit of $150. How many bike sales, once again, do you expect to make? 180, right?

$$\$350 \text{ X } 180 = \$63,000 \text{ Gross Sales}$$
$$\$150 \text{ X } 180 = \$27,000 \text{ Gross Profit}$$

In other words, from your first year in business, you get $27,000 in gross profit from sales of $63,000.

Now, what other ways can your bike shop make money? How about those repairs? What about accessories? Based on the industry guidelines that you read about in the trade journals, you figure that for every thousand dollars in new bike sales, you will have $200 in service calls and accessories.

$$\$63,000 \text{ / } 1,000 \text{ X } \$200 \text{ new sales} = \$12,600$$
$$\$63,000 + \$12,600 = \$75,600 \text{ Gross Sales or Revenue}$$

Sixty-three (for $63,000 in gross sales) multiplied by 200 equals another $12,600 in revenue per year.

Not bad for a beginner! At least, that's the way it looks right now. Gross profit is the difference between the cost of the goods you sold and your selling price. It does not take into account your overhead costs. We will discuss this relationship a little later in this chapter when we look at budgeting expenses.

NOW COMES THE FORECAST

Now comes the crystal-ball part of forecasting. When during the year are you actually going to see the money for those 180 bikes? Now you have to think about all of those variables that can affect sales during the year, including the weather and the competition. What if the weather is great, but the old man gets his act together and starts to advertise like crazy? What difference will that make to your sales?

Sales are sure to be healthy during the spring, for example, with the anticipation of the warmer, bike-riding months of summer in the air. Summer sales should be good, too, although not as high as those during the spring rush. It is during this period, however, that riders get the most use of their bikes, even though school is closed. The greater the use of bikes means more flat tires and other repair jobs. Income from repair jobs, you hope, will see you through to the fall, when the students return eager to spend their summer savings. In this season of falling leaves, you expect to see your profits rise.

Finally, there is no getting around slow sales in winter -- or is there? As it looks now, the winter months will be tough to weather. You will have to keep this in mind during those peak periods of healthy earnings. Instead of buying that new compression pump you may want, it may be wiser to save those peak season profits for the rainy (or snowy) days of the off-season.

It's time now to put your sales forecast for the upcoming year on paper. Using a ruler (neatness is important because you want to be as precise as possible), prepare a grid as shown.

The precise numbers of the sales forecast can be assigned month-by-month to a "spread sheet" like the following:

My Bicycle Shoppe

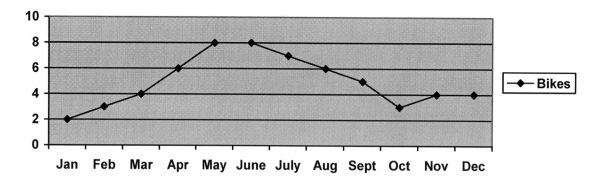

Congratulations! You have just completed a model sales forecast! You can do this for your real business, too, just by following these simple guidelines:

a. Base your forecast on "hard" information about your ACTUAL prospects.
b. Anticipate changes in your sales levels during the year, taking as many variables as possible into consideration.
c. Be conservative.

One decision you can already make for your imaginary bike business based on your sales forecast is when to open for business. Since winter is so slow, you should put as much of that time behind you as possible. You should probably open just in time to advertise your spring sales and the new models so you can be in the right place, ready and waiting, when the best sales season begins. DO NOT open in the fall unless you have enough cash to carry you through three or four months of overhead expenses without sales. And why would you want to do that anyway?

BUDGETING YOUR EXPENSES

Money flows in when you sell your bikes or other products or services, and money flows out when you pay your expenses. What stays behind -- the difference between the two -- is your net profit. This is what you are working for: cash to use as you please. This is "new money" that your business has earned for you. You can and should be very proud of this amount.

Of the hard earned $8,000 that you have in your imaginary savings account for your imaginary bike shop, you had better plan on spending most of -- perhaps $6,000 -- before you even open your doors for business. This is typical; you usually have to spend some money and take a financial risk before you take in any money.

There are two kinds of expenses -- variable and fixed.

VARIABLE EXPENSES

Your sales projections are based on how much you sell. Depending on how much you sell, you are going to have variable expenses that are a percentage of your sales revenue. These variable expenses are often referred to as "costs of sales".

Your largest single variable expense, if you are a retailer, will be your inventory. Logically, you have to buy something before you can sell it. If you are going to have an **inventory** in your imaginary bike shop, you have to purchase it from a wholesaler or a distributor. The faster you sell the inventory (called "sell-through" or "turning the inventory"), the faster you get your costs back plus your profits. That's why it's so important to select merchandise that people want to buy.

Labor may be your single largest expense if you are in a service business, unless you put all of your employees on salary, in which case they become a fixed expense. Most of the time, small businesses link their personnel needs to the amount of work to be done. As a plumbing contractor moves into his busy season, for example, he hires more plumbers to service all the calls. When the business dies down, the extra help are laid off.

Variable expenses, of course, are not as predictable as fixed ones. But you CAN make good guesses because VARIABLE EXPENSES ARE LINKED DIRECTLY TO SALES. Take an average month's sales and calculate what percentage of the selling price was made up of variable expenses. That percentage is a useful tool in projecting what your expenses will be in the following months. Presuming that you meet or come close to your sales projections, you should hit your variable expense estimates very closely as well.

When they are graphed, variable expenses should look similar to the sales forecast curve.

Notice that the variable expenses came due slightly before the money from sales. This is because you usually will have to actually pay for the merchandise (or labor) before you can collect the selling price. The closer these two curves are to each other, the healthier the business is because it has less money sitting idle in the form of "owned" inventory. Ideally, a small business should buy on credit as far into the future as possible -- say, 60 or 90 days -- and sell it all before the bill comes due.

This is what the spread sheet looks like after the variable expenses are added.

My Bicycle Shoppe

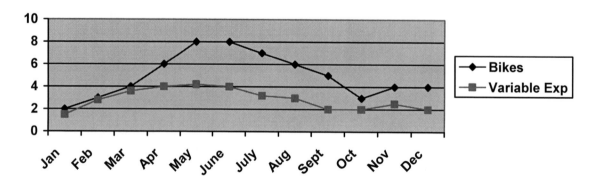

FIXED EXPENSES

As the name suggests, fixed expenses are those that remain fairly steady and predictable. These expenses may rise with the tide of inflation, but they will not fluctuate as your sales will. Nor are they influenced by your volume of sales.

Your fixed expenses are those overhead essentials you need to stay in business. For example, the rent money you pay for that prime corner location (which, you believe, will give you the edge over your side-street competitor) is a fixed expense. In the case of your bike shop, this will cost you, say, $750. Your phone is another fixed expense. So is your salary; although you may want to base that on how strong your sales are. Whether you sell one bike, no bikes, or a hundred, fixed expenses are going to stay the same and HAVE to be paid.

Fixed expenses are very easy to portray visually. All you need is a straight line. This shows up on your forecast or spread sheet like this:

My Bicycle Shoppe

Now we can combine the variable expenses with the fixed expenses to get a clear picture of total expenses.

Here's what this combination of sales and expenses looks like on the spreadsheet.

2009 © Copyright of the American Institute of Small Business

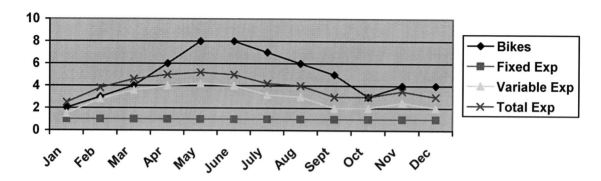

My Bicycle Shoppe

PROJECTING YOUR CASH FLOW

Up to this point, we have discussed the money you expect to make (from your sales) and the money you think you will have to spend (on expenses). To get the most accurate picture of your cash position and your financial health, however, we must link the two together. All those wavy lines add up to a cash flow projection -- a prediction, in fact, of where your money is coming from, where it's going, and what you're left with in the end. On paper, in black and white, where you can read it and understand it, this is called the CASH FLOW STATEMENT. It is, perhaps, the most useful planning tool you will ever have (or need) to monitor the health of your business.

Each month on your spread sheet reflects what you think your Income Statement (also known as a Profit and Loss Statement) will look like for those months in the future. Side by side, they give you a very good idea of what the trends are in your business.

Here's one of the ways to use your forecast: look at the next-to-the-bottom line on the cash flow statement. These are your projected profits (or losses) on a month-by-month basis. By adding them together horizontally and keeping a running total on the last line of the spread sheet, you can tell how far ahead -- or into the hole -- you really are. This is called the Cumulative Total, and is THE REAL bottom line.

Projecting your cash flow in this way would not be of much use to you, however, if you discovered your business was in financial trouble and on the verge of bankruptcy. For this reason, you probably will want to chart the difference between what you THOUGHT would happen (this is your projection) and what will ACTUALLY happen (these would be your actual sales and expense figures as they occur).

This can be done using a form similar to the one below as a kind of early warning system. Each month you can see at a glance what your actual sales, expenses and cash position are, compared to what you thought they would be.

	February				Year to Date		
	Actual	Forecast	Difference		Actual	Forecast	Difference
Beg Cash	4.2	4.5	-0.3		5.0	5.0	0.0
Sales	2.7	2.5	0.2		4.3	4.5	-0.2
Expenses							
Variable	2.3	2.2	-0.1		3.7	3.7	0.0
Fixed	1.0	1.0	0.0		2.0	2.0	0.0
Total	3.3	3.2	-0.1		5.7	5.7	0.0
Net Profit	-0.6	-0.7	0.1		-1.4	-1.2	-0.2
End Cash	3.6	3.8	-0.2		3.6	3.8	-0.2

The first set of three columns shows the current month, and the second set shows the year-to-date figures. The first column, called "actual", is how you actually did. The second column, "forecast", is your earlier estimate of how sales and expenses would go. The third column, "difference", is just what it says - the difference between what you did and what you thought you would do. It could show the difference in terms of dollars or percentages.

By preparing and evaluating comparisons each month, you'll be able to detect problems before they get out of hand. The third column tells you how accurate and/or realistic your projections are. And, hopefully, you'll get better and better each month at forecasting the future.

Forewarned is forearmed. And preplanning, based on what your forecasts reflect, will go a long way toward keeping you out of trouble.

For example, imagine that in five years your bicycle business has grown to the point where you have four full-time employees on the payroll. Not surprisingly, your cash flow chart has grown considerably, too. Now, you have three lines for repair supplies alone. One of these is reserved for expenses involved in purchasing tire patching kits. Since your time is now almost always spent in the back room with the books of the business, these particular expenses come to you from the employee responsible for such purchases. Three months into the new year, you realize (by comparing "Actuals" with "Estimates", the third column shows "+100%") that you are spending twice as much each month for patching kits as you thought you would.

This would not be a problem if these unexpected expenses were offset by unusually high sales in the area of patching kit sales. You check and see that this is not the case. You have a problem: your business is leaking cash and the leak must be patched as quickly as it is discovered. Now you can ask the right person some straightforward questions, such as: "Have you switched to a different wholesaler? Are you purchasing a more expensive kit? Has the price of patching kits increased since last year? WHY are we spending MORE on flat tire patching kits than I PROJECTED we would?" If there is a good reason, you can change your projections -- and the rest of your plans -- accordingly to accommodate the new information. If there isn't a good

explanation, you can nip the problem before it gets out of control and does real damage.

Your cash flow statement can be as long or as short as you wish to make it. You may choose, for example, not to list every item you stock separately, but group them together in categories instead.

A FEW CLOSING WORDS ABOUT BUDGETS

Whether it is for a complex business or for a family of four, there is really no mystery to it. A budget is not money itself, but it is about money. A budget is made up of a lot of assumptions. For you, the bicycle businessman, it is whether or not you will be able to buy that new compression pump, whether or not you will be able to put the neighbor boy on your payroll for the summer, whether or not you can open a branch store, whether or not you can pay off a debt (or take out another bank loan), whether or not you can take a vacation this year -- or give yourself a raise. Your budget is the financial well-being (or ill health) of your business. And your cash flow statement is none other than the visual representation, on paper in black and white, of your budget.

A budget is no longer a luxury, if ever it was. For businesses, large or small, it is a necessity.

Now you are prepared. Your forecast is your budget. You can run your future business by getting yourself "on plan" or "on budget" today. If you aren't on budget, your forecasts tell you where to make the changes. What's out of balance? If one "actual" is significantly higher than the "projected", your objective should be clear: do what you have to do to lower it.

There are those owners of small businesses who have very little to say about budgets, and there are those who do not even have them. But they are hard to find. There are many, on the other hand, who could probably talk your ears off about the merits of a budget.

In this chapter, you have learned:

1.   A budget *PRESENTS YOU WITH A DEFINITE BUSINESS OBJECTIVE.* It gives you an idea of where you are headed financially.
2.   It *ACTS AS A SAFETY SIGNAL.* If there is trouble ahead because your buyer is spending too much for a new kind of flat tire patching kit, you will know about it in advance to do something about it.
3.   It *PLACES RESPONSIBILITY.* If there is a problem, you will know where to look to correct it.
4.   A budget *HELPS YOU PREVENT WASTE.* More than any other tool you have at your disposal, your budget tells you where you are paying too much or getting too little.
5.   Sales forecasts, cash flow statements, and budgets will keep you moving steadily toward your long-term success. They keep both of your feet firmly planted in reality. What you don't know can put you out of business. But if you plan with good projections, you can succeed even faster.

Websites You May Find Useful

Sales Plans - http://www.businessknowhow.com/marketing/sales-plan.htm
About.com -
http://sbinformation.about.com/od/businessplans/a/salesforecast.htm

Step To Success
One Action a Day Will Move You Forward

It is time to move forward. Complete the **Step to Success** Action and feel your progress.   No matter where you are going, you can get there one step at a time.

A sales plan is different than a marketing plan. Try to plan out the sales you expect for the next year. Then match it to you marketing plan to make sure they work together.   Do it NOW!

Chapter 16

50+ Simple Ways to Find The Money Your Need

"Happiness is not in the mere possession of money; it lies in the joy of achievement, in the thrill of creative effort."
- Franklin D. Roosevelt

In this chapter you will learn:

1. *How much money will you need to start?*
2. *Four steps to obtaining a loan.*
3. *The two general categories of financing.*
4. *Where can you borrow money?*
5. *How to prepare a loan proposal.*

MONEY is obviously important to starting a business. You have to want it in order go get more of it, and you have to be organized enough to keep it and manage it once you get it. Unless you have successfully managed a small business before, brace yourself -- because you are going to learn a whole new way to think about money!

First and foremost, forget all those discouraging words you heard from the pessimists in your life. You CAN get the money you need to start and successfully run your business -- IF you follow the plan we lay out for you in this chapter. It may be of interest to you that more than 500,000 new businesses get started each year. Each one of them started the same way -- with an idea and a little money.

WHAT WILL YOU USE THE MONEY FOR?

Few people have difficulty spending money. Every entrepreneur, however, should be familiar with and prepared for some very important uses of money. Below are typical uses of money.

Working Capital

This money is used to buy inventory, pay salespersons, make lease payments and handle unexpected costs until customers buy and pay up in large enough amounts to keep your business up and running on its own.

Inventory

Because inventory can consume large amounts of working capital, make sure you buy the right amount of inventory. In retailing, for example, too small quantities may lead to empty shelves and lost customers. Too large a stock, on the other hand, can raise your costs due to excess inventory and obsolete merchandise.

Excess inventory is a nonworking asset. As long as it sits on shelves, inventory ties up cash while producing no return. If your inventory is financed, you're actually paying someone for your stock to gather dust. To reduce inventory, some companies are turning to "just-in-time" systems. Instead of overstocking raw materials to ensure fast delivery, a just-in-time system shifts the burden to vendors through contracts that guarantee rapid shipments to fulfill customer orders.

Capital Equipment Purchases

Whether you start a business, buy one or get into a franchise, some of your largest expenses will be capital equipment. One important consideration when building a budget is that loans for machinery, technology including telecommunications systems and computers and other types of capital equipment are generally easier to get because they are secured by the equipment itself as the collateral. Because of that, loans are based on the life of the equipment but generally not for more than ten years.

Research and Development

Ideas form the basis for most businesses, large and small. One idea may be enough to start an enterprise, but it is not enough to maintain growth. The importance of improving existing products and developing new ones has never been more evident than it is today. Campbell Soup Company never stops developing new varieties and uses for their soups; Hershey Chocolate eventually diversified into other candy products, building on the success of its original Hershey Bar to keep its share of an increasingly competitive market.

The lesson to be learned is that research and development is a continuing need for many businesses and that funds must be allocated or found for product development on a continuing basis.

Expansion

A good idea can't be held down. If a retailing idea is good in one location, two stores will be even better and ten stores will create a commanding purchasing situation. The same holds true in other marketing fields. If you=ve put together a hot selling organization for one line of products, chances are you can take on another line or two and be that much more successful.

Naturally, expansion always brings with it extra costs, but additional financing should be easy to come by if you have a successful record to show for your efforts.

Purchasing a Business

You never know when the opportunity to acquire a good company will come

---

along, whether in your own business or in an allied field. Many entrepreneurs have made a career of going from success to success by keep keeping their eyes open for the right opportunities. Naturally the better record you establish in your main business, the easier it will be to get financing for a new acquisition.

HOW MUCH MONEY WILL YOU NEED TO START?

The answer to this question is easy to understand, but hard to calculate. A new business needs:

1) Enough to buy the equipment, tools, raw materials, inventory or whatever else it needs to build the products or provide the service it sells;

2) enough to pay the day-to-day operating expenses until the profits begin.

Most entrepreneurs are proud, resourceful people; they feel uncomfortable asking for money. Their initial tendency is to ask for too little money. Being as optimistic as they are about the future of their enterprise, they assume that they can make everything work the way they want it to. As a result, they start their business with less money than they need.

 Buck's painting service is a sad, but true, case of poor planning. He thought he could get started on the money he planned to make from his first job. He bought the business cards he needed and his first order of paint on credit, figuring that he could collect the money before the bills were due in 30 days. He didn't plan on having to buy an extra ladder, but he felt pretty good about the amount of money he was making; so he went ahead anyway and put it on his charge account with the paint supplier.

The job went reasonably well: he finished on time, even though he had to go back and get two more gallons of paint to get the right coverage. The

---

customer paid him in full when he was finished, too. Unfortunately, on the way back from the job, his truck finally lost the exhaust pipe he had been patching together for the past few months. It took $187 to get it replaced, and that was $187 he didn't have. Since he wasn't working his regular job anymore, all of his regular expenses had to be picked up by his business in addition to the expenses for his first job. He was too tightly budgeted, and all it took was a bad bump on the road to throw him off.

In less than a month of business, Buck had already dug himself into a hole that looked deeper every day. He got so worried, he went back to his old job because of its regular income. Because he wasn't out soliciting new customers and he wasn't available to answer the phone or make estimates, what little business he did have trickling in dried up almost immediately. By the third month, Buck was out of business, vowing never gain to do anything that crazy.

Imagine another small business -- this one a word processing service -- that started with a good deal of planning up front. Judy thought carefully about where her customers were going to come from, how much they probably would spend with her each month and what kind of equipment she would need to service them. She took time to shop the market, get the right equipment to begin with and even approached a few of the customers to find out what kind of jobs they were interested in. She was pleasantly surprised to

find a small publishing company that had overload work every July for about six weeks, and they needed it done in a special typeface. She said she would prepare to handle the work at a pre-arranged price if they could assure her of the contract.

As a result of doing her homework, Judy was able to predict very accurately what her monthly income was going to be. She felt very confident about her figures for the first six months, and reasonably confident about the second six months. Based on these estimates, she was able to calculate her start-up costs and her operating expenses. The moral of the story is simple: when she got the biggest projects of the year - as planned - she was ready for them. She had the cash she needed to pay an extra typist to work overtime on a rented word processor and she could afford to buy the new typefaces she promised the customer to get the job in the first place.

What is the difference between Buck and Judy? Very simply, one planned the financial side of the business, and the other didn't. One is still in business, and the other isn't.

You CAN do it! There is nothing magical about financial planning, and you don't need a lot of formal training to do it. All you need to do is look ahead and imagine what is going to happen in your business, and then use your common sense!

Buck is statistically more typical than Judy. Planning the finances for a business is hard work, and not everyone likes to do it. Not everyone realizes how important it is. Then, four or six or twelve months later, just as things are starting to get going, they run out of money. Instead of concentrating on delivering products and services to their customers, they're running around town trying to arrange financing to pay their suppliers and the phone bill so they can stay in business. Since they can't take care of the customers at the same time, the customers get frustrated and begin to drift away. Sales and cash flow go down. As the situation gets more desperate, the small business owner runs faster and faster, trying to keep it all together. It becomes increasingly difficult to reverse this downward spiral; ultimately, the business runs out of time with the creditors and the entrepreneur runs out of energy and excuses. The poor management decisions lead to the initial undercapitalization, and the undercapitalization finally causes the business to fail.

It doesn't have to end this way, however. Undercapitalization is just "under-planning"; with a little more planning at the beginning, the small business can get a little more money up front, and that can make all the difference.

Here's how to do it: to calculate how much you will need, you must construct a CASH FLOW PROJECTION, sometimes referred to as a PRO FORMA by your banker. **This tool is better than a crystal ball!** It is a wonderful planning tool because it can help you imagine the future. By imagining, or projecting, what you think you are going to sell and spend during the upcoming months, you can see problems coming while there is still enough time to do something about them. Losing money on paper is a lot easier to take than losing real money -- especially when it's your own!

To construct a cash flow projection, all you need to do is estimate what it is going to cost to keep your business going month-by-month during the next year or 18 months. You can think of it as all of your monthly income statements side by side. (Your income statements are the statements that list your sales income, sales costs and overhead expenses, thereby giving you a monthly profit or loss figure.)

By adding together all of the "bottom lines," that is, the monthly profits or losses, you will be able to see your cumulative cash flow. Look at how the bottom line changes in the example which follows.

Frank's Snow Plowing and Lawn Care Service
Pro Forma Cash Flow Statement
For the Twelve Months Ended December 31, 20XX

	Apr	May	June	Jul	Aug	Sep
Sources of Cash:						
Sales	**2,500**	**3,000**	**3,500**	**500**	**500**	**1,000**
Uses of Cash:						
Cost of Sales	1,175	1,350	1,575	275	275	450

Operating Expenses	1,443	1,555	1,668	893	893	1,055
Total Uses:	**2,618**	**2,905**	**3,243**	**1,168**	**1,168**	**1,505**
Increase (Decrease)	(118)	95	257	(668)	(668)	(505)
Cumulative Cash Flow	**(118)**	**(23)**	**234**	**(434)**	**(1,102)**	**(1,607)**

	Oct	Nov	Dec	Jan	Feb	Mar
Sources of Cash:						
Sales	**1,000**	**6,000**	**6,000**	**12,000**	**6,000**	**6,000**
Uses of Cash:						
Cost of Sales	450	900	900	1,800	900	900
Operating Expenses	1,455	2,380	2,380	3,530	2,180	2,330
Total Uses:	**1,905**	**3,280**	**3,280**	**5,330**	**3,080**	**3,230**
Increase (Decrease)	(905)	2,720	2,770	6,670	2,920	2,770
Cumulative Cash Flow	**(2,512)**	**208**	**2,928**	**9,598**	**12,518**	**15,288**

What does this cash flow projection tell us about Frank's business? First, it tells us a lot about how he spends his money and is very helpful in determining how much he will need to run his business.

Here is a list of the equipment Frank's company will need before he even gets started:

	Cost
Truck (4-wheel drive) for snow plowing and hauling mowers	$0
Snow plow attachment	1,700
Snow blower	1,000
Gasoline tank for extra gasoline	50
Snow shovels (2)	200
Ice axe	75
Lawn mowers (1 riding, 1 push)	2,000
Grass bagger	100

Rakes	50
Shovel	30
Chemical sprayer	150
Hoses (3)	95
Pruning shears	50
Total	$5,500
Fertilizer	800
Office Equipment	1,000
Total	$7,500

In addition to the $5,500 for equipment, Frank needs $800 for fertilizer and insecticides, $1,000 for office equipment and $200 for office supplies. Thus, his total start-up expenditures will be $7,500.

Frank's start-up costs could have included the amount of his original equipment investment to get his truck but since he was able to buy it over time and pay cash, it does not have to be counted as a start-up expense. He sold the truck to his company for $10,000 and enjoys some very nice tax benefits.

This was a smart way to get himself some of the equipment he needed because he can now count it as an asset without debt, but it wasn't the only way. The truck could have been financed through a local banker.

What else can we learn from Frank's pro forma cash flow? We can see just when he gets his income, and at what levels. Notice that Frank's cash flow has dramatic seasonal fluctuations: in the winter and spring, he is taking in a lot of cash. However, there a few months between seasons when the grass isn't growing and the snow isn't falling, so he isn't making much money. Actually, during these months, he is taking in very little and must live off what he has already earned.

So how much does Frank need to start? It's simple: he needs enough to pay his start-up costs plus the extra amount he needs to get himself through the slow months of low income.

The lowest point of Frank's cumulative cash flow is in the seventh month (October) when he is "down" $2,512. At this point, he has paid all of his bills, but still has more money going out than coming in. If it kept up like this, Frank would soon be out of business. However, Frank knows that it takes this long to establish himself in the market and build up his accounts.

Now, most entrepreneurs would say, "It looks like I need about $10,000 to start my business -- $7,500 for start-up costs and $2,500 to cover expenses that exceed my income through October." But Frank is a little smarter than that -- he knows that if it doesn't snow as expected, the money from his plowing contracts will start late.

Instead of getting "just enough" to get started, Frank uses a good rule of thumb he learned from his banker: he is going to begin his company with enough money to purchase his initial equipment and supplies ($7,500), plus one and one-half times the amount he thinks he needs to cover his expenses in the early months.

$$1.5 \times \$2,500 = \$1,250$$
$$\$1,250 + \$2,500 = \$3,750 \text{ for operating expenses.}$$

Rather than getting "just enough" -- which was probably just enough to get himself into trouble -- he is getting enough money to succeed. He has planned extra money for those unexpected problems that come up. Now, if he needs to make repairs on his truck, or if the price of gas goes up, or if it doesn't snow as planned, he will be able to ride out the situation and be around to profit another day.

You **must** do this for your business, too. Before you start looking for ways to cut corners or start operating on less than you should, find out how much it would realistically cost to run your business the right way. Remember -- multiply the lowest point in your cash flow by 150% (1.5) or even 200% (2) and you will be very near the actual amount you will end up spending. This is the ACTUAL amount of money you need to get your business started. If you follow this rule, and you have carefully thought through all of the expenses to include on your cash flow projections, you will not suffer from undercapitalization.

Frank's goal now is to raise the $7,500 he figures he needs for start-up and the $3,750 he needs for operations, a total of $11,250.

$$\$7,500 + \$3,750 = \textbf{\$11,250}$$

FOUR STEPS TOWARD A LOAN

Unless you are able to write your own check to start your business, you will have to get at least a few other people involved. Even if you are able to do your own financing, you may want to get someone else involved anyway because of their skills, business contacts or experience.

One of the principles of small business that you should become familiar with now is the notion of using other people's money to begin a new venture.

Remember, this is the third key to understanding money that we discussed at the beginning of this chapter. This is referred to in the financial community as 'sharing the pie'. When you use other people's money, you are saying to them, "If you let me use your money in the beginning to get started, I'll share my profits with you later." In this way, you both make more money. Economists call this the creation of wealth, and it's one of the fundamental components of our free enterprise system.

Getting someone else involved is a decision that you must think about carefully. The easiest or the cheapest source of money is not always the best. There may be "strings" attached or unreasonable conditions.

Once you have decided how much you need, you will be almost ready to start discussing your situation with people who can help you. First, you have to **PACKAGE** your idea. In a way, you have to sell someone else on your dream -- and in order for them to be persuaded to part with their cash, you have to convince them that you are worth the investment.

Where you get your money is largely dependent upon how much you need. Different sources are comfortable with different amounts. Generally, the more money you want, the more "packaging" you need and the more lengthy your written proposal.

Yes, you **will have to write your proposal**. For obvious reasons, this is still the best way to get your story in front of a lot of people quickly, professionally and in a consistent way. But don't despair if you aren't the world's greatest writer or a born "typewriter jockey" -- you can get plenty of help from secretarial services, someone you know with a word processor or a student

 looking for part-time work. The important parts are your ideas; so if you can't do it alone, find someone with whom to work. Look at it this way: being able to meet this challenge is one of your first managerial tests!

There are basically three stages in financing a business. These reflect the three basic life cycles in a business.

First, there is **seed money** that is used in the very preliminary stages of a business. The amount of money needed here can be quite small. It is used to organize and plan the project. Frank used his personal money for this stage to drive around town talking to building owners about his contract plowing service. It cost him several hundred dollars in travel expenses, lost wages from his regular job, lunches, letters, postage, letterhead and the like. A restaurant entrepreneur might use this time and money to make a site selection and have an architect do some preliminary drawings of the restaurant.

The second stage of financing is the **start-up** financing. This is the money it will take to get the doors open and get the business started. Frank needed his $11,250 for this stage.

The third stage is **growth** financing, and is usually needed after a year or so of successful operation. Frank might want to buy a few more trucks or set up a similar type of operation in a nearby community once he's got all the bugs worked out and has turned the corner of his one-truck operation. ("Turning the corner" means he is showing consistent profits.) The restaurant entrepreneur might want to open another location or two, or even start franchising his idea if it turns out to be profitable.

HERE'S HOW YOU PACKAGE OR PRESENT YOUR SITUATION TO A POTENTIAL INVESTOR OR LENDER:

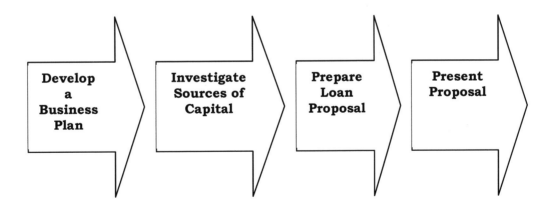

STEP 1: Develop a business plan. In the financial community, this is THE tool you need. It is a typewritten report that tells the investor or lender that

---

you have thoroughly planned your business. It is designed to give them confidence in you. IF you don't need very much money, say $15,000 or less, you may not need to write a complicated plan, but you should have at least thought enough about each of the aspects of the business plan to be able to discuss them with an investor or lender. The Business Plan is discussed in detail in the last chapter of the book.

Basically, the business plan answers the following questions in a logical order:

1. What is a business?
2. Which will be the most profitable products?
3. What are the major markets and competitors?
4. How will you pay back the monies you borrowed?

It also presents the budget and cash flow projections for at least the next 12 months.

The details of writing a business plan are presented later in this book.

Frank's proposed loan of $11,250 was a relatively small amount of money for relatively straightforward needs. Although he did not write a long formal business plan, he did think about each of the components thoroughly because he knew that some people would push him just enough to find out how much he really knew about his business.

STEP 2: Investigate potential sources of capital. After you have done your basic planning and have prepared your loan proposal of up to 10 pages, you can start looking for the best source for the amount of money you need. Frank's snow removal and lawn care business needed $11,250; this is a lot of money to some people and not enough to trouble with for others. We will discuss several of the best sources of money a few pages from now.

STEP 3: Prepare a loan proposal. This is ABSOLUTELY REQUIRED for all but the informal financing arrangements. It is like a mini-business plan, is about 10 pages long, and is tailored specifically to a single investor or lender. Because it is short, each one can be customized to show each prospective lender or investor the information that is needed or requested. This becomes the "talking tool" in your negotiations for money. It has the following information:

1.   A very brief summary of your business, including what your business is, what products you sell and the general types of competition you have.

2.   A brief history of yourself and your business to date, including any other financing.

3.   An explanation of the proposal: what amount of money you need, what terms are preferred, repayment preference, collateral available, equity options available and any other information that is relevant to your specific request for funds.

4.   The appropriate financial statements must be included: balance sheet, earnings history (if any) and financial projections for three years.

5.   Credit, personal and business references.

Frank put together a very successful financing proposal for his business. It did its job -- it got him the money he needed on terms that made sense for him. Later in this chapter, we will take a close look at a typical loan proposal so you can see exactly how to put yours together.

STEP 4:   Present your materials to your prospective lenders or investors. This can be a formal presentation or an informal discussion, depending upon who you are meeting with. One of the people who expressed interest in Frank's business turned out to be his barber -- he was interested in investing the whole $11,250. When Frank made his presentation, he did it over coffee at a restaurant near the barber shop. Later, when he made a presentation to a loan officer at a bank downtown, it was much more formal.

That's all there is to it: 1-2-3-4, and you've got the money you need to start and run your business. YOU can do this, too -- literally hundreds of thousands of people are getting millions of dollars to start and run their dreams every year.

For the rest of this chapter, we will concentrate on filling in the rest of the "how's" related to getting money, such as:

- How do you find people who are able to lend money or invest?
- How do you approach them and ask them if they are interested in your proposition?
- How do you make a successful presentation?

By the time you have finished this chapter, you will be fully prepared to get the money you need. You will be able to hold your own in conversations with other business people, investors and lenders. In short, you will have learned what it takes to put money behind your dreams. Rather than just being a bystander, you can be an active contender.

THE TWO CATEGORIES OF FINANCING

Obviously, there are as many different ways to structure a deal as there are people to make the deals, but they all fall into two general categories: debt financing and equity financing.

DEBT FINANCING is the simplest way to raise money. Basically, it describes any kind of loan. The person or organization loaning you the money makes his money on the interest you pay. As long as you continue paying the loan payments, he will leave you alone and let you run the business as you see fit. The interest rate is agreed to in advance. The loan-maker knows how much he will make on the deal before he loans you the money, and his chief concern is whether you will be able to pay back the loan on time.

Your ability to repay makes the difference when you convince someone to loan you money. Depending upon whether it's your bank or your brother, you have to satisfy different criteria. Your prior history of repayment (your credit record) and the viability of the business are key elements. Obviously, if you still owe your brother from the last $500 he loaned you and he thinks your business idea is pretty shaky, he is going to doubt your ability to repay. If the business goes bad, how will you pay him back?

If you talk to your bank, the same concerns are present. What assurances and evidence can you give that indicate that you can pay back tomorrow what you borrow today? If your business idea seems shaky, the bank may ask you to pledge your car or even your house as collateral in case you can't make the payments. You may want to think twice about what you pledge and how much you pledge. If the unthinkable happens and you lose the money in the business, you risk losing some of your own assets. Sometimes bankers ask you to pledge collateral to lower their risk by taking on more of it yourself; in essence, they are saying, "We will let you use our money so you don't have to sell your assets to raise the money. But we want to be sure of getting our money back and we want to see how committed you are to this new business of yours. We want you to put up your personal property as security for us."

EQUITY FINANCING is different. Selling equity means you sell a part of the business to someone else. What they are purchasing by investing in you is the possibility that you will make a success of the business. They are gambling that, in the long run, their share of the business will be worth many times more than the amount of their original investment.

You have to decide two things: what you WANT (in other words, what would be the best deal for you) and what will WORK. You may have to settle for a "less than ideal" arrangement. You must think through beforehand how much risk you want to take yourself, how much you want to share with an outside investor, how much control of the day-to-day operations you want to share and how much of the "pie" you want to share, if any. Many small business people eventually conclude that sharing a larger pie and sharing the risk is worth giving up part of the profits and some control.

The right investor can be an angel, but the wrong kind can have a very negative influence. If the investor brings valuable management expertise or skills to the business, everyone wins. However, if the investor is a 'meddler' or egomaniac, it may be better to look for another investor - a silent partner - who will stay in the background.

Sometimes you can combine debt and equity financing. This is called a convertible debenture. This begins as a loan, and then is converted to a share in the ownership of your business, if and when the business is successful. It is particularly attractive to friends and relatives and certain business investors. If the deal goes sour, they fall back on the provisions of the loan. If it is successful, they can convert their loan into stock  or part ownership of the business at probably a much better profit or gain than through an ordinary loan with interest.

WHERE CAN YOU BORROW MONEY?

There are many different sources of money. Each of them can be considered a possibility for the person who will need money to either start a small business or to help an existing business. These sources can be divided between traditional and nontraditional sources.

Traditional Sources

Yourself.   For the individual businessperson the most logical place to look for financing is his or her own assets. These sources include money in bank accounts, certificates of deposit, stocks and bonds, cash value in insurance policies, real estate, home equity, value of hobby collections, automobiles, pension fund, Keogh or IRAs.

Obviously, if you had sufficient capital, there would be no need to turn to other sources for your needs. But, as noted before, in order to be successful in a business, most people must know how to use other people's money to finance the new or expanding business.

One word of caution. In today's fast moving economy, most of us have one or more credit cards. It is tempting to take advantage of the availability of money simply by using these cards. Remember, most credit card companies advance money at a much higher rate of interest than you could normally pay a bank or some other financing source. Equally important, although your monthly payments may appear to be small, because of the high interest, your debt compounds and rises quickly.

Family or Relatives. If you are fortunate enough to have family or relatives who have money to invest or loan, then sometimes they represent an excellent lending source. Exercise great caution, however, when borrowing money from a relative. There is an old saying: NEVER MIX BUSINESS WITH PLEASURE.

For every family loan that goes sour, there are probably two sweet ones. Before seeking out a loan from a relative, consider what future effect a loan may have on the relationship.

One source of money often used is family and relatives. Too often, however, money gets in the way of good family relationships. Therefore, extreme care must be used in determining whether or not a family member or relative should be approached.

One way you can avoid future problems and disagreements with relatives who lend you money for your business is to have a written agreement. Spell out clearly what you and your relatives have agreed:

* Date of the loan
* Loan amount
* Date the loan will be repaid in full
* Dates of loan payments
* Frequently of payments? Monthly, quarterly, etc.
* Amount (percent) of interest
* Collateral, if any.
* Signatures by both parties

One important note: It may be wise to make sure the relative from whom you are borrowing has notified his or her spouse. That way, you can ensure that no future problem arises due to any miscommunication.

Friends. Friends, by their very nature, trust one another. And they often are in a position to aid in a financial situation.

Again, as with relatives, one has to be careful to assure that the friendship will not be put into jeopardy in the event the friend will require a sudden payback. Use the same caution as you would borrowing from a relative.

Your Own Company. If you already have an established company and are in need of money, one of the first places to turn is to the company itself. An established company or business has several options available. These include taking a first or second mortgage on any real estate or property that it owns, borrowing money against machinery or hard assets such as equipment or motor vehicles; borrowing against inventory that is considered liquid.

Pledging Accounts Receivable

A common method by which companies can obtain a loan is by pledging the firm's accounts receivable in return for a loan. This means that your receivables are pledged or turned over to the bank or loan company that makes the loan. Then, as the receivables are paid, the firm deducts a certain amount of each payment until the loan is paid. Essentially, what the bank or loan company is doing is using your accounts receivable as collateral against the loan.

Factoring

Factoring is another way of using your receivables in order to raise badly needed cash. In factoring, one goes to a factoring company which actually buys your accounts receivables.

Assume, for example, that you have $50,000 in accounts receivables and it is a particularly slow time of the year in which you have very little cash flow. The factor will buy your $50,000 in receivables. Possibly they will give you $30,000 or $40,000 for them. The factor then owns the receivables. The amount of discount that the factor takes depends on such things as how old your accounts receivables are, who owes you the money, what you sell, how long you have been in business and so on. You can find a listing of factors in the Yellow Pages. You can also get a list of such companies from your banker.

Commercial Banks. Commercial banks are the largest single source of loans to both small and large businesses. Banks are in the money business. They make money by lending money. Many banks have a special department that focuses on small business loans.

At the end of this loan source listing we will describe in considerable detail how to prepare a BANK LOAN PROPOSAL.

Savings and Loan Associations. These are like banks, but are organized under a different type of charter. Originally established to facilitate the lending of money for home mortgages, they have gradually evolved into full-service banking operations. There are some government restrictions on where and how they can operate as compared to commercial banks. Like banks, their charge for loans is based on the prime rate or some variation of it.

During 1991 and 1992, the savings and loan industry was rocked by a great number of scandals involving poor-risk loans. As a result, the remaining savings and loans are taking a very careful look at any business loan application. Many are now requiring any loan to be backed up by an equivalent amount of collateral.

Loan Companies.   Loan companies, which exist in most U.S. cities and communities, represent one of the largest sources of money in the country. Unlike banks which obtain their funds from many different sources, loan companies have to rely upon their own capital or raising money, just as other businesses do. Thus, their interest rates are usually higher. In some instances they can be several percentage points above the prime rate.

Loan companies are considered collateral lenders, that is, they rely heavily upon the borrower's ability to back up every dollar of their loan with an asset. For example, a borrower may have to pledge accounts receivable, put up the mortgage on the company's building, or assign the value of an insurance policy, stocks or bonds.

Loan companies often have different operating policies, and the interest rate they charge may vary as much as five percent from one firm to another. Therefore it is prudent to shop around before you settle on a particular loan company. A listing of the loan companies for your area can be found in the Yellow Pages.

Small Business Investment Companies (SBIC). These are privately owned companies licensed and insured by the Small Business Administration (SBA) to provide capital to small firms. SBICs focus on specific industries such as medically-oriented high technology enterprises, or agricultural, manufacturing or real estate companies. Normally these firms have proprietary and high growth potential products.

Community Development Companies. These are companies that have been established by local communities to attract business into their community. The most popular type of CDC is one which develops a shopping mall or business development center. An example of the latter would be a geographic area set aside in a community for a commercial or industrial park.

Insurance Companies. An often overlooked source of money is your own insurance company. You may find that you can use your life insurance policy as collateral in obtaining a loan. Insurance companies often have a large reserve of cash and are constantly looking for good investment opportunities.

Nontraditional Sources

Nontraditional sources are unlimited in number and type, but you need to be creative to acquire the necessary funds from them for your start-up or expanding business.

Customers. Customers or potential customers can be an excellent source of funding. Consider the following examples: Two engineers work together at the same company. On their own time, they develop a new plastic, the manufacturing of which require a very large capital investment. When used as raw material their plastic is one-third the cost of the product companies or customers are currently using. The engineers contact a  very large potential user, who realizes that the new plastic can reduce her raw material costs significantly. Subsequently, she lends the two engineers the necessary money to start their own business. In return for her investment, the user receives a contract assuring her company of getting 75 percent of the manufacturing output of the new plastic.

Another typical example, is that of a cosmetologist who wants to open her own salon. In conversations with a customer, it turns out that the customer likewise wants to have her own business. The customer invests in the salon and the two form a partnership. The cosmetologist manages the salon and the other employees; her partner participates in the day-to-day affairs of the salon, handling bookkeeping, advertising and customer service.

Suppliers. Depending on the type of business you plan, your suppliers could be an excellent source of money.

For example, a family in a medium-size southern city decided to open a convenience food store. They went to their food wholesaler who made arrangements to borrow enough money to pay for their shelving in exchange for a promise from the store owner that he would make at least 80% of his purchases from the firm, providing the prices were fair.

This same small businessman also went to his meat supplier who made arrangements for him to borrow money to purchase his refrigerated meat display cases.

Thus, he was able to purchase all of his display cases and shelving with money borrowed on a promise to purchase a certain percentage of his needs. Further, he signed agreements assuring that he would not be overcharged when making his purchases.

Leasing Companies. One way people have been able to finance their business is through a leasing company. Instead of actually borrowing money, you would make arrangements with a leasing company who would purchase items you need for your business, such as a truck, office furniture or computer equipment.

Then, you lease the items from the leasing company over a certain period of time. Title to the goods or property is retained by the leasing company.

Business Brokers and Investors. Some individuals specialize in making small business loans either on a straight interest basis or a shared equity basis. Often these people will advertise in the classified section of the Sunday newspapers and in the yellow pages of the telephone book.

If you elect this method of financing, be certain you are dealing with someone who is reputable and has a good track record with such loans. If they want a piece of your business, would you want them as a "partner"?

Invoice Discounting and Factoring. There are many companies out there to help you with your short term financing needs. If you have or can generate invoices to customers for future services, there are companies that can help you. Look in your local yellow pages for factoring companies or search the Internet. For invoice discounting services contact the Interface Financial Group at 972-562-8512. They are the leaders in invoice discounting.

Advertise for Money

You can actively seek funding by running a display advertisement in the business section or under the appropriate heading in the classified ads of your local newspaper. Specify the amount of money needed and the type of business for which it will be used. Check the "Business Opportunities" in your local paper for samples. Confidentiality for both parties can be maintained through the use of a post office box or newspaper box number.

Grants

Grants for FREE money to start businesses are hard to find. There are a few people out there that would make you think that grants are easy, but it is just not the case. Most grants from the U.S. government are for non-

---

profit entities, high technology companies or other government agencies. Grant programs come and go frequently and it is hard to keep up on all of them by state. To find grants, call your local city hall, county offices, state office and economic development agencies and ask if they have any current grant programs. Be aware that applying for grants can be a long and complicated process. If they have an application form, be sure to fill it out completely. Many grant providers will reject your request if you don't fill it correctly.

ASKING FOR YOUR LOAN

Now that Joe and Doris Smith have completed their Loan Proposal, they are ready to meet with their banker. Prior to this time they had done one other very important thing.

Eight years before they even considered having a business of their own, they opened a joint CHECKING ACCOUNT at the local branch office of the First National Bank of Anywhere.

Over the past eight years, they had taken out two small loans from the bank. The first was to finance their automobile purchase of three years ago. Then last year they had taken out a $5,000 loan to remodel their kitchen and breezeway.

While doing this, they became well acquainted with Ted Benson, the bank's vice-president.

When they first considered going into their Snow Plowing and Lawn Care Service, they casually mentioned to Mr. Benson that they might see him for a business loan. Thus, they had paved the way to set an appointment with their bank for a business loan. If your banking experience has been limited, consider taking all or some of the following steps:

1. Open a personal checking account with a commercial bank.

2. Ask to meet a bank officer when you open your account. Even the president is not too high on the ladder. If he is not available, ask to meet a vice president.

3. Ask to see this same person from time to time when you come into the bank to make a deposit or to cash a check. Simply go over and say "HELLO".

4. If you already have a checking account open, consider opening a savings account.

5. Take out a loan, even if it is a small one, in order to establish a LOAN HISTORY with your bank.

In short, if at all possible, attempt to establish a personal relationship with a specific individual at your bank. This relationship is best established over a period of time. However, if it is not possible, then when you ask for a loan, you simply have to meet with a loan officer.

Make an appointment to discuss your loan and state that you wish to present your loan proposal. DO NOT DISCUSS THE PROPOSAL AT THIS TIME.

Once you appear at the appointed time, present your loan proposal to the bank officer. At that time he will probably ask you some clarifying questions and then indicate that your loan request will be presented to a loan committee.

Or, if you have a loan history with the bank, you may hear immediately. Naturally, the higher the amount of the loan request, the greater the number of questions you may be asked.

> *In this chapter you have learned:*
>
> 1. *In order to be successful in a Small Business, you have to WANT to MAKE MONEY.*
> 2. *In order to be successful in a Small Business, you have to know how to spend money properly in order to maximize your profits.*
> 3. *In order to be successful in a Small Business, you have to know how to borrow money.*
> 4. *There are numerous places to borrow money. You have to identify the best option for you.*

Websites You May Find Useful

Small Business Administration – www.sba.gov

Wells Fargo – www.wellsfargo.com

Government Benefits & Grants – www.benefits.gov

Step To Success
One Action a Day Will Move You Forward

It is time to move forward. Complete the **Step to Success** Action and feel your progress. No matter where you are going, you can get there one step at a time.

Before you can ask anyone for money, you need to understand how much you will need. Take out a piece of paper and write down all the items you will need to get your business up and running. Remember to add in additional amounts as working capital until your business becomes profitable.

Chapter 17

Small Business Administration Loan Programs

"Formal education will make you a living; self-education will make you a fortune."
- Jim Rohn

There are those who argue that big businesses, profiting from "economies of scale," can produce far more efficiently than small businesses. But small business is where the innovations take place. Swifter, more flexible and often more daring than big businesses, small firms produce the items that line the shelves of America's museums, shops and homes. They keep intact the heritage of ingenuity and enterprise and they help keep the "American Dream" within the reach of millions of Americans. Every step of the way, SBA is there to help them.

SMALL BUSINESS ADMINSTRATION PROGRAMS

Small Business Administration (SBA). In most states the SBA has a Lender Certification Program. Under this program, participating certified banks accept the loan application, investigate credit, establish loan limit and approve the loan which is guaranteed by the SBA. The procedure takes three to six days. Non-certified banks may take four to six weeks, if they participate at all in the SBA program. The bank will help you decide what SBA loan programs may fit for your needs.

The U.S. Small Business Administration is dedicated to providing customer-oriented, full-service programs and accurate, timely information to the entrepreneurial community. All of the SBA's programs and services are provided to the public on a nondiscriminatory basis.

Basic Conditions of SBA Financing Programs

1. SBA **DOES NOT** loan money or give grants to small businesses. The SBA guarantees loans for banks or other agencies.
2. A business must be a for-profit entity.
3. Small business must have less than $2 million net profit and fewer than 500 employees.
4. Business owner must be of good character and demonstrate ability to run a successful business.
5. Loan applications must discuss how the loan will be repaid.
6. Typically the SBA requires the business owner to put in monies equal to 1/3 of the total amount of financing.
7. Maximum loan limit is $2,000,000.
8. Maximum SBA loan guarantee is $1,000,000
9. The guarantee fee on the loan is between 2-3.5%
10. Loan may be used for working capital, inventory, machinery and equipment, improvements.
11. Loans can be made for 5-7 years for working capital, 10 years for equipment or 25 years for property.
12. Interest rates are discussed by you and the banker, but can not be more than the SBA guidelines permit.
13. Personal guarantees will be required from owners with 20% or more ownership in the business.

7(a) Guaranteed Loan Program

Its function is to provide short- and long-term loans to eligible, credit-worthy start-up and existing small businesses that cannot obtain financing on reasonable terms through normal lending channels. The

SBA provides financial assistance through its participating lenders in the form of loan guaranties, **not direct loans**. The SBA **DOES NOT provide grants or loans** for business start-up or expansion. The SBA Office of Capital Access administers the 7(a) Loan Guaranty Program. Loans under the program are available for most business purposes, including purchasing real estate, machinery, equipment, and inventory, or for working capital. The loans cannot be used for speculative purposes. The SBA can guarantee a maximum of $1,000,000 under the 7(a) program.

Those that use this program are start-up and existing small businesses.

Certified and Preferred Lenders

Its function is to designate the most active and expert SBA participating lenders as either Certified or Preferred. Certified lenders receive a partial SBA delegation of authority to approve loans. Preferred lenders receive full delegation of lending authority. A listing of participants in the Certified and Preferred Lenders Program is available from SBA district offices.

LowDoc Loan Program

Its function is to reduce the paperwork involved in loan requests of $150,000 or less. The SBA uses a one-page application for SBALowDoc that relies on the strength of the applicant's character, business experience and credit history. Under the LowDoc Program, the SBA will guarantee 80% of the loan made by a banker to an existing business, a business purchase or business start-up.

SBA Express Program

Its function is to encourage lenders to make more small loans to small businesses. Participating banks use their own documentation and procedures to approve, service and liquidate loans of up to $150,000. In return, the SBA agrees to guarantee up to 50% of each loan. SBA Express can be used as a revolving line of credit up to seven years. An example of a revolving line of credit has the same characteristics of a loan, except you do not have to take all the money at once. On a

$10,000 loan, you can borrow $2,000 this month and $3,000 next month and $5,000 in month 3. The interest that you pay on the loan is calculated on the amount of the loan you have borrowed. In the previous example, you would pay interest on $2,000 for one month, $5,000 for two months and $10,000 for the balance of time you make payments.

CAPLines Loan Program

Its function is to finance small businesses' short-term and cyclical working-capital needs. Under CAPLines, there are five distinct short-term working-capital loans: Seasonal, Contract, Builders, Standard Asset-Based, and Small Asset-Based lines. The SBA generally can guarantee a maximum of $1,000,000 or 75% of the amount needed. Owners must meet the same requirements as any other SBA 7(a) business loan.

Those that use this program are start-up and existing small businesses

Export Working Capital Program (EWCP)

Its function is to help small businesses for short term export financing when financing is not available on reasonable terms. The program enables the SBA to guarantee up to 90% of a secured loan, or $1,000,000, whichever is less. Loan maturity may be for up to three years with annual renewals. Loans can be for single or multiple export sales and can be extended for pre-shipment working capital, post-shipment exposure coverage or a combination of the two.

Those that use this program are export-ready small businesses

Defense Loan & Technical Assistance (DELTA), 7(a) Loan Program

Its function is to help defense-dependent small firms that are adversely affected by defense cuts diversify into the commercial market through financial and technical assistance. Loans must be used for the following: to retain jobs of defense workers, create new jobs in impacted communities, or modernize/expand in order to remain in the national technical and industrial base. DELTA uses the following loan programs:

7(a), with a maximum total loan of $2 million; and/or 504, with a maximum guaranteed debenture of $1.3 million. 7(a) loans carry a maximum guaranty of 80%. Federal, state and private-sector resources provide a full range of management and technical assistance.

Those that use this program are defense-dependent small firms adversely impacted by defense cuts. Small businesses must have 25% of their sales from Department of Defense or defense-related Department of Energy contracts.

Funding is established through SBA resource partners.

International Trade Loan (ITL), a 7(a) Loan Program

Its function is to offer long-term financing to small businesses engaged or preparing to engage in international trade, as well as to small businesses adversely affected by import competition. The SBA can guarantee up to $1.25 million for a combination of fixed-asset financing and working capital. The working-capital loan guaranty portion cannot exceed $750,000 and the fixed asset portion cannot be greater than $1,000,000.

Those that use this program are export-ready small businesses

Certified Development Companies (CDCs), a 504 Loan Program

Its function is to provide long-term, fixed-rate financing to small businesses to acquire real estate, machinery or equipment to expand or modernize. Typically at least 10% of the loan proceeds are provided by the borrower, at least 50% by a non-guaranteed bank loan, and the remainder by a SBA-guaranteed debenture. The maximum SBA debenture is $1 million for meeting the job creation criteria or a community development goal. Generally, a business must create or retain one job from every for $35,000 provided by the SBA. The maximum SBA debenture is $1.3 million for meeting for meeting a public policy goal.

Those that use this program are small businesses requiring "brick and mortar" financing

Funding is established through certified development companies (private, nonprofit corporations set up to contribute to the economic development of their communities or regions). To find a certified development company go to:

http://www.sba.gov/gopher/Local-Information/Certified-Development-Companies/cdcall.txt

Community Adjustment and Investment Program (CAIP), a 7(a) Loan Program

Its function is to create new sustainable jobs and preserves existing jobs in businesses at risk due to changed trade patterns with Canada and Mexico following the National American Free Trade Agreement (NAFTA) was signed. Business applicants must be located in a CAIP-eligible community. They also must demonstrate that within 24 months and as a result of the loan they will create or preserve at least one job per $70,000 of federally guaranteed funds they receive. CAIP is a partnership between the federal government (primarily the SBA and U.S. Department of Agriculture) and the North American Development Bank.

Those that use this program are Businesses in communities with significant job losses related to the North American Free Trade Agreement.

Funding is established through Certified Development Companies.

MicroLoan, a 7(m) Loan Program

Its function is to provide short-term loans of up to $35,000 to small businesses for working capital or the purchase of inventory, supplies, furniture, fixtures, machinery and/or equipment. Proceeds cannot be used to pay existing debts or to purchase real estate. Loans are made through SBA-approved nonprofit groups. These lenders also receive SBA grants to provide technical assistance to their borrowers. Additional entities also receive grants to provide technical assistance to other businesses selecting non-SBA-backed financing.

Those that use this program are small businesses needing small-scale financing and technical assistance for start-up or expansion

Funding is established through intermediary lenders (nonprofit organizations with experience in lending and technical assistance).

The Facts About . . . The MicroLoan Program for Entrepreneurs

The MicroLoan Program combines the resources and experience of the U.S. Small Business Administration with those of locally based nonprofit organizations to provide small loans and technical assistance to small businesses.

Under the MicroLoan Program, the SBA makes funds available to qualified nonprofit organizations, which act as intermediary lenders. The intermediaries use these funds to make loans of up to $35,000 to new and existing small businesses. The intermediaries also provide management and technical assistance to help ensure success.

INVESTMENT

www.sba.gov/inv

Small Business Investment Companies (SBICs)

Its function is to provide equity capital, long-term loans, debt-equity investments and management assistance to small businesses particularly during their growth stages. The SBA's role consists of licensing the SBICs and supplementing their capital with U.S. government-guaranteed debentures, participating securities or low-interest loans. SBICs are privately owned and managed, profit-motivated companies, investing with the prospect of sharing in the success of the funded small businesses as they grow and prosper.

Those that use this program are small businesses seeking long-term capital. Almost 75% of the businesses that were funded in 2001 were in the manufacturing, information, or professional, scientific or technical services. Over 75% of the businesses received $25 million or greater.

Funding is established through small business investment companies. To find a small business investment company go to: http://www.sba.gov/gopher/Local-Information/Small-Business-Investment-Companies/sbicall.txt

Angel Capital Electronic Network (ACE-Net)

Its function is to provide an Internet-based secure listing service for entrepreneurs seeking equity financing of $250,000 to $5 million from accredited "angel" investors. The "angels" using ACE-Net can negotiate directly with listed companies to provide equity capital funding and advice for a stake in the entrepreneur's corporation. ACE-Net is operated as a partnership between the SBA's Office of Advocacy and a number of nonprofit organizations nationwide. It will ultimately be turned over to a private nonprofit organization.

Those that use this program are entrepreneurs and "angel" investors.

SURETY BONDS
www.sba.gov/osg

Surety Bond Guarantee

Its function is to guarantee bid, performance and payment bonds for contracts up to $1.25 million for eligible small businesses that cannot obtain surety bonds through regular commercial channels. By law, prime contractors to the federal government must post surety bonds on federal construction projects valued at $25,000 or more. In addition, many states, counties, municipalities, and private-sector projects and subcontracts also require surety bonds. Contractors must apply through a surety bonding agent, since the SBA's guaranty goes to the surety company.

Those that use this program are small construction and service contractors; surety and insurance companies, and their agents; federal and state agencies; state insurance departments -- federal, state and other procurement officials

Funding is established through surety and insurance companies and their agents; four SBA area offices: Atlanta, Denver, Philadelphia, and Seattle. To find out which office to call go to: http://www.sba.gov/osg/contacts.html

FEDERAL PROCUREMENT
www.sba.gov/gc and pronet.sba.gov

The function of the SBA in federal procurement that all small businesses have the maximum practicable opportunity to participate in providing goods and services to the government. Each year the SBA negotiates procurement goals with each Federal agency.

The most current goals are as follows:

1. 23% of prime contracts for small businesses;
2. 5% of prime and subcontracts for small disadvantaged businesses;
3. 5% of prime and subcontracts for women-owned small businesses;
4. 3% of prime contracts for HUBZone small businesses;
5. 3% of prime and subcontracts for service-disabled veteran-owned small businesses.

To identify Federal opportunities that may be available, go to: http://www.fedbizopps.gov/ or http://www.pronet.sba.gov/

Natural Resources Assistance Program

Its function is intended to help small businesses receive a fair share of the large quantities of natural resources and surplus real property that the Federal Government sells on an annual basis. The program covers timber and related forest products, strategic materials (go to: http://www.gsa.gov/Portal/home.jsp to get a list of products), royalty oil, leases involving rights to minerals, coal, oil and gas and surplus real and personal property.

Certificate of Competency (CoC)

Its function is to help small businesses secure government contracts by providing an appeal process to low-bidder businesses denied government contracts for a perceived lack of ability to perform satisfactorily. SBA is authorized by the Congress to certify as to a small company's "capability, competency, credit, integrity, perseverance and tenacity" to perform a specific government contract. A COC is valid only for the specific contract for which it is issued. A business concern which is capable of handling one contract may not be qualified to handle another.

Those that use this program are small businesses that have been denied government contracts for perceived lack of ability.

Office of Federal Contract Assistance for Women-Owned Business Owners (CAWBO)

Its function is to use a multifaceted outreach and educational program to teach women business owners to market to the federal government.

This program is for women-owned businesses. To find out more or if you qualify as a women-owned business go to: www.womenbiz.gov

Procurement Marketing & Access Network (PRO-Net)
www.pronet.sba.gov

Its function is to serve as a search engine for contracting officers, a marketing tool for small firms, and a "link" to procurement opportunities and other important information. Pro-Net; contains business information on almost 200,000 small firms. The Pro-Net project is a cooperative effort among SBA's offices of <u>Government Contracting</u>, <u>Minority Enterprise Development</u>, Advocacy, Women's Business Ownership, Field Operations, Marketing & Customer Service, the Chief Information Officer, and the National Women's Business Council. Registration for this database is free.

HUBZone Empowerment Contracting

Its function is to encourage economic development in historically underutilized business zones — "HUBZones" — through the establishment of federal contract award preferences for small businesses located in such areas. After determining eligibility, the SBA lists qualified businesses in its PRO-Net database.

Those that use this program are Small businesses located in historically underutilized business zones

See the SBA Office of HUBZone Empowerment Contracting Program, www.sba.gov/hubzone

RESEARCH & DEVELOPMENT

Small Business Innovation Research (SBIR)

Its function is to provide a vehicle for small businesses to propose innovative ideas in competition for Phase I and Phase II awards, which represent specific R&D needs of the participating federal agencies. These awards may result in commercialization of the effort at the Phase III level.

Small businesses must meet certain eligibility criteria to participate in the SBIR program.

- American-owned and independently operated
- For-profit
- Principal researcher employed by business
- Company size limited to 500 employees

Each year, ten federal departments and agencies are required by SBIR to reserve a portion of their R&D funds for award to small business.

- Department of Agriculture
- Department of Commerce
- Department of Defense
- Department of Education
- Department of Energy
- Department of Health and Human Services
- Department of Transportation
- Environmental Protection Agency
- National Aeronautics and Space Administration
- National Science Foundation

For more information on SBIR go to:
http://www.sba.gov/sbir/indexsbir-sttr.html#sbir

Small Business Technology Transfer (STTR)

Its function is to require each small firm competing for an R&D project to collaborate with a nonprofit research institution. This program is a joint venture from the initial proposal to the project's completion. STTR's most important role is to foster the innovation necessary to meet the nation's scientific and technological challenges in the 21st century.

Small businesses must meet certain eligibility criteria to participate in the STTR Program.

- American-owned and independently operated
- For-profit
- Principal researcher need not be employed by small business
- Company size limited to 500 employees

Funding is established through five federal agencies with extramural research and R&D budgets of $1 billion: NASA, the National Science Foundation, and the departments of Defense, Energy, and Health & Human Services.

Tech-Net is an electronic gateway of technology information and resources for and about small high tech businesses. It is a search engine for researchers, scientists, state, federal and local government officials, a marketing tool for small firms and a potential "link" to investment opportunities for investors and other sources of capital. To learn more about Tech-Net, go to: http://tech-net.sba.gov/index2.html

BUSINESS COUNSELING & TRAINING

The SBA provides most business counseling and training programs through its resource partners.

Small Business Development Centers (SBDCs)

Its function is to provide high quality, low-cost management and technical assistance, counseling and training to current and prospective small business owners. Administered by the SBA, the program is a cooperative effort of the private sector, the educational community, and federal, state and local government.

Those that use this program are pre-business, start-up and existing small businesses

There are more than 1,000 locations, including universities, colleges, state governments, private-sector organizations. To find an office near you, go to: http://www.sba.gov/gopher/Local-Information/Small-Business-Development-enters/

SCORE Association (SCORE)

Its function is to offers counseling and training for small business owners who are starting, building or growing a business. SCORE services also include going into business seminars, and specific business topic seminars, including sales and marketing, finance, or international trade. Most seminars and one-on-one counseling is either free of charge or a small nominal fee.

There are more than 12,000 volunteers in 389 chapters with 700 locations, www.score.org

To find a SCORE office near you or to sign up for e-mail counseling, go to: http://www.score.org/

BUSINESS INFORMATION SERVICES

Answer Desk

Its function is to help callers with questions and problems about starting and running businesses. The computerized telephone message system is available nationwide 24 hours a day, seven days a week. Counselors are available Monday through Friday, 9:00 a.m. to 5:00 p.m. Eastern Time.

This is open to the general public

Toll-free telephone number: 1-800-U-ASK-SBA

Farmers Home Administration. This government program guarantees loans up to 90% of loan value for businesses located in towns of less than 50,000 population. Amounts borrowed are normally larger than under the SBA, and the borrower must show how his new or expanded business will benefit the community.

> *In this chapter you have learned:*
>
> *1.   The Small Business Administration has many loan programs through banks to help you fund your business.*
>
> *2.   The SBA also provides counseling to entrepreneurs through their two organizations: SCORE and the Small Business Development Center, in addition to email counseling through its main office.*

Websites You May Find Useful

Small Business Administration Financing – www.sba.gov

SCORE – www.score.org

Small Business Development Centers -

http://www.sba.gov/aboutsba/sbaprograms/sbdc/index.html

Step To Success
One Action a Day Will Move You Forward

It is time to move forward. Complete the **Step to Success** Action and feel your progress.   No matter where you are going, you can get there one step at a time.

Research the different types of loan programs to see if you qualify. Then set up a meeting with a banker to see what loan programs they offer. You can also take a minute to find the local SCORE or SBDC in your area.

You can do it. Get going!!

Chapter 18

"For Every Benefit You Receive A Tax Is Levied"
                                   - Ralph Waldo Emerson

OR

"There is no such thing as a good tax"
                                   - Winston Churchill

For all of us the classic quote is:

"In this world nothing is certain but death and taxes"
                                   - Benjamin Franklin

Whatever your view of taxes, they are a part of owning a small business. Managing your tax setup and on-going payment of taxes can be complicated. Information in this chapter is provided from the Internal Revenue Service.

IS YOUR BUSINESS A HOBBY OR A BUSINESS?

It is generally accepted that people prefer to make a living doing something they like. A hobby is an activity for which you do not expect to make a profit. If you do not carry on your business or investment activity to make a profit, there is a limit on the deductions you can take.

You must include on your return income from an activity from which you do not expect to make a profit. An example of this type of activity is a hobby or a farm you operate mostly for recreation and pleasure. You cannot use a loss from the activity to offset other income. Activities you do as a hobby, or mainly for sport or recreation, come under this limit. So does an investment activity intended only to produce tax losses for the investors.

The limit on not-for-profit losses applies to individuals, partnerships, estates trusts, and S corporations. For additional information on these entities, refer to business structures. It does not apply to corporations other than S corporations.

In determining whether you are carrying on an activity for profit, all the facts are taken into account. No one factor alone is decisive. Among the factors to consider are whether:

1. You carry on the activity in a business-like manner,
2. The time and effort you put into the activity indicate you intend to make it profitable,
3. You depend on income from the activity for your livelihood,
4. Your losses are due to circumstances beyond your control (or are normal in the start-up phase of your type of business),

5. You change your methods of operation in an attempt to improve profitability,
6. You, or your advisors, have the knowledge needed to carry on the activity as a successful business,
7. You were successful in making a profit in similar activities in the past,
8. The activity makes a profit in some years and the amount of profit it makes, and
9. You can expect to make a future profit from the appreciation of the assets used

in the activity.

For details about not-for-profit activities, refer to Publication 535, Business Expenses.

FEDERAL EMPLOYER ID NUMBERS (EIN)

About EINs: An Employer Identification Number (EIN), also known as a Federal Tax Identification Number, is a nine-digit number that the IRS assigns to business entities. The IRS uses this number to identify taxpayers that are required to file various business tax returns. EINs are used by employers, sole proprietors, corporations, partnerships, non-profit organizations, trusts and estates, government agencies, certain individuals and other business entities.

Do You Need One?

If you answer YES to any of the following questions, you will need to apply for a Federal Employer ID Number.

Do you have employees?	YES	NO
Do you operate your business as a corporation or a partnership?	YES	NO
Do you file any of these tax returns: Employment, Excise, or Alcohol, Tobacco and Firearms?	YES	NO
Do you withhold taxes on income, other than wages, paid to a non-resident alien?	YES	NO
Do you have a Keogh plan?	YES	NO
Are you involved with any of the following types of organizations? • Trusts, except certain grantor-owned revocable trusts, IRAs, Exempt Organization Business Income Tax Returns • Estates	YES	NO

- Real estate mortgage investment conduits
- Non-profit organizations
- Farmers' cooperatives
- Plan administrators

APPLYING FOR AN EIN

On-line

This Internet EIN (I-EIN) application opens another avenue for customers to apply for and obtain an employer identification number. Once you have completed all necessary fields on the online form, preliminary validation is performed and will alert you to information IRS needs that you may not have included. An EIN will be issued after the successful submission of the completed Form SS-4 online. There are some entities that may not apply for their EIN online. They are:

Foreign Addresses (including Puerto Rico), Limited Liability Company (LLC) without entity types, REMICs, State and Local Governments, Federal Government/Military, Indian Tribal Government/Enterprise.

For U.S. entities, please call the toll-free Business and Specialty Tax Line at 1-800-829-4933 should you need assistance applying for an EIN.

Foreign Addresses (addresses outside the continental USA, Alaska and Hawaii) call 215-516-6999.

To apply online go to: https://sa.www4.irs.gov/sa_vign/newFormSS4.do This will give you the SS-4 form online to be filled out and then submitted through clicking NEXT at the bottom of the page.

If you don't want to fill out the form on the Internet you can print a copy of the SS-4 form from:

http://www.irs.gov/pub/irs-pdf/fss4.pdf

To Apply By Phone, Fax or Mail:

First you should print out the SS-4 form from the file listed above.

If your principal business, office or agency, or legal residence in the case of an individual, is located in:	Call the Tele-TIN or Fax-TIN number shown or file with the "Internal Revenue Service Center" at:
Connecticut, Delaware, District of Columbia, Florida, Georgia, Maine, Maryland, Massachusetts, New Hampshire, New Jersey, New York, North Carolina, Ohio, Pennsylvania, Rhode Island, South Carolina, Vermont, Virginia, West Virginia	Attn: EIN Operations Holtsville, NY 00501 Business & Speciality Tax Line (Obtain an EIN from 7:30am-5:30pm local time only: (800) 829-4933 Fax-TIN: (631) 447-8960
Illinois, Indiana, Kentucky, Michigan	Attn: EIN Operations Cincinnati, OH 45999 Business & Speciality Tax Line (Obtain an EIN from 7:30am-5:30pm local time only: (800) 829-4933 Fax-TIN: (859) 669-5760
Alabama, Alaska, Arizona, Arkansas, California, Colorado, Hawaii, Idaho, Iowa, Kansas, Louisiana, Minnesota, Mississippi, Missouri, Montana, Nebraska, Nevada, New Mexico, North Dakota, Oklahoma, Oregon, Puerto Rico, South Dakota, Tennessee, Texas, Utah, Washington, Wisconsin, Wyoming	Attn: EIN Operations Philadelphia, PA 19255 Business & Speciality Tax Line (Obtain an EIN from 7:30am-5:30pm local time only: (800) 829-4933 Fax-TIN: (215) 516-3990
If you have no legal residence, principal place of business, or principal office or agency in any state:	Attn: EIN Operations Philadelphia, PA 19255 Business & Speciality Tax Line (Obtain an EIN from 7:30am-5:30pm local time only: (800) 829-4933 Fax-TIN: (215) 516-3990

HOW LONG WILL IT TAKE TO GET A NUMBER?

You should apply for an EIN early enough to have your number when you need to file a return or make a deposit. You can get an EIN quickly by applying online, or by calling the Tele-TIN phone number for your state. If you prefer, you can fax a completed Form SS-4 to the service center, and they will respond with a return fax in about one week. If you do not include a return fax number, it will take about two weeks. If you apply by mail, send your completed Form SS-4 (PDF) at least four to five weeks before you need your EIN to file a return or make a deposit.

If you don't have your EIN by the time a return is due, write "Applied for" and the date you applied in the space shown for the number. Do not use your social security number.

If you don't have your EIN by the time a deposit is due, send your payment to the service center address for your state. Make your check or money order payable to Internal Revenue Service and show your name (as shown on the SS-4), address, kind of tax, period covered, and the date you applied for your EIN.

Need more information?
Read Publication 1635, Understanding Your EIN (PDF).

STATE TAX ID NUMBERS
To find out if you need to file for a different number for your state go to the following website for links to all the state tax authorities or find your own department of commerce website:
http://www.irs.gov/businesses/small/article/0,,id=99021,00.html

BUSINESS TAXES
The form of business you operate determines what taxes you must pay and how you pay them. The following are the four general types of business taxes.

- Income Tax
- Self-Employment Tax
- Employment Taxes
- Excise Tax

Income Tax

All business except partnerships must file an annual income tax return. Partnerships file an information return. The form you use depends on how your business is organized.

The federal income tax is a pay-as-you-go tax. You must pay the tax as you earn or receive income during the year. An employee usually has income tax withheld from his or her pay. If you do no pay your tax through withholding, or do not pay enough tax that way, you might have to pay estimated tax. If you are not required to make estimated tax payments, you may pay any tax due when you file your return. For additional information refer to Publication 583, Starting a Business and Keeping Records.

Self-Employment Tax

Self-employment tax (SE tax) is a social security and Medicare tax primarily for individuals who work for themselves. Your payments of SE tax contribute to your coverage under the social security system. Social security coverage provides you with retirement benefits, disability benefits, survivor benefits, and hospital insurance (Medicare) benefits.

You must pay SE tax and file Schedule SE (Form 1040) if either of the following applies.

1. Your net earnings from self-employment were $400 or more.
2. You had church employee income of $108.28 or more.

What is Self-Employment Tax?

Self-employment tax (SE tax) is a social security and Medicare tax primarily for individuals who work for themselves. It is similar to the social security and Medicare taxes withheld from the pay of most wage earners. You figure SE tax yourself using Schedule SE (Form 1040). Refer to "What is Self-Employment

Tax?" in Publication 533, Self-Employment Tax.

Who Must Pay Self-Employment Tax

You must pay SE tax and file Schedule SE (Form 1040) if either of the following applies.

1. Your net earnings from self-employment (excluding church employee income) were $400 or more.
2. You had church employee income of $108.28 or more.

Refer to "Who Must Pay Self-Employment Tax?" in Publication 533, Self-Employment Tax.

Figuring Earnings Subject to Self-Employment Tax

Generally, you need to figure your total earnings subject to SE tax before you can figure your net earnings from self-employment. This section will help you figure these total earnings. Refer to "Figuring Earnings Subject to Self-Employment Tax" in Publication 533, Self-Employment Tax.

Estimated Taxes

Federal income tax is a pay-as-you-go tax. You must pay the tax as you earn or receive income during the year. There are two ways to pay as you go: withholding and estimated taxes. If you are a self-employed individual and do not have income tax withheld, you must make estimated tax payments.

Methods of Figuring Net Earnings

There are three ways to figure your net earnings from self-employment: the regular method, the non-farm optional method, the farm optional method. Find out which method is appropriate for your situation. Refer to "Methods of Figuring Net Earnings" in Publication 533, Self-Employment Tax.

Reporting Self-Employment Tax

Use Schedule SE (Form 1040) to figure and report your SE tax. Then enter the SE tax on line 53 of Form 1040 and attach Schedule SE to Form 1040. Refer to "Reporting Self-

Employment Tax" in Publication 533, Self-Employment Tax.

Filled-In Form Examples

The "Filled-in Form Examples" section of Publication 533, Self-Employment Tax provide examples that illustrate the use of the short and long forms of Schedule SE (Form 1040).

Publications:
- Publication 15 (Circular E), Employer's Tax Guide
- Publication 15-A, Employers Supplemental Tax Guide
- Publication 225, Farmer's Tax Guide
- Publication 505, Tax Withholding and Estimated Tax
- Publication 517, Social Security and Other Information For Members of the Clergy and Religious Workers
- Publication 541, Partnerships
- Publication 570, Tax Guide For Individuals With Income From U.S. Possessions
- Publication 911, Direct Sellers

Forms:
- Form 1040, U.S. Individual Income Tax Return
- Schedule ES (Form 1040), Estimated Tax for 2004
- Schedule C (Form 1040), Profit or Loss From Business
- Schedule C-EZ (Form 1040), Net Profit From Business
- Schedule SE (Form 1040), Self-Employment Tax

Employment Taxes

When you have employees you as the employer have certain employment tax responsibilities that you must pay and forms you must file. Employment taxes include the following:
- Social security and Medicare taxes
- Federal income tax withholding
- Federal unemployment (FUTA) tax

What Are Employment Taxes?

If you have employees, you are responsible for Federal Income Tax Withholding, Social Security and Medicare taxes and Federal Unemployment Tax Act (FUTA).

Independent Contractors vs. Employees

Are you or your help independent consultants or employees? Before you can know how to treat payments you make for services, you must first know the business relationship that exists between you and the person performing the services.

e-file for Business and Self-Employed Taxpayers

IRS e-file and electronic payment options for employment taxes, information returns, partnerships, corporations, estates & trusts and returns for charities and nonprofit organizations.

Federal Tax Deposits

You generally have to deposit employment taxes, certain excise taxes, corporate income tax, and S corporation taxes before you file your return. If you don't make the deposits electronically, deliver deposits with completed deposit coupons to an authorized financial institution or a Federal Reserve bank serving your area.

Employment Tax Requirements

This page describes the basic requirements for tax and wage reporting compliance. Covers topics such as determining if an EIN is necessary, calculating withholdings, making deposits, and keeping tax and reporting records.

Employment Tax Forms

This page provides a listing of the common employment tax forms that a small business or self-employed person would need

Employment Tax Publications

This page provides a listing of the common employment tax publications that a small business or self-employed person would need

Employment Tax Notices
This page provides a listing of IRS notices that would be interest to a small business owner or a self-employed person

Self-Employment Tax
The Self-Employment Tax is a social security and Medicare tax for individuals who work for themselves.

How To Use the Income Tax Withholding and Advance Earned Income Credit (EIC) Payment Tables
There are several ways to figure income tax withholding. This explains methods of withholding based on information you get from your employees on Form W-4.

Excise Tax
Excise taxes are taxes paid when purchases are made on a specific good, such as gasoline. Excise taxes are often included in the price of the product. There are also excise taxes on activities, such as on wagering or on highway usage by trucks. Excise Tax has several general excise tax programs. One of the major components of the excise program is motor fuel.

Excise taxes are taxes paid when purchases are made on a specific good, such as gasoline. Excise taxes are often included in the price of the product. There are also excise taxes on activities, such as on wagering or on highway usage by trucks. Excise Tax has several general excise tax programs. One of the major components of the excise program is motor fuel.

Find out more about the various databases and programs listed below for Excise Tax:
- Excise Summary Terminal Activity Reporting System (ExSTARS)

- Terminal Control Number (TCN) Database
- 637 Registration Program
- Excise Tax On-line Exchange (ExTOLE)
- Motor Fuel Excise Tax Electronic Data Interchange (EDI)
- Additional Resources for Excise Tax

Hot News

Online Form 637 Registration Status Check - This new web application provides the ability for businesses to confirm whether individuals/companies have a valid IRS registration. Click on the above link for additional information on the 637 registration program.

Recordkeeping

Why should I keep records?

Good records will help you monitor the progress of your business, prepare your financial statements, identify source of receipts, keep track of deductible expenses, prepare your tax returns, and support items reported on tax returns.

What kinds of records should I keep?

You may choose any recordkeeping system suited to your business that clearly shows your income. Except in a few cases, the law does not require any special kind of records. However, the business you are in affects the type of records you need to keep for federal tax purposes.

How long should I keep records?

The length of time you should keep a document depends on the action, expense, or event the document records. You must keep your records as long as they may be needed to prove the income or deductions on a tax return.

How long should I keep employment tax records?

You must keep all of your records as long as they may be

needed; however, keep all records of employment taxes for at least four years.

How should I record my business transactions?
Purchases, sales, payroll, and other transactions you have in your business generate supporting documents. These documents contain information you need to record in your books.

What is the burden of proof?
The responsibility to prove entries, deductions, and statements made on your tax returns is known as the burden of proof.. You must be able to prove (substantiate) certain elements of expenses to deduct them.

Additional Resources
- Publication 583 , Starting a Business and Keeping Records
- Farm Business Expenses section of Publication 225, Farmer's Tax Guide

Tax Years

You must figure your taxable income and file an income tax return based on an annual accounting period called a tax year. A tax year is usually 12 consecutive months. There are two kinds of tax years.

Calendar year - A calendar tax year is 12 consecutive months beginning January 1 and ending December 31.
Fiscal year - A fiscal tax year is 12 consecutive months ending on the last day of any month except December. A 52-53-week tax year is a fiscal tax year that varies from 52 to 53 weeks but does not have to end on the last day of a month.
-

IIf you file your first tax return using the calendar tax year and you later begin business as a sole proprietor, become a partner in a partnership, or become a shareholder in an S corporation, you must continue to use the calendar year unless you get IRS approval to change it or are otherwise allowed to change it without IRS approval.

You must use a calendar tax year if:

- You keep no books.
- You have no annual accounting period.
- Your present tax year does not qualify as a fiscal year.
- You are required to use a calendar year by a provision of the Internal Revenue Code or the Income Tax Regulations.

For more information, see Publication 538, Accounting Periods and Methods.

First-time filer

If you have never filed an income tax return, you adopt either a calendar tax year or a fiscal tax year. You adopt a tax year by filing your first income tax return using that tax year. You have not adopted a tax year if you merely did any of the following.

- Filed an application for an extension of time to file an income tax return.
- Filed an application for an employer identification number
- Paid estimated taxes for that tax year.

Changing your tax year

Once you have adopted your tax year, you may have to get IRS approval to change it. To get approval, you must file Form 1128, Application To Adopt, Change, or Retain a Tax Year.

Accounting Periods and Methods

Accounting Periods

Each taxpayer (business or individual) must figure taxable income on an annual accounting period called a tax year. The calendar year is the most common tax year. Other tax years include fiscal, 52-53-week, and short tax years. For information on how to choose your tax year, refer to Accounting Periods in Publication 538.

Accounting Methods

Each taxpayer must also use a consistent accounting method, which is a set of rules for determining how and when to report income and expenses. The most commonly used accounting methods are the cash method and the accrual method. Under the cash method, you generally report income in the tax year you receive it and deduct expenses in the tax year you pay them. Under the accrual method, you generally report income in the tax year you earn it, regardless of when payment is received, and deduct expenses in the tax year you incur them, regardless of when payment is made.

Cash Method Example

Frances Jones, a farmer, was entitled to receive a $10,000 payment on a contract in December 2001. The contract was not a production flexibility contract. She was told in December that her payment was available. At her request, she was not paid until January 2002. She must include this payment in her 2001 income because it was constructively received in 2001.

Accrual Method Example

James is a farmer who uses a calendar tax year and an accrual method of accounting. He enters into a turnkey contract with Waterworks in 2001. The contract states that James must pay Waterworks $200,000 in December 2001 and that they will install a complete irrigation system, including a new well, by the close of the year 2003. He pays Waterworks $200,000 in December 2001, they start the installation in May 2003, and they complete the irrigation system in December 2003. Economic performance for James' liability in the contract occurs as the property and services are provided. James incurs the $200,000 cost in the year 2003.

Refer to Accounting Methods, in Publication 538, for information on how to choose your accounting method.

Inventories
An inventory is necessary to clearly show income when the production, purchase, or sale of merchandise is an income-producing factor. If you must account for an inventory in your business, you must use an accrual method of accounting for your purchases and sales.

Changing Your Accounting Method
Once you have set up your accounting method and filed your first return, you must generally get IRS approval to change the method. If your current method clearly shows your income, the IRS will weigh the need for consistency in reporting against the need for change.

Additional Resources
• For additional information on accounting methods, refer to Publication 538, Accounting Periods and Methods
• Read the following articles in PDF format on Cash vs. Accrual Accounting.
o Letter from SB/SE Commissioner to Stakeholders (PDF)
o Action on Decision (AOD 2000-5) (PDF)
o Revenue Procedure 2001-10 (PDF)
o Chief Council Notice CC 2001-010 (PDF)
o Summary Points (PDF)

Checklist for Starting a Business
Most businesses start out small. The checklist below provides the basic steps you should follow to start a business. The list

should not be construed as all-inclusive. Other steps may be appropriate for your specific type of business. Refer also to the Small Business Administration's Checklist for Going into Business (PDF).

- Select a business structure. Consulting SBA's Small Business Startup Kit may help you decide which structure works best for your business.
- Determine if you need to apply for an Employer Identification Number (EIN).
- Write a business plan and investigate business financing and marketing.
- Start your tax year, choose your accounting method, and keep records. Get business tips and consultation services by contacting a small business expert.
- Learn about the types of federal business taxes.
- Consult (Publication 557) Tax-Exempt Status for Your Organization, if you are a nonprofit organization.
- Learn about your social security reporting requirements before hiring any employees.
- Learn about workplace requirements for small businesses with the Department of Labor's Employment Law Guide, which addresses workplace requirements for small businesses.
- If you have employees:
  1. Prepare to meet federal employment tax requirements by reading IRS (Publication 15) Employer's Tax Guide, and (Publication 15a) Employer's Supplemental Tax Guide, or (Publication 51) Agricultural Employer's Tax Guide.
  2. Ask employees to complete withholding certificates:
     - Form W-4, Employee's Withholding Allowance Certificate (PDF), and Form W-5, Earned Income Credit Advance Payment

(PDF)

3. Comply with state and federal regulations regarding the protection of employees. For information on state labor laws, work force availability, prevailing wages, unemployment insurance, unionization, benefits packages, and employment services, contact your state government.

4. Investigate the federal minimum wage, overtime, and child labor laws from the U.S. Department of Labor, Wage and Hour Division.

5. Review the federal health and safety standards employers must provide for the protection of employees as specified by the Occupational Safety and Health Administration (OSHA). Many states have similar standards. For a particular state's information, contact your state government or go to OSHA's list of approved state plans.

6. Check your State Board of Workers' Compensation to see if you need workers' compensation insurance by contacting your state government .

7. Complete U.S. Citizenship and Immigration Services Employment Eligibility Verification Form I-9 for every employee, citizen and non-citizen alike. If you have any questions, contact the U.S. Citizenship and Immigration Services.

- Determine your estimated federal tax payments and begin making payments:
  - Form 1040-ES, Estimated Tax for Individuals (PDF), or Form 1120-W, Estimated Tax for Corporations (PDF)

RECOMMENDED READING ABOUT TAXES FOR SMALL BUSINESSES

A comprehensive list of helpful publications for small businesses. Most are available to browse online. All may be downloaded in Adobe PDF format and printed.

Publication	Description	PDF File	Available As Web Pg
Publication 334	Tax Guide for Small Business (For Individuals Who Use Schedule C or C-EZ)	609K	Web Page
Publication 535	Business Expenses	829K	Web Page
Publication 547	Casualties, Disasters, and Thefts (Business and Nonbusiness)	129K	Web Page
Publication 560	Retirement Plans for Small Businesses (SEP, Keogh, and SIMPLE Plans)	311K	Web Page
Publication 583	Starting a Business and Keeping Records	196K	Web Page
Publication 587	Business Use of Your Home (Including Use by Day-Care Providers)	220K	Web Page
Publication 598	Tax on Unrelated Business Income of Exempt Organizations	263K	Web Page
Publication	Understanding Your EIN -	112K	No

1635	Employer Identification Numbers. This publication is designed to educate the public about the Employer Identification Number (EIN). It explains what an EIN is, how to know if you need one for your business and provides application criteria.		

TAX ASSISTANCE

The IRS publishes the Guide to Free Tax Services (PDF), Publication 910, which identifies the many IRS tax materials and services available to you, and how, when, and where you can get them. Most of the materials and programs are free and available year-round through the IRS. Internet, telephone, and fax access of tax materials, filing options, tax publications, tax education and assistance programs, and tax tips are covered in this guide. The guide also lists telephone numbers for recorded tax information, automated refund information, and IRS mailing addresses.

In this chapter you have learned:
1.   The IRS has many programs for small business owners.
2.   Depending on your business, you need to determine which taxes apply to you.
3.   Filing an EIN is mandatory if you have employees.

Websites You May Find Useful

IRS Small Business – http://www.irs.gov/businesses/small/
About.com
http://sbinformation.about.com/od/taxes/Small_Business_Tax.htm

Step To Success
One Action a Day Will Move You Forward

It is time to move forward. Complete the **Step to Success** Action and feel your progress. No matter where you are going, you can get there one step at a time.

Taxes can be intimidating to some people but it is really because they don't understand it. Find out if there are tax classes given by your local IRS office and sign up for one if possible. Understanding taxes will help you become more comfortable with your accounting and bookkeeping processes.

Do it now!

INDEX